From Persons to People

Also by William Petersen

Planned Migration: The Social Determinants of the Dutch-Canadian Movement (1955)

American Social Patterns (1956; editor)

University Adult Education: A Guide to Policy (1960; with Renee Petersen)

Population (1961, 1969, 1975)

Social Controversy (1963; co-editor with David Matza)

The Realities of World Communism (1963; editor and contributor)

Nevada's Changing Population (1963; with Lionel S. Lewis)

The Politics of Population (1964, 1970)

Japanese Americans: Oppression and Success (1971)

Readings in Population (1972; editor)

Malthus (1979)

The Background to Ethnic Conflict (1979; editor)

Dictionary of Demography (1985-86; with Renee Petersen; 5 volumes)

Ethnicity Counts (1997)

Malthus: Founder of Modern Demography (1999)

From Birth to Death: A Consumer's Guide to Population Studies (2000)

From Persons to People

Further Studies in the Politics of Population

William Petersen

Transaction Publishers
New Brunswick (U.S.A.) and London (U.K.)

Library of Congress Catalog Number: 2002072146
ISBN: 0-7658-0170-1
Printed in Canada

Library of Congress Cataloging-in-Publication Data

Petersen, William.
   From persons to people : further studies in the politics of population / William Petersen
        p. cm.
   Includes bibliographical references (p.) and index.
   ISBN 0-7658-0170-1 (cloth : alk. paper)
   1. Population. 2. Ethnicity. I. Title.

HB851 .P45   2002
305.8—dc21   2002072146

For Renee

Contents

Introduction   1

Part I. Population

1.   The Fundamentals of Demography   9
2.   Population Structure   19
3.   Population in History   35
4.   Malthus   45
5.   Marx and Early Marxists   53
6.   Lenin and His Successors   67
7.   Parents versus the State   79
8.   Efforts to Reduce the Fertility of Less
     Developed Countries   87
9.   A State in the Desert   105
10. The Abortion Controversy   113

Part II. Ethnicity

11. Concepts of Ethnicity   125
12. Political Influences on Ethnicity   145
13. Europe's Nations and Subnations   171
14. Names in Population Records   185
15. Jews as a Race   195
16. Chinese Americans and Japanese Americans   201
17. Social Consequences of Religion   227
18. A Closing Word   237
Appendix   239
Index   241

Introduction

This book contains some of the conclusions I have drawn from work over the past several decades concerning issues in the study of population and ethnicity. The title, *From Persons to People,* reflects the underlying theme, the logical and technical problems associated with aggregation and classification. Virtually all the data used in the social disciplines are gathered from individuals, who may or may not be members of the groups that are consolidated in the eventual statistics. Whether census enumerators classify persons according to some characteristic or whether they are grouped following their own self-identification, summing these persons into a grouping typically ignores the problems associated with such an aggregation. Usually neither the author nor the reader is consciously aware that this journey needs a map.

Analysts of languages differentiate between bilingualism, which is a characteristic of individuals, and diglossia, which is one of populations. A simple aggregation would lead one to assume that where one exists the other must also, but in an interesting essay Joshua Fishman exemplified the distinctions to be made. There are four possible combinations: (1) A monolingual population made up of monolingual individuals, the simplest case, is restricted to very small and isolated speech communities. (2) A country with both diglossia and bilingualism is approximated in Paraguay. The rural population there once spoke only Guarani; but a substantial portion, particularly of those that moved to the towns, learned Spanish, which in the countryside is also the language of education, the courts, and other government institutions. As a consequence, more than half of the population use both languages. (3) In a society with distinct social classes and little movement between them, it sometimes happens that each class has its own language. In pre-1914 Europe, for instance, the elites often spoke French and the mass of the common people another language. The small amount of low-level communication required between master and servant was likely to be in a sharply curtailed version of either language—that is, a pidgin. (4)

Bilingualism without diglossia, finally, can be exemplified by the United States during the period of mass immigration from Europe. Newcomers to the country who spoke their native languages had a strong motivation to learn English, but their bilingualism was usually transitory, seldom lasting as a mass phenomenon beyond the immigrant generation or, at most, the second generation.

As a broader illustration of the dilemmas to be weighed, consider how classification developed in biology, beginning with the taxonomy of the Swedish botanist who was known as either Carolus Linnaeus or Karl von Linné (1707-1778). He classified plants and animals (and minerals!) using their external characteristics to define the units. He also initiated the binomial nomenclature still in use, and this is the one element of his pioneering contribution that has remained. Revisions in his schema have concentrated on two points, how to define a species, and what criterion one uses to arrange species into larger categories.

In his authoritative *This Is Biology,* Ernst Mayr responds to both these questions painstakingly. The species that Linnaeus concocted shared a common "essence," were sharply distinguished from other species, were constant through time and space, and had within each of them little or no variation. As with almost everything else in biology, the addition of evolutionary theory made all these characteristics obsolete. Nature has no "essences." The basic propositions of Darwinism are that living things evolve; thus, that lines between related species are not sharp but often ambiguous, and that a change in speciation typically starts with variation within a single species. As redefined, a species is a group of interbreeding beings that is reproductively (that is, genetically) isolated from other species because of physiological or behavioral barriers. As Mayr points out, it is "only incidental" that a species may also have such other properties "the occupation of a separate niche and certain species-specific morphological or behavioral characteristics," similar to those that earlier biologists had used to define a species. Specialists in systematics are often in contention about the details of the present taxonomy, but there is absolute consensus on the link between the theory of evolution and the way that species and higher divisions are formed. Species developed as they did because they have a function: to protect well balanced, harmonious genotypes from dilution. In short, biologists have a over-all theory by which their aggregations and classifications can, at least to some degree, be validated.

Illustrative Classification

The closest analogy to the biological classification in the social disciplines is the breakdown by race. In demographic statistics such as the census, the division between whites and blacks has been a contentious and imprecise process. The definition of "race" has been continuously changed, and with each revision challenged anew. In population counts various devices have been used to approximate reality. In past censuses of the United States, the enumerator designated each person's race by physical characteristics and presumed genealogy, sometimes (but unofficially) by the place where the person lived. In the segregated South, a person living in a black neighborhood was a black, and this was usually the case also in the rest of the country. In recent enumerations, in which the respondents themselves identified their race, the prior system fell apart. In 1980, for example, groups as small as the 14,000 Aleuts were distinguished, while more than 6.7 million persons placed themselves in the "Other" category. This half-rejection of ethnic classification was reinforced in the 1990 and 2000 counts, when many of those of mixed blood insisted on listing the supposed races of all their antecedents. There has been substantial pressure to drop the question on race from the next census.

Worse than the various definitions of "blacks" in population counts has been the association of this clumsily aggregated collectivity with not only biological but also cultural characteristics. There is a large literature on prejudice and discrimination, some of it merely self-serving but much of it valid. The main issue is how to cope with probability: if young black males constitute a high percentage of convicted criminals, is it unreasonable of law-enforcement officials—and the public—to regard all young black males with greater suspicion? Most of the decisions that everyone has to make are based on assessing the probability of alternative choices, and in general this is accepted as reasonable behavior. Are "race profiles" also logical and therefore acceptable?

As another example, consider "the old." Setting off the category by an arbitrary line—those aged 60+, 65+, or whatever—is just as frustrating as trying to make ethnic or racial distinctions. Of the characteristics of old people that everyone "knows," most are dubious or false, or true only on the same probabilistic basis. Yet it is routine to ignore the percentage, whatever it is, that deviates from the norm and speak of "the old" as a unit, or to divide the old into several subcategories—each of which has the same faults. The main difference from similar statements about blacks is that old age is usually a less sensitive subject.

Race and age are similar in that there is a biological underpinning, which may help an analyst in making reasonable choices when he fashions his categories and arranges them in a taxonomy. Other distinctions that those in the social disciples habitually use have no external affinities; they are completely human inventions. Take as an example—one totally lacking any ideological content—the way the United States is divided into regions. How persons living in "the Middle West" or "the South" differ statistically from other Americans depends in large part on how these places are delineated. The regions of the United States were drawn following the 1870 census by one Henry Gannet, and with minor revisions his schema has been maintained ever since. However useful the partition into four regions (and, within them, nine divisions) may have been at the time, it is relatively meaningless today. The principal fault is that the regions as defined are composed of whole states, which very often are too heterogeneous to make useful building blocks. Far better units are, for example, the so-called BEA (from Bureau of Economic Analysis) economic areas, each of which consists of a Standard Metropolitan Statistical Area or similar core and the surrounding counties. A total of 183 economic areas so drawn covers the entire country, and by combining them one can fashion larger units that are relatively homogeneous in specific cultural or economic attributes.

Another example is the seemingly obvious pair employed-unemployed. In the United States a sample of the civilian noninstitutional population aged 14+ are asked each month whether they worked for pay during a specified week. Variation in data so collected becomes apparent when American statistics are compared with those of other industrial countries. If we calculate by the American criteria used before 1980, the British rate of 1.9 percent unemployed would rise to 2.8 percent, the Italian rate of 6.3 percent would fall to 3.2 percent. In Japan those temporarily laid off are "employed," in the United States "unemployed." The "self-employed" are characterized as employed in the American system but not in many others. In 1979 a commission that had been established to propose reforms of labor force data submitted its report, and if its recommendations are ever fully accepted, this will mean that comparisons over time will be as puzzling as those over space.

As another instance, "urban" relates either to large aggregates of people or to their typical institutions and way of life. The inherently complex contrast between a city and the countryside, formalized as one between urban and rural, is aggravated by inconsistent terminology, particularistic theorizing, and poor statistics. For the first century of the Republic, "urban" was used to define a place that had been granted a charter by the state government, with minimum populations ranging among the states from 100 to 1,000. Subsequently definitions changed every decade or two, with adaptations to such new (or newly recognized) phenomena as metropolitan areas, suburbs, urban fringes, and so on. To what degree is there such an entity as "urbanism," the manner of living specific to city dwellers? Certainly the contrast with family farms was sharp, but farmers later adopted many of the ways once associated with towns.

In subsequent chapters, I will describe features of populations or ethnic groups with the conventional divisions that had been contrived as I have suggested with these several examples. Occasionally, I will remind the reader of the limitations of the analysis, but I hope that he will keep them in mind throughout. It would be a vast improvement in his understanding of all works in the social disciplines if he learns be constantly aware of how the entities had been aggregated and classified.

Part I

Population

1

The Fundamentals of Demography

The word "population" derives from the Latin *populus,* people. Like most verbal nouns, a population once designated either a process or a state. One of the charges made against King George III in the Declaration of Independence was that he "endeavored to prevent the population of these states," but in this sense of "growth in numbers" the word has become archaic. The English language never developed a full equivalent of the French *peuplement.*

There is also an obsolete word, "population," derived from a different Latin root, which means devastation or laying waste. With the word in that sense, the last reference in the *Oxford English Dictionary* is from 1747, but it is surprising that it has not been revived by one of the more zealous proponents of controlling the increasing number of the world's human beings.

As demographers understand the term, the population of a designated area is the number of persons who, by specified criteria, are there on a particular date. In counting the members of any areal unit, one can enumerate either all who in some sense belong there (whether or not they are currently present) or all who are physically in residence (whether or not that is their legal domicile). The first is called the population de jure, the second the population de facto. Some nations count one, some the other.

Population Statistics

In a strict sense the census is a product of modern times. The counts made by various ancient peoples were only of the portion of a population that, for example, paid taxes or could be conscripted for military service.

What is the population of the United States? To this seemingly simple query, there is no single correct answer. There are three official totals: the civilian population, the total resident population, and

9

the total population including Americans living abroad. The practice of the United States in distributing census forms abroad is to use whatever facilities seem to be useful, such as Army and Navy auspices for their personnel and airlines and passenger ships for others. American consulates have the forms available, but persons not on the public payroll who live abroad are recorded only if they themselves take the trouble to register.

The most general supplement to periodic counts of all the people in a designated area is one or another form of vital statistics. These are made up of a continuing registration of births and deaths (or of the religious ceremonies accompanying them), as well as changes in civil status marked by a marriage, divorce, annulment, or separation; an adoption or legitimation; as well as sometimes fetal deaths, the state of health, moves from one residence to another, and so on.

In the Western world such data were compiled first by churches, only later by secular institutions, and there are serious deficiencies concerning the accuracy and completeness of especially the earliest records. In the United States the so-called registration areas comprised all states in which the numbers of births and deaths listed were judged to be at least 90 percent complete. It was not until 1933 that, with this rather casual definition of completeness, both the fertility and the mortality of the whole country were designated as fully measured.

International migration, formally defined as a movement across the border between nations, has been recorded in modern times, but with much ambiguity and sloppiness. Many analysts have omitted those who cross borders without permission, but illegal migrants have constituted a very high proportion, perhaps in some years even a majority, of those who have moved across international borders since the Second World War.

The fact that data on international movements are an adjunct of state control means that national concerns largely determine the statistics. Thus, the countries' far lesser interest in those departing than in those arriving has meant that the expected parity between the two figures is generally not even approximated. In 1977, the UN Economic Commission for Europe published a study of how migrants were counted at both ends of the 342 paths between any two ECE countries. The number of recorded immigrants was 57 percent greater than that of emigrants. With that much inaccuracy in the documentation of legal migration within a region with the world's best population statistics, one must be wary of conclusions about recorded movements anywhere else.

Errors

Errors occur in every type of demographic data, and a good deal of professional demographers' expertise is concentrated on pinpointing deviations from accuracy, estimating their probable size, and making suitable adjustments. An undercount is generally more frequent and larger than an overcount. Sectors at a society's periphery—the homeless, casual laborers, criminals, and near-criminals—are always the most difficult to count and therefore the most likely to be overlooked. Throughout the world, census bureaus often exclude (or, at best, enumerate with less precision) such marginal sectors of the population as residents of the shantytowns that ring cities of less developed countries, the Indian jungle population in parts of South America, or the nomads in some countries of northern Africa.

Since an enumeration of residents is almost always divided between citizens and aliens, the accuracy of a count may be affected by the complicated legal definitions of nationality, which differ considerably from one country to another. In the United States, the 1940 census was the first in which a comparison was made of the census count of aliens with the registration by the Immigration and Naturalization Service. There was a disconcertingly large difference between the enumeration (based on each person's self-identity) of about 3.5 million and the registration (a summation of persons defined as aliens in a legal context) of about 5 million. One can assume that in every census many aliens report themselves as citizens.

One common source of error is that some respondents misunderstand the instructions concerning census questions. The Bureau of the Census tests each query in several locations before it is included in the schedule, but even so the wording sometimes generates bizarre replies. Haley Barbour, formerly the chairman of the Republican National Committee, likes to recall an incident when he was director of the Mississippi census:

> One day a bunch of us were sitting around the office in Jackson looking at some business census forms. I'll never forget, we got one response from a little mom-and-pop operation up in Iuka, Mississippi. As they went down the questionnaire they came to the question, "Number of employees broken down by sex." And they answered that question, "None broken down by sex, but we have two with a drinking problem."

In 1970 the United States census schedule asked persons to identify themselves as of Mexican, Puerto Rican, Cuban, South or Central American, or other Spanish origin. The total count of all these
Hispanics or Latinos was 1,508,886, contrasted with fewer than
600,000 in both the 1969 and the 1971 Current Population Surveys.
As the Bureau later noted, "Some respondents apparently interpreted
the category 'Central or South American' to mean central or southern United States."

When the 1920 census reported that there were only 81,338
foreign-born Japanese in the United States, some racist newspapers
questioned the accuracy of the datum. Ten years earlier the census
count had been 67,655, and during the decade the net immigration
amounted to 67,108. Seemingly, if one took into account the probable death rate of a population with many old people, the 1920 figure represented an undercount of some 55 percent. In fact, the apparent error was due to the different ways that two federal agencies
defined "the United States." By the usage of the Bureau of the Census, the territory of Hawaii, with its sizable number of Japanese
Americans, was excluded, but the Commissioner of Immigration
included territories. When the figures were assigned to the proper
populations with estimates of the probable changes during the decade, the count in 1920 proved to be not lower but slightly higher
than an extrapolation from 1910.

The residence, the place where one customarily or legally lives,
can be interpreted in various ways, which affect not only the stated
size of a population but also how its characteristics are recorded.
Occasionally, persons establish a pseudoresidence in order, for instance, to gain a tax advantage or to run for electoral office. When
unmarried college students, previously counted as residents of
their parents' homes, were redefined as residing where they were
temporarily living, this increased the official populations of college towns. For example, the population of Chapel Hill, the site of
the University of North Carolina, jumped from 3,654 in 1940 to
9,177 in 1950. Not only the number of people but also their median
age, income, occupations, sex ratio, and so on changed radically
when a redefinition of a technical term brought about a large influx
of teenagers.

Whenever it is possible, statisticians try to find a quantitative measure of each qualitative attribute. In United States censuses, for example, education is measured by the years of schooling completed.

Over the decades this index has risen appreciably, though by more meaningful measures the population's learning has not improved nearly so much and during some periods may have declined.

Editing and Imputation

The returns in an American census are edited in various ways before the data are printed. The 1990 census schedules, which each person was to send in by mail, were then reviewed in the field against lists of local residences in order to pick out those lacking any information about the people supposedly living in them. In that year I took a temporary job as such a field editor to pursue these no-shows in two towns in California. In Pebble Beach many houses are the second homes of well-to-do families who actually live, say, in San Francisco; the dwellings were often empty, and neighbors knew little or nothing about the owners. In Carmel, which prides itself on maintaining a village-like ambiance, such routine urban conveniences as house numbers are verboten. On the list I was given, homes of presumably missing residents were identified as, for instance, "a green house catty-cornered from the two-story brick building." Though sometimes I could not find such places, I was able to fill in many gaps and correct some errors. I was also made aware as never before in my professional career as a demographer why it is impossible to compile a fully accurate record of a population of several hundred million.

Once this field editing has been completed, the data are processed at one of the offices of the Bureau of the Census. When data are fed into a computer, it is programmed to perform a so-called validation check, detecting such errors as coding "3" for sex when only "1" or "2" is permissible. The program also fills in some information omitted on the form but unambiguously implied in other responses. If the space specified for sex is left blank, for example, it can be indicated by a given name or a self-identification as a wife. The computer can also correct such impossible combinations as a male "housewife," a "widow" aged 10 years, a native-born "alien," and the like—though it may not always be obvious which half of the contradiction is in error.

The computer is also programmed to use bits of evidence from the rest of the questionnaire or from other sources to make a plausible, but not necessarily correct, addition to the reported responses. Even more dubiously, data on supposedly similar components of the neighborhood are used to produce not only the characteristics but even the existence of persons or households. In the 1960 census, for instance, some "occupied" housing units had no one reported living in them; and a total of 776,665 persons, or 0.4 percent of the official count, were "imputed" by replicating nearby households on which there were data. In 1970, the census form asked a sample of households to give the 1969 income from wages or salaries for each person in the household who had worked, but for 11 percent of the households some part of the total income was similarly imputed. In many critics' view, such a difference between 0.4 percent and 11 percent is one between editing to which they do not object and so great a revision that the user of the resultant tables cannot be sure what they mean.

These issues were given a thorough public airing when lawsuits were brought to challenge some of the results in both the 1980 and the 1990 censuses, especially statistics that had been based on such imputations. Several large cities claimed to have lost millions of dollars in federal funding because of inaccurate counts of the poorer sectors of their populations. Though in both instances the Bureau of the Census won the court cases, in the second round of suits the matter was closed only when, in March 1996, the Supreme Court declined to review fresh appeals.

For the 2000 count the Bureau announced tentative plans to enumerate only about 90 percent of the population--that portion that would present fewest problems—and then to complete the census using sample surveys. Whether this procedure would conform with the provision in the Constitution prescribing the decennial count was also tested in federal courts. Republicans feared that, with this approximation of the actual number, the Democratic administration might increase the proportion of those sectors of the society that typically vote Democratic. A special three-judge panel, with two members who had been appointed by President Reagan and one by President Clinton, decided unanimously that using sampling would not conform with the law setting census procedures.

An alternative to imputation might be to revert to the practice the Bureau of the Census used before computer techniques were fully developed—that is, to include in each table a residual proportion labeled "Not stated" or "Unknown." This procedure would give users of the data a more honest, as well as more accurate, representation of what we really know about the population.

Demography

The word demography is derived from two Greek words meaning "people" and "description of." It was coined by the French political economist Achille Guillard in his *Éléments de Statistique Humaine, ou Démographie Comparée* (1855). Earlier writings about births and deaths, the growth in numbers, and the relation of population to other social processes went by different names: "political arithmetic" (used to denote the pioneer efforts of such mercantilist writers as the English professor of anatomy William Petty, who coined the phrase); "political economy" (the term current at the time of Thomas Robert Malthus to designate the study of population, among other topics); and "human statistics" or simply "statistics" (used particularly by German analysts of the early modern period).

In some ways demography is a fully developed discipline, with its own national and international professional societies, a wide range of journals, and many persons who identify themselves as demographers. Yet it has also been and still remains a rather amorphous congeries, made up of bits and pieces of other disciplines that everyone in the field assembles for himself. As the late American demographer Frank Notestein wrote in his last published paper, "Since the major part of our scientific equipment lies in our background professions, all of us tend to come to the subject with modes of thought, orientation, and prejudices of our background disciplines."

This kind of haphazard training, more or less inevitable for a pioneer of Notestein's generation, has largely continued, at least in the United States. Demography is usually taught in departments that offer advanced degrees not in that discipline but in sociology, economics, geography, statistics, or public health; and most aspiring demographers are thus required to become adept also in another set of skills. The consequence is that their training in mathematics and economics may often be less than optimal for population studies, and in biology and history typically close to nil. It means also that members of the discipline, with their diverse points of view, may find it difficult to cooperate or even to communicate fully.

If each American demographer, as Notestein remarked, evolves along a partly unique path, the same must be said a fortiori of each national school of demography. Since the last quarter of the nineteenth century, the dominant social issue related to population studies has differed from one country to another: in the United States, for many years, immigration and race relations; in Britain, historical demography and the statistics of less developed countries; in France, the low birth rate and how to raise it; in Italy, what is termed "constitutional demography," whose practitioners have stressed biological factors far more than in population studies elsewhere; in Central Europe, multinational populations; in the former Soviet Union, economic productivity; and, more recently, in most less developed countries, excess fertility and measures that might reduce it. In each context such emphases, while setting priorities for the most significant work, have also impeded the exchange of findings between one locale and another.

The subject matter of the discipline is conventionally divided between "formal" and "social" demography. There is a more or less fixed interrelation among fertility, mortality, and the structure of a population by age and sex. What is called formal demography, which often is based on technical and mathematical intricacies that laymen may not follow, is essentially the analysis of that interrelation and its effects. So-called social demography or population studies, on the other hand, comprises analyses of how population interacts with social, economic, political, geographic, and biological factors. As the nineteenth-century Belgian statistician Adolphe Quetelet pointed out, there is a polarization between practitioners who believe that demography is a natural science with the same kinds of discoverable laws as physics and chemistry and, on the other hand, those who hold that life and death can be truly understood only in relation to their enormously varied cultural and social settings. The regularity to be found in what he termed "moral statistics" (including data on marriage, divorce, crime, etc., as well as population per se) he saw as a social law comparable to a law of physics. The characteristics of "*l'homme moyen*," the average man, is based on "constant," "perturbative," or "accidental" causes that together set a central point and the dispersion around it.

The French economist and demographer Paul Vincent, who helped compile the first multilingual demographic dictionary, wrote an eloquent article describing how difficult he found it to ferret out an acceptable definition of demography and thus an appropriate list of its main terms and concepts. Participating in the compilation of such a work, he found, forced him to rethink matters that he assumed he already knew. For four years Renee Petersen and I worked to write another *Dictionary of Demography,* with again the same series of perplexities about the nature of the beast we were trying to describe.

In each case the basic dilemma, as Vincent put it, was whether to define demography in a "restrictive" or an "extensive" manner. In arguing for the second alternative, he asked the reader to imagine the reaction of someone who, "in order to translate a work on *demography*, had to resort to a whole series of technical dictionaries—sociological, juridical, medical, economic, etc.—after having vainly searched his 'demographic' dictionary for terms currently used in demography." To satisfy fully the supposed user of a dictionary, in short, would require at least brief excursions into all the fields associated with population: biology in relation to birth and death; medicine and epidemiology; law in its regulation of such matters as euthanasia, abortion, international migration, and so on; mathematics, statistics (in particular, vital statistics), and computer science; large slices of sociology, political science, economics, anthropology, geography, and psychology.

From the 1950s on, moreover, there was a marked shift from earlier description or analysis to a frequent emphasis on recommended policies, with important consequences on how demographic data and techniques were regarded. About the same time a new approach emerged called "demographics," meaning the analysis of population data as these relate, for example, to the markets for particular commodities. Since obviously no single discipline can be all-inclusive over so vast a range, to some degree the limits of demography remain indeterminate and mutable.

Open or Secret Data

International statistics encompass a basic contradiction. For scholars, the cold quantitative record of nations' achievements and failures is the neutral subject matter of their discipline. Those more concerned with what they deem to be the national interest, however, have often objected to the public display of such facts, and many have used their countries' publications to broadcast misleading or false data.

In 1853, at a statistical congress meeting in Brussels, representatives of twenty-six countries tried to establish the definitions and procedures that would make the data collected by all governments fully comparable. The permanent commission that evolved out of that congress, however, could get no more than partial and reluctant cooperation from the several nations. Over the years Germans objected even to the convention that the proceedings were published in French, at the time the standard language of diplomacy. The commission lasted until the Franco-Prussian War, and its successor, which met at irregular intervals between 1878 and 1912, almost foundered during the First World War. Yet the International Statistical Institute did survive, and its serial *Aperçu de la Démographie des Divers Pays du Monde* became for a period the most important source of international population data. Eventually it was superseded by the several series of the United Nations and other international agencies established after the Second World War.

Though such works reflect the substantial improvement in professional demographic standards over the past several decades, they also display the spread of statistical recording—of a sort—to a wide array of countries with neither the ability nor usually the will to maintain reasonable standards of accuracy. How should a responsible reference work deal with the publications of a country that combines in some technical work of a high quality with a frequent indifference to scholarly objectivity? The issue is fundamental to a large body of publications in various disciplines that are often accepted unquestioningly. Specialists express doubt about the statistics of the former Soviet Union or of Communist China, but the usual practice is to cite population figures of African countries, for instance, as given, with no warning to the uninformed reader that these are estimates at best and, in many cases, figures that have been falsified in order to present the regimes with the best image possible.

A more general deficiency of population statistics is analyzed in the various works of the American demographer Eugene M. Kulischer, especially in his principal book, *Europe on the Move: War and Population Changes, 1917-47*. In his view, history is a continuous battleground. Though, as demographic institutions ordinarily define their task, "the role of cataclysms is minimized," in fact changes take place "not only by 'normal' fertility and mortality but also by wars, epidemics, and other forms of excess mortality, as well as by the uprooting of peoples." When I introduced into an elementary textbook on population a detailed account of politically sponsored mortality in totalitarian states, this new departure was criticized by several more traditional demographers. In my opinion, my implied definition of the discipline represented not only a fuller but also a more realistic view of twentieth-century conditions.

2

Population Structure

For a demographic analysis the most important classification of any population is one by age and sex, for which the term is population structure. The reason, of course, is that almost all behavior patterns diverge along those two dimensions, partly because of physiology, partly because everywhere cultural norms differ between males and females and between children, adults, and the old.

Changes in the age and sex structure affect everything. If the market for toys contracts, the one for rock music will expand. When the number of American women aged 40 to 54 was forecast at 30 million by the turn of the twentieth century, a magazine called *Quarante*, designed to appeal to American women over 40 who have "arrived," got a competitor called *Lear's*, which would concentrate on how women of a certain age could resolve conflicts between traditional and innovative values. Projected demand for housing involves marriage (and mating) trends, the probable size of families, and the range of home prices most likely to fit the available incomes, and an underlying factor—the age structure. In short, no matter what social phenomenon we want to analyze from politics through the market for consumer goods, the sex ratio and the relative sizes of age groups are relevant.

One might suppose that the age of a person is so unambiguous an attribute that it could be recorded with a full assurance of its accuracy. In fact, the concept is defined differently in various cultures. In China a child, assigned the age of 1 year at birth, becomes a year older at the beginning of each successive lunar year, so that by the Chinese reckoning everyone is between 1 and 3 years older than by the Western convention. In Bangladesh there is a confusion between Western, Bengali, and Muslim calendars, all of which are in current use. Many persons in less developed countries do not know how old they are; and in literate populations age is often misstated, because the respondents do not know it, report it only approximately, or refuse to respond altogether.

If we arrange the elements of a bar graph to represent successive ages from the lowest at the bottom to the highest at the top, each divided between males at the left and females at the right, the typical shape of the graph will be a pyramid. For of those born in, say, 1900, some will have died each year since then, gradually reducing the length of the bars representing successively higher ages. Usually, however, the shape is not a perfect pyramid, for mortality varies by sex and from one age to the next, and because fertility and migration also affect the population structure. A depletion caused by a past famine or epidemic, or by a period of especially low fertility or large emigration, is represented by an indentation from a smooth pyramid; and a period of exceptionally high fertility or of large immigration is represented by a corresponding bulge. These irregularities remain on population pyramids of successive dates, gradually moving up to the top of the graph and disappearing only when the persons concerned finally die off.

Connections between various parts of the age structure are analyzed by cohorts. Until rather recently dictionaries defined the word "cohort" as one of the ten divisions of a Roman legion or, by extension, any band of warriors, with citations in both senses back to the fourteenth century. Among demographers, "cohort" is used to mean all those who during a single year (or other period) have gone through a particular demographic experience, such as being born (a birth cohort), getting married (a marriage cohort), and so on. We have all become familiar with the use of the concept in commercial or political writings—the Young Marrieds; the Gray Panthers; the baby boomers, who grew up to become the Yuppies and then moved into post-Yuppydom. In Britain, journalists labeled a group around an extravagantly produced leftist magazine, which features its own regular wine column, the Yummies, or Young Upwardly Mobile Marxists.

Problems of Innumeracy

We Americans, it would seem, are unduly impressed by statistics, and we are constantly fed figures of all kinds. A periodical called *Harper's Index* compiles such bits of information—for example, that 42 percent of Americans regularly attend religious services, that 150 schools invited Lee Iacocca to speak at their graduation ceremonies, and so on. Advertising agencies, presumably following tests of relative effectiveness, insistently inform us, for instance, that 83.2 percent of health professionals recommend a certain product. Many such figures are, if not made up, then based on so slight a foundation that we should automatically dismiss them. But to assure ourselves that a count is reasonably accurate is only the first step toward understanding what the statistics mean.

Absolute numbers used to compare entities of grossly different dimensions are almost always misleading, and it may not help to convert the absolute figures into percentages. During the Soviet Union's first two five-year plans, when published statistics on industrial production were very sparse indeed, comparative percentages appeared relatively often: in the United States, production of steel, say, rose by 3 percent, in the Soviet Union by 17 percent—but, as we were not told, from widely divergent bases. In an example discussed by Galileo, if a horse worth a hundred dollars is appraised at ten dollars by one person and at one thousand dollars by another, who deviated more from the true value? Galileo held that the two were equally in error, since $1,000:100 = 100:10$, but that is not the only "correct" answer.

A rate is a device for comparing the actual with the potential. We put the number of births in a year in the numerator and the population in which they occurred in the denominator and get a figure, called the crude birth rate, that generally ranges from around 10 to 50 or more. It is called "crude" because some portion of those in the denominator designated as potential mothers are, in fact, children, males, or women beyond the age of childbearing. So in a first adjustment, we change the denominator to females aged, say, 15 to 44. But both the physiological ability to bear a child and the cultural stimuli to family formation vary greatly over that age range, and to be more precise we calculate separately birth rates for females aged 15–19, 20–24, and so on and then sum them up. As this familiar example illustrates, perhaps the most useful refinement of a crude rate of any activity is to break it down by sex and by age group.

It may be enlightening to exemplify from several actual cases how misleading it can be to interpret statistics that have been offered without taking population structure into account:

- In a 1905 Massachusetts state census, married women were asked how many children they had borne (an average of 2.77) and how many their mothers had borne (an average of 6.47). There had been, in other

words, a disastrous decline in family size over only one generation—
the consequence, undoubtedly, of one or another deleterious custom.

But the fertility-in-process of the respondents, who ranged in age
from 18 up, was compared with the completed fertility of the respondents' mothers, all of whom were past the childbearing period.

> • During the Spanish-American War, the Secretary of War used his an-
> nual report to respond to public criticism about the large number of
> soldiers dying in the Philippines. Their death rate, he pointed out, was
> almost identical with that of the civilian population of Washington.

But the soldiers were all in the age group with normally the lowest
mortality; the civilians were of all ages.

> • Proponents of the restrictive immigration laws that were enacted in
> the 1920s often contrasted immigrants' birth and crime rates with the
> much lower ones of the native population (and a similar restrictive
> policy is now being advocated with the same argument).

But immigrants are mainly in the age group from which both parents and criminals come; in the first decades of this century well
over half of those convicted of crimes were young males, who are
everywhere more likely to be arrested.

> • The family income of various ethnic groups in the American popula-
> tion ranges from well over one and a half times the national average
> (Jews) down to under two-thirds of the average (American Indians). Of
> the many reasons that could be given for the differences, the one most
> often cited is discrimination.

But an important factor is the median age—ranging from the mid-
30s to the mid-40s (Jews, Poles, Irish, Italians, and Germans) or
from 18 to the low 20s (blacks, American Indians, Puerto Ricans,
and Mexicans). Men and women of whatever ethnicity who are well
along in their careers generally earn more than those who recently
entered the work force.

> • During the 1970s, baby boomers flooded the labor market, but for the
> next ten years or so only about half as many people, the products of
> the baby bust, would enter the labor force each year. This was ex-
> pected to bring about a fall in unemployment and a possible rise in the
> wages of young workers.

But because black fertility rates remained high, blacks made up about
a fifth of new entrants, or double the percentage a decade earlier.
Many were less educated and unskilled, aggravating the unemployment problem rather than the contrary. In this case, a breakdown by

age had to be supplemented with one by race to avoid misunderstanding.

> • The last census of the Soviet Union, in 1979, included the usual question on age, as we know from the enumeration schedule. In a nontotalitarian country such a basic datum would be in the very first publications of census results. However, except for a few partial citations of minor importance, no age data were published. How is it that even after the era of Soviet "openness" had been proclaimed, officials somehow overlooked this omission?

Murray Feshbach, the most knowledgeable of the American sovietologists on such matters, acquired a set of age and sex data for four republics of the USSR. The change in the sex ratio of children from 1970 to 1979 indicated that infant mortality had increased during the intercensal period by between a third and a half. Statistics for the four republics, which approximate four ethnic components of the USSR, showed that the Russian, Ukrainian, and Latvian sectors were declining relative to the Uzbek—and presumably other Muslim sectors. Because of shifts in age structure, the growth of the work force would be much slower and also concentrated in the non-Slavic population. In short, the publication of merely age and sex statistics can inform such a demographer as Feshbach about changes in the population with highly significant economic, social, and military implications.

Population Structure and Growth in Numbers

Several decades ago, at the height of the movement to usher zero population growth (ZPG) into the United States, a student asked me to sign a petition endorsing that goal. To realize his objective, I tried to explain to him, was more complex than its sponsors seemed to realize: zero growth would mean that more than half the population would be aged over 30—the sector that the same student was denouncing as untrustworthy. He thought I was pulling his leg. What did growth in numbers have to do with the relative size of age sectors?

The campaign that the student supported was conducted vociferously by his organization, Zero Population Growth, Inc. It reflected the well publicized views of its first president, Paul Ehrlich, author of such works as *The Population Bomb* (2nd ed., 1971) and the most persistent of the country's antinatalist zealots. The most striking characteristic of the organization's members was their youth, with a median age under 30 and full-time students constituting well over a third of the total. To the extent that this organization can be taken as typical of the antinatalist movement, the pressure in the United States for ZPG was generated largely by male college students and young men who had recently graduated from college. These were the boom babies on the threshold of maturity, whose recommended policies reflected their experiences with overcrowded schools and, after graduation, shortages of attractive job opportunities.

The term "zero population growth" has been used with several meanings, and the phrase hardly represents the *mots justes* for several of them. The brochures of the ZPG organization, like most popular accounts of attempts to cut the birth rate, ignored a key determinant of population growth—namely, the age structure. If efforts to reduce fertility focus only on cutting the number of children per family, and if the number of families increases, the population may continue to grow. And, vice versa, if the number of families is small, even a sizable progeny per family will not reverse a trend toward depopulation. The same slipshod logic has permeated much of the propaganda advocating assistance to antinatalist programs in less developed countries. The boom babies who reached childbearing age could form so many new families that even if each couple had only 2.1 offspring (the approximate number needed to replace the parents and make up for sterility and deaths at early ages), the total number of children in the United States would have grown by a considerable number. That is why virtually every demographer then believed that the baby boom would have an "echo"; the actual decline in American fertility was the unexpected consequence of a fall in family size so great that it more than made up for the larger number of young people entering the prime reproductive ages. Because American women postponed longer than had been anticipated in both getting married and, subsequently, starting a family, the echo came later than expected. By the late 1990s, thus, there were some 72 million boys and girls of school age, with again an especially heavy crowding in the country's high schools.

In several interesting publications, the American economist Richard Easterlin has used the details of this cycle to build a theory of family formation. When the national birth rate is high (as during the baby boom and, again, during the delayed echo), the competition within the large cohorts will tend to result in a higher rate of unemployment, lower wages, and slower advancement. Therefore, members of that generation will tend to marry later and put off longer having children, and more of the women will seek jobs outside the home. Economic strains will result in higher rates of divorce. When, on the contrary, cohorts entering the work force are relatively small, economic opportunities will be abundant and young people will marry earlier and have more children.

A second meaning given to "zero population growth" is also simplistic—that, with no regard to age structure, the total population remains constant from one year to the next. But the slogan calling on Americans to achieve zero growth by the year 2000 was visionary, for the continuous shifts in age structure would generally result in significant changes in the subsequent rate of growth. If there is no migration and if age-specific birth and death rates remain constant for as much as a century, the fluctuations in the population's rate of growth will finally end. In the so-called stable population that is thus brought into being, both the age structure and the rate of growth (which can be negative, zero, or positive) remain fixed. A stable population with no growth is called stationary, and this is the meaning that demographers assign to what the antinatalists term "zero population growth."

Males and Females

A person's sex is obviously a major determinant of his or her behavior. Both biology and culture set many differences between males and females, and often a distinction is made between "sex," related to physiological impulses and constraints, and "gender," the comparable effects of the culture. However, some in the social disciplines are so inclined to understate biological factors that they use "gender" to denote the whole range of characteristics: there have been journal papers in which the authors discuss what they term "gender hormones."

The sex ratio is defined as the number of males per 100 females. The primary sex ratio (or the number of males conceived per 100 females) has been the subject of much speculation, but with no conclusive resolution; it is not known. The secondary sex ratio (or the number of males born per 100 females) has ranged worldwide between 104 and 107. In the United States it fell from 105.3 in 1969 to 104.9 in 1995, and the breakdown of this change is interesting, because it is more than a bit puzzling. When controlled for maternal and paternal ages and the infant's birth order, the sex ratio at birth fell among white mothers but rose among black mothers. The shift is significant: a change of 1 per 100 females represents nearly 4,000 newborns per year. Among the possible reasons cited, perhaps the most likely is that black females typically have higher levels of estrogen than whites.

In most cultures parents generally prefer a boy to a girl, especially as their first child. Two gynecologists devised a method based on the relative acidity/alkalinity of the uterus that may enable a couple to realize that preference by timing the conception at a particular point in the menstrual cycle. If this procedure works and if many parents were to adopt it, the changed sex ratio of children would alter various characteristics of the population. For example, if a population with a typical sex ratio at birth of 105 doubled in 118 years, raising this sex ratio to 116 would increase the doubling time to 178 years.

A grossly skewed sex ratio has effects that permeate the entire culture. Of the early Chinese immigrants to the United States, for instance, virtually all were young males; the more than 100,000 Chinese enumerated in the American censuses of 1880 and 1890 included only about 4,000 females. Since in most of the country racial intermarriage was then illegal, usually men could satisfy their sexual urge only with prostitutes: a civil society built on normal family life was unachievable. Similarly, the culture of the Old West, or of most European colonies during their heyday, or of almost any other frontier area, reflected the effects of a surplus of males and the consequent dearth of family life.

When the sex ratio is close to parity, according to the conventional view, men and women in a Western society pair off and form families. The actual process is likely to be more complex, as suggested by the fact that the word "family" has been ambiguous since it entered the language. It derives from *famulus*, a servant, and the route to its present meaning has been circuitous. The earliest definition of "family" given in the *Oxford English Dictionary*, with citations going back to the fifteenth century, is "the servants of a house or establishment; the household." The primary present-day meaning is "the group of persons consisting of parents and their children, whether living together or not; in a wider sense, the unity formed by those who are connected by blood or affinity"; but in this sense the earliest citation is from a 1667 work of John Milton. That is to say, the confusion between a household and a family, a frequent problem in interpreting demographic statistics, is found also in the etymological history of the word. Since data are often not available to distinguish precisely between a family and a household, the stated size of a "family" may be no more than a rough indicator of fertility.

What anthropologists term the "nuclear family," or a married couple and their minor children living together apart from other kin, was until recently taken to be the universal norm in Western societies. Variations resulting from different patterns of marriage and remarriage, or from the adoption of children, or from sharing the residence with other kin, boarders, or servants, were regarded as aberrations or extensions of the standard. In recent publications, reflecting a shift in cultural norms, the Bureau of the Census has defined a family as any two or more members of a household who are related by blood, marriage, or adoption—a definition that has little relation to the earlier notion that the institution, comprising two parents and their children, was one key to measuring fertility. This statistical imprecision has been aggravated by pressure to include in the concept such anomalous types as one-person households, single mothers and their children, and two homosexuals sharing a residence.

The Adult and the Old

Relations between generations partly depend, of course, on how age groups are defined. Physiology sets a sequence of periods in the human life cycle, but it is difficult to decide at what ages the most important transitions take place. For example, the American psychologist Daniel Levinson approximated the stages with overlapping ages: childhood (ages 0–22), early adulthood (17–45), middle adulthood (40–65), late adulthood (60–85), and very late adulthood (80–?). The American demographer Jacob Siegel divided those at or close to retirement into several subclasses, often with markedly different physical and social characteristics: "the older population" (60+), "the elderly" (65+), "the aged" (75+), and "the extreme aged" (85+).

As defined by various criteria, "maturity" has often been postponed long beyond what it is either by physiological criteria or by the cultures of most less developed countries. Of 25-year-olds in the United States, at a recent date more than one-fifth lived with their parents. About four out of ten young men, having once left their parents' home, returned to it. Many were free to spend their wages on themselves and pay no rent. As pointed out in an interesting paper in *American Demographics* (April 1996), "Children may become adults anywhere between 12 and 25 years, [depending on what criterion is used, whether] a person can drive or rent a car, vote, be drafted, drink or purchase alcohol, get married, have an abortion without parental consent."

Problems of the old are concentrated among those aged 85+. In the United States as in other developed countries, data concerning them are poor. Their ages as reported in the census are notoriously inaccurate, and statistics on income, health, and other conditions of life are certainly no better. The number of the oldest old is estimated at 2.6 million, or only 1 percent of the population; and even if that sector of the population doubles in the next few years, which is quite likely, this roughly 2 percent of the population will not in itself constitute a serious burden. The problem would arise by a change in the ratio between the proportion of the population in the labor force and the proportion that has either not yet entered it or has retired from it.

Age Structure and Dependency

The convention among demographers is to divide the whole age range into three sectors—persons aged, respectively, 0–14, 15–64, and 65+. Thus, the dependency ratio, or dependents compared with producers, is defined as those aged 0–14 plus those aged 65+, compared with those aged 15–64. In the United States (assuming unrealistically that all persons between 15 and 64 were in the labor force), every three persons who were working in 1980 supported two persons either below or above those productive ages. As the boom babies (those born in the surge of high birth rates in the late 1940s and most of the 1950s) move into retirement, this relatively comfortable ratio will be cut substantially. The precise ratio will depend on the average age of retirement and other mutable factors, but at best the age structure will present the producers in the population with sharpening dilemmas.

In most countries of the West the two types of dependency have moved in opposite directions, with fewer dependent children and somewhat more dependent aged. Every one of the fifteen countries of the European Union, in spite of the many significant differences among them, is undergoing a rise in the median age, and extrapolations to the year 2020 suggest that the trend will continue. Despite such programs in the United States as the former Aid to Families with Dependent Children and school lunches, most American children are cared for privately in a family setting. Most elderly persons receive at least partial governmental care, ranging from Social Security and Medicare as a minimum to public institutionalization. Put another way, the taxes used to provide for the old partly determine the size of after-tax incomes, and this remnant is one factor in potential parents' decisions about how many children they will have.

This thesis is often framed in reverse, that in less developed countries, which typically have few or no social security benefits, parents depend on their children to care for them in their old age and therefore have a strong motive to propagate lavishly. In Poland there is (or there used to be) a folk custom called *dozywocie*; parents distribute their property not in a will but at retirement, giving the most reliable son an extra share in return for a commitment to support his parents for the rest of their lives. Analyses of advanced economies are often based on cross-national studies of "the value of children" as measured by how much they cost the parents to raise and how much return the parents can expect from their offspring once they mature.

In a primitive society one way of dealing with the unproductive aged is politely labeled geronticide, whether by killing off infirm old people or exposing them to the elements. The custom was reportedly so well established among Eskimos that a person too old to contribute to the always precarious economy of the household took off himself (or herself) to die and thus gave the remaining family members a better chance of surviving.

In advanced civilizations before the modern age, on the other hand, often the elderly were revered. In *Japanese Things*, a delightful account of nineteenth-century Japan, Basil Hall Chamberlain summarized an ethical primer, "Four and Twenty Paragons of Filial Piety," that was used in both that country and China to train the young in the proper respect for the old. One Paragon slept uncovered so that any mosquitoes would attack him and leave his parents undisturbed; another, though 70 years old, crawled about in baby's clothes in order to delude his 90-year-old parents into believing that they could not be so old after all. In a society with a relatively unchanging culture whose traditions are held in great esteem, it is appropriate that the old exercise great authority. Granting them special deference and honor, moreover, entails relatively little sacrifice, for in such a society the proportion who survive to anything approaching three score and ten is always very small.

At first, the aging of Western populations was mainly the result of declining birth rates, but in the last several decades the trend has been reinforced by successful therapies for some of the diseases from which old people are most likely to die. It is worth stressing such contrary instances to counter the persistent emphasis on ailments like Alzheimer's disease, which brings about a loss of organic functions and intellectual acuity.

When serious gerontological studies began a generation or two ago, researchers looking for subjects typically used those conveniently assembled in "old people's homes." This subsector, though quite atypical of the whole age group, was long used to characterize the old, and we may still be in the process of correcting the false impressions we were all taught. As late as the 1950s, it is true, more than a third of the elderly in the United States were living in poverty, but since 1982 the poverty rate of the older population has been under that of the general population. Today the age bracket of Americans with the greatest wealth per capita, those aged 55 to 64, is followed by the next older, those aged 65+. Those who retire with a private pension and Social Security generally maintain the same level of living as when they were working; more than 90 percent live either alone or with a spouse. According to recurrent Harris polls, most old people report that they are better off than the country believes them to be.

Generational Conflict

In developed societies, the elderly, generally, have come to be viewed as a social problem. One of the many translations of population structure into popular folklore is the familiar "conflict of generations," of which the most critical facet is what Germans call the *Rentenberg*, the mountain of taxes that in every Western country all others have to climb in order to fund welfare programs for the old.

The problem first became acute in France: the country's perennially low fertility, by reducing the percentage of children in the population, had increased that of the elderly. Moreover, many workers retired in late middle age, wanting no more than a modest home in a village and the opportunity to spend their evenings playing cards at the local café. As Alfred Sauvy, the principal French demographer of the past generation, once remarked, in his country the class conflict between capitalists and workers was being supplanted by one between those in the labor force and the growing number who had retired from it.

In 1889, when as chancellor of Germany Otto von Bismarck introduced the world's first state pension, he opened a Pandora's box that neither he nor any of his contemporaries had dreamt of. This was the beginning of the welfare state. When Bismarck opened the floodgates, life expectancy was 45 years; today, in the countries of the OECD, it is 76 and rising. Yet state pensions in all these countries can still be claimed either at 65, the age originally set, or in some countries at a lower age.

In the United States the American Association of Retired Persons (AARP) conducts one of the most powerful and effective lobbies in the national capital. Its Washington headquarters is ten stories high and almost a block long. The annual budget of half a billion dollars pays for a video production room, a well-stocked research center with many researchers, legions of lawyers and policy analysts. Only one member of Congress, Alan Simpson, a Republican Senator from Wyoming who was about to retire, has dared attack this "eight-hundred-pound gorilla," as the AARP is known among members of Congress. The hearings that Simpson conducted in 1995 concentrated on the well-based allegation that many of AARP's activities are commercial and that its tax-exempt status is therefore fraudulent.

Each year the AARP publishes a Public Policy Agenda, which forms the basis of activity by both its staff and the many volunteers who further its efforts. In 1999, as a typical year, the goals were concentrated on issues of most concern to the older sector of the American population: Social Security, Medicare, managed care, utilities, pensions, consumer protection, job equity. Several of these issues—in particular, those related to Social Security—have become among the most contentious that members of Congress hope to resolve. The AARP also conducts research on the characteristics of its target population and organizes its members locally to encourage voting and pressure on legislators.

Countering the AARP is the first lobbying group to represent young adults, a tiny organization called Americans for Generational Equity (AGE). A David opposed to a Goliath, AGE has championed "the long-term welfare of younger and future generations of Americans" through such reforms as a means test for Social Security benefits and tax incentives to induce persons to buy private retirement programs.

The contrast between the old and the adult, as indicated by that between AARP and AGE, omits a significant sector of the population. While the welfare of old people has improved considerably over the past several decades, that of the youngest has declined. In the early 1980s the age category with the highest incidence of poverty was the old; then it became children. It is not that the two sectors of the population compete directly for the same funds, but rather that various social trends, driven in part by political forces, have benefited one and not the other. One can reasonably question policies that ignore the welfare of future citizens, even while applauding those that raise the retired sector out of poverty.

How pervasive the preparation for old age has become in the United States can be seen from the succession of automatic or permitted steps from birth on:

Age, 1 day   May apply for Social Security number.

18 or 21   Depending on state law, acquire full control over assets in one's name.

19   No longer a dependent unless attending school, in which case the cutoff is postponed to age 24.

30   Under regulations guiding automobile insurance, an adult with reduced premiums.

50   Eligible to join AARP, with discounts on various goods and services.

62   Eligible for early-retirement benefits from Social Security. For those reaching this age in 2000 or later, the benefits were slightly smaller.

65   Eligible for full Social Security benefits and a wide variety of "senior citizen" discounts. For persons born in 1960 or later, the age for Social Security benefits was raised to 67.

70   Eligible for considerably larger Social Security benefits if one deferred application to this age.

70.5   Legal deadline for starting distribution of funds invested in retirement plans.

100   Insurance companies pay off on all life policies.

Though most members of Congress hesitated long before attacking an organization with 32 million members, in the mid-1990s for the first time Washington dared to cut back "entitlements," long deemed to be untouchable by any federal politician who wanted to remain in office. While most older citizens were satisfied with the status quo, younger ones were beginning to find the steep tax burden too onerous to be sustained, particularly since the trend in the age structure suggested that retirement benefits might no longer be available when their turn came to receive them.

In 1998 the largest annual cohort among the American baby boomers (4.6 million persons) had its 40th birthday. More American adults are putting away childish things and concentrating on such prosaic matters as job security, family stability, the safety of their home and children, the taxes on their incomes and property. The maturing of the baby-boom generation has meant also that input to the Social Security system, based on the number of persons in the labor force, is adequate for the present. However, from 1980 to 1996 the number of Americans aged 15 to 19 fell off by about 2.5 million, or 12 percent; as these cohorts of the baby bust move into the labor force, their smaller numbers will start a crunch in the funding of the system. With minor differences, this is also the status of old-age pensions in other industrial countries.

In sum, the age structure and, to a smaller degree, the sex ratio of any population have important effects on the country's economy and politics. In order to understand fully virtually any important policy debate, one should ask what is the population structure of the two sectors that are affected, one of which pays the costs of the proposed program, and the other that receives the benefits.

3

Population in History

Long-term trends in population are often discussed with what is termed the demographic transition. The phrase has acquired several meanings, of which the simplest can be briefly stated: the shift accompanying modernization is from Stage I, a relatively static population with high fertility and mortality, to Stage II, a rapid population growth based on a continuing high fertility and falling mortality, and then to Stage III, a relatively static population based on a new balance between low fertility and low mortality. In short, the initial dynamic factor was the control of mortality at early ages, which propelled the population surge of modern times, followed by efforts to control fertility.

In the extensive polemics about the demographic transition, several key points have been emphasized. As originally applied to the West, it oversimplified the complex interaction of social factors influencing population; and when the same schema was applied to less developed countries with the expectation that European history would be repeated stage by stage, the faults of the theory became more obvious. Even so, it is a convenient framework with which to discuss long-term shifts in population growth and its determinants.

Decline in Mortality

Deaths of children and particularly of infants are relatively common for two reasons. A baby, if born with defects, may not be able to remain alive very long; and any baby, even if born healthy, is especially susceptible to infectious disease and accidents. For a population lacking modern medicine, if we plot the percentage of deaths against the ages at which they take place, we construct a U-shaped curve, with very high rates in infancy and early childhood declining to a low point in early maturity and then gradually rising again in old age.

According to historical analyses of several regions of France, the expectation of life for the period 1680–1720 was about 25 years. This does not mean, of course, that everyone died by that age, but rather that the large proportion of deaths early in life, when balanced against the relatively few who survived to old age, averaged out at 25 years. Using these statistics as a base, the French economist Jean Fourastié spelled out the kind of life people led at that time. He invited the reader to consider an average family head, a man who had married for the first time at age 27. Born into a family of five children, of whom only half reached age 15, he also, like his father, had five children, of whom again only two or three were still alive when he died. Living to age 52, this man moved into the venerable elite, for only one in five males reached that advanced age. In his immediate family (not to speak of uncles and aunts, nephews and nieces, and first cousins), he survived an average of nine persons: one of his grandparents (the other three having died before his birth), his two parents, three siblings, and three of his children. He had lived through two or three famines as well as three or four periods of poor harvests and high-priced grain, which recurred every decade or so. He had lived also through sicknesses of his brothers and sisters, his children, his wife (or successive wives), his parents, and himself, having survived two or three epidemics as well as the more or less endemic whooping cough, scarlet fever, diphtheria, and so on. He had often suffered from such ailments as toothaches and slow-healing wounds. Poverty, disabilities, suffering were constantly with him. Death was the center of life, just as the cemetery was the center of the village. This was a representation of life not only of France at that time but also of the rest of the West and, until rather recently, of most of the less developed world.

A century or so later, around 1800, expectation of life from birth in the West had risen to around 35 to 40 years, about half of what it is today. In spite of the extension of the average age by 10 years or a bit more, life was still in some ways similar to Fourastié's reconstruction. Out of every five children born, one died before its fifth birthday and another before it reached maturity.

Falling Death Rates

The breakthrough to the modern control of mortality took place during the period from the last decades of the nineteenth century to the First World War. Infections that attack mainly infants were checked, so that the U-shaped curve lost most of its left leg, changing into a J-shaped curve. The remarkable cut in death at early ages was more or less equivalent to a sharp increase in fertility; babies survived that a few years earlier would have died, and for several generations, as a direct consequence, the population of industrial nations grew by unprecedented proportions.

There was also a marked change in the relative mortality of the two sexes. According to a United Nations' publication, in thirty-four less developed countries most of the sex ratios of deaths during the first year of life were between 100 and 119, but in thirty-one developed countries the comparable figures were between 120 and 139. Similarly, in industrial countries female mortality fell far more than male also at 15 to 24 years. Risks increased much more as male adolescents became young adults than among females of the same ages: as boys adopted adult roles, they entered the military, suffered many more accidents, and died more often from violence.

In a society without modern medicine, the greatest hazards for females are associated with pregnancy and childbirth, but in industrial countries significant developments in obstetrics reduced this prime risk considerably. Thus, the difference between men's and women's life expectation has widened throughout the West. In the United States, females live some 7 years longer than males; in the 65–74 age bracket, men's death rates are twice those of women. Moreover, in first marriages, grooms are on the average 2 years older than brides, and in the increasingly common remarriages, the average difference in age is 4 years. The cumulative effect is a vast production of widows, whose number in the United States increased over the past generation or so from fewer than 6 million to more than 10 million, while the far smaller number of widowers fell off.

For a period, this historic improvement in death control was restricted to the West, but from the time of the Second World War it spread to the rest of the world. The most startling early instance of a new pattern was in Ceylon, where the estimated expectation of life at birth rose from 43 years in 1946 to 52 in 1947. In most Western countries, the 9 years of longer life realized in twelve months had taken half a century to achieve. The amazing drop in mortality seemingly derived mainly from one factor—DDT, an insecticide that had been developed during the war; when sprayed from airplanes over low-lying areas, it all but eliminated malaria, the principal cause of death in Ceylon. Soon the same control was exercised elsewhere—

in India, Mauritius, portions of the Near East—wherever mosquitoes bred in large numbers. Before the war, malaria had been the most potent single cause of sickness and death, and within a few years the World Health Organization felt it appropriate to institute a campaign to eliminate it altogether. It did not succeed, partly because several species of mosquitoes became resistant to the insecticides being used, and partly because zealots, especially in the United States, tried to ban the use of DDT. Most of a special issue of the *WHO Chronicle* (May 1971) was devoted to that campaign; in the opinion of a wide range of health experts, the cost of withdrawing DDT before the development of an equally effective substitute would have been a disastrous worldwide resurgence of malaria.

Other ailments were brought under control by sulfa compounds and antibiotics. The threat of smallpox, a scourge for centuries, was so much reduced with mass vaccinations that in the mid-1970s several countries repealed the laws compelling everyone to be vaccinated. Such measures, from spraying insecticide to mass vaccinations, could be applied to the whole populations of less developed countries with minimum cooperation from the people affected. Expensive antibiotics and other supplies, as well as medical and administration personnel, were furnished mainly by Western taxpayers through the funding of international agencies and bilateral relief programs. Peasants all over the world who knew nothing of modern medicine in any other sense became quite familiar with penicillin. As before, the main effect was on infant and child mortality, and its decline was again equivalent to a rise in the birth rate—a rise, moreover, that was not accompanied by a change in the country's technical equipment, familial values, or any other of the supposed determinants of fertility.

Many infant deaths in nonindustrial countries, however, were caused by infections not susceptible to easy mass control, such as those caused by food contamination. But very few persons in those countries died of heart disease, stroke, and cancers, which attack mainly the old and are therefore the main causes of death in developed countries. Mortality fell in less developed countries to levels more or less the same as those in nations with the best health systems. By 1970, crude death rates in industrial countries ranged from, say, 6.8 in Japan to 10.5 in Sweden, and in nonindustrial countries from 6.8 in Venezuela to 16.7 in India. This near parity developed in spite of a continuing sharp contrast in the deaths of infants; according to United Nations' estimates for 1980–85, the difference in average infant mortality rates was between 17 for more developed regions and 91 for less developed ones.

In other words, the most publicized population problem of recent decades, the explosion of people in Latin America, the Near East, and Asia has been the result principally of the successful application of life-saving techniques and personnel, funded at great cost and with the best intentions, mainly by the United States and other Western powers.

Less developed countries (apart from those that have oil to export) also are poor. How to specify the poorest among them is not an easy task, and international agencies use different criteria. The United Nations defines "least developed countries" as those with a combination of low income per capita, low literacy rates, and little manufacturing industry. Of the 36 such countries in 1982, 26 were in Africa and 8 in Asia, plus Haiti and Samoa. The population under age 15 ranged from over a third to not quite half, with most of the countries around 43 to 47 percent (compared to 22 percent in the United States). In contrast, only 2 to 5 percent were aged 65+ (in the United States 12 percent). Even though in these very poor countries children become productive at early ages, the burden of dependency on young adults is heavy. Crude birth rates were in the 40s, crude death rates close to 20; this means that, with no change in the rates, the population would double every 25 to 30 years. With such a population structure, campaigns to reduce the size of the average family would have to be successfully maintained for several generations to counteract the effect on fertility of the constant large flow into the prime reproductive ages. Cutting the number of children per family avails little when the number of families remains constant at a high level or even keeps growing.

People and Their Sustenance

The successful control of much of the mortality in poor countries has not generally been viewed as a benediction, for the consequence was a larger increase of humans than the world had seen previously. Everyone has to eat if he is to remain alive, and over the centuries one of the most contentious of debates concerning population has been about whether the growth of the human species was outpacing the increase in the food supply. Views on the subject have alternated periodically between opposed extremes, often with only a slight dependence on the real balance between people and sustenance. During the two generations following the First World War, a double reversal took place in opinion on whether civilization was facing disaster because of too many people, or too few. Both shifts encompassed virtually every scholarly, official, and lay commentary in all Western countries.

The successive moods can be exemplified for the 1920s by Paul Mombart's *Die Gefahr einer Übervölkung für Deutschland* (The Danger for Germany of a Surplus Population), and for the 1930s by Enid Charles's *The Menace of Underpopulation.* The Second World War distracted the zealots, but they came back with the Club of Rome's *The Limits of Growth* and similarly oriented works. These were declarations by distinguished persons and influential commissions. Until he was ousted by the Nazis, Mombart was Germany's leading demographer, the author of that country's most significant text, *Bevölkerungslehre.* Enid Charles worked with her husband Lancelot Hogben at the London School, and then, after their divorce, she was with the Dominion Bureau of Statistics in Ottawa and later with the World Health Organization in Southeast Asia. The Club of Rome was an international study group of prestigious businessmen; in 1981 there were 75 members from 35 countries.

If today's militants took the time to read these no less fervent pronouncements of yesterday and the day before yesterday, they might learn that the cycle of opinion was largely self-generated: the exaggerations of one decade stimulated a counterhyperbole some fifteen years later. As a prime example, the imminent worldwide famine prophesied by doomsayers of yesterday became instead a worldwide grain glut. From 1975, cereal production per capita rose worldwide by about 15 percent; in less developed countries, the production of all foods increased by almost 12 percent. Bangladesh, among the poorest and most densely populated of less developed countries, has been able to cut its grain imports drastically. Chinese corn was flooding the markets of neighboring countries. Saudi Arabia was giving away wheat it no longer wanted to store. In Finland farmers were turning surplus wheat into vodka, mink fodder, and glue.

The new balance between population and resources can be aptly illustrated by a worst-case example. India's 1987 drought was the most destructive in 125 years. The two chief grain-producing states, Punjab and Hayana, had almost no rain, and most other states only between 40 and 80 percent of the average. In Uttar Pradesh, the most populous state, half the land was not even sown. Hope that the monsoon would arrive in time to save the rice crop lasted till late July and then was proved futile. Until very recently such a natural disaster would have been the precursor to a major famine. On this occasion the government had in reserve enormous stores out of past surpluses. From 1950 to 1983–84 total domestic production of food grains had tripled, and in mid-1987 the stocks on hand totaled twice the estimated amount needed to tide the country over the drought. The dread prospect of famine was replaced by concern about the strain on the transport and distribution systems.

The overflow of staples did not mean that all peoples around the globe were eating well, but rather that the problem of hunger was often misconstrued. The causes were sometimes partly economic or environmental, but political factors, though usually ignored, were in many instances more important. To gain a preliminary understanding of the 1973–74 famine in Ethiopia, for instance, the best background reading would not be a work on dessication south of the Sahara but an account of the civil strife that led to the ouster of Haile Selassie. Mozambique, designated the poorest country in the world, has a fertile soil, valuable ores, and a fine coastline. That over 5 years its GNP fell by half and its foreign debt rose to $2.3 billion one can ascribe only to its Communist government and the destabilizing reactions of neighboring South Africa. Of the population of roughly 14 million, more than one person in ten was a would-be refugee, on the road fleeing the civil war but finding no refuge anywhere.

Population Forecasts

Predictions of a gross disparity between food and population turned out to be false mainly because of the stupendous rise in productivity effected by the green revolution. But demographers have been wrong also in their forecasts of population. As has been shown time and again, statements about the future by population experts are no better than those by meteorologists or economists. In the real world there are no seers. "A demographer," the demographer Joel Cohen once explained, "is somebody who guesses wrong about the future of populations. A mathematical demograper is somebody who uses mathematics and computers to guess wrong about the future of populations." Indeed, as the British demographer John Hajnal once remarked to a group of his professional peers, it matters not whether population forecasts prophesy well or poorly, for their true function does not depend on their accuracy. Statesmen, business-men, and administrators of all types must plan for an assumed num-ber of citizens, customers, and clients; and without a prod from a suitably authoritative source, they find it difficult to begin opera-tions. Given a figure, any figure, for the near future, they get under way, and if the projection proves to have been wrong they make adjustments. Hajnal's novel interpretation was meant as an in-joke, but by now demographers' fallibility is no longer an in-secret. Yet the demand for population projections continues even though many of those who use them have come to suspect their trustworthiness.

Population projections concerning persons already alive can in one sense be fairly accurate, for age-specific death rates are unlikely to change appreciably over a few years. If a school superintendent, for example, wants to know how many pupils will attend each grade 10 years from now, he would seem to need as base figures only the preschool and school populations plus the unreliable fertility esti-mates for only some 5 years. In fact, however, even this simplest case is a bit more complicated. Families move from one school dis-trict to another; immigration includes a variable proportion of school-age children; and for college enrollments, administrators must try to guess what percentage of the usual age range will attend and how many older students will also take courses.

Fertility Trends

The momentous decline in infant and child mortality was accom-panied not, as one might expect, by a fall in fertility but often, so far as we can tell from deficient statistics, by a probable initial rise in the number of children born. Everything favored a high birth rate: the population structure set a large proportion in the reproductive ages; the reduced incidence of certain debilities improved fecundity; and nothing had altered the pronatalist norms appropriate to the time when many had to be born for a few to survive to maturity.

As part of the new nations' élan, a myth evolved that all social and economic ills, the consequence of colonial maladministration, would miraculously be cured by political independence. In 1948, Nehru termed India "an underpopulated country." In the first years after the Communist victory in China, the country's leaders declared its vast population to be its main economic asset; in the words of one Party official, "Man should be viewed as a producer rather than a consumer." Among an influential sector of Latin American politicians and intellectuals, an increase in numbers was applauded with an almost mystical faith in the benefits they would bring; under Juan Perón, for example, the Argentine government hoped to double its population within a generation. Often these nationalist sentiments merged with the Marxist dogma that, given a just and efficient society, a country's population was an irrelevancy. Less extreme asseverations that population growth is, or may be, of benefit to a people's welfare remained an acceptable point of view in the continuing debate. Meanwhile Western demographers, newfangled social workers, and zero populationists were starting a massive effort to furnish contraceptive means to the people of less developed countries.

Concern about the population growth in less developed countries spread to a demand, especially in the United States, for zero population growth also in the industrial West. From President Eisenhower's declaration that he could not imagine anything more emphatically not a proper governmental function than providing birth control, only 10 years passed to President Nixon's complete reversal of this policy. Nixon recommended that the domestic family-planning services supported by the federal government be expanded and integrated, and as a direct consequence of this message, Congress set up the Commission on Population Growth and the American Future to lay a foundation for antinatalist programs. Its report, *Population and the American Future*, was published in 1972, when fertility in the United States had fallen below the replacement level. This does not mean that the population was decreasing, but rather that the increase was the fortuitous consequence of the temporary high proportion in the childbearing ages. American women aged 18 to 24 reported that they expected to have an average of under 2.0 children, but 2.1 are needed as a minimum to replace the two parents and make up for early deaths and sterile marriages.

Over the past several generations, one of the most important factors in reducing fertility has been the possibility of rising in the social scale. Still today we have the paradox that the poorest parents, those least able materially to care for large families, often have the most children, for many of them see little chance of bettering themselves no matter what they do. Ethnic groups that have taken full advantage of the opportunities in America—such as Jews, Japanese, and Chinese—generally restrict their family responsibilities in order to move up faster.

This association between family size and upward mobility, a routine element of population dynamics for well over a century, has been intensified by the expanded ambitions of many women. Physiologically, the prime childbearing ages are the 20s, especially the early 20s; but a woman who wants both to establish herself in a profession and to have children, is inclined to put off beginning her family (as the phrase goes) until her early or even middle 30s. In her presidential address to the Population Association of America, Jane Menken posed the question, "How late can you wait?"

4

Malthus

Malthus's Essay on the *Principle of Population* was written as a short polemical pamphlet in 1798. Then, in a 1803 second edition that was four times as long, Malthus responded to criticisms and incorporated much new material based on his travel and wider reading. All together, there were six editions of the *Essay* during Malthus's lifetime and a posthumous seventh. All the study, reflection, and writing that went into the periodic revisions have been ignored by many of those who have commented on the principle of population. Almost without exception they cite the first edition, the preliminary version of a theory that underwent fundamental changes in its gradual development. Moreover, the principle of population is almost never compared with the theories that Malthus opposed. That the First Essay (as Malthus's biographer James Bonar termed the 1798 edition) was written in a polemical context is evident from its very title, which depicts the work as "remarks on the speculations of Mr. Godwin, M. Condorcet, and other writers." In 1795, while in hiding from the Jacobins' sentence of death, the French revolutionary the Marquis de Condorcet wrote *Esquisse d'un tableau historique des progrès de l'esprit humain*, a history of progress from its earliest beginnings to its imminent culmination in human perfection. Following from achievements brought about by the French Revolution, the human race would soon attain universal truth, virtue, and happiness. All inequalities of wealth, of education, of opportunity, of sex, would disappear. All would speak the same language, and the earth would be bountiful without stint. In his *Enquiry Concerning Political Justice*, the English anarchist William Godwin depicted the same flawless future and went even farther:

> [Since] one tendency of a cultivated and virtuous mind is to diminish our eagerness for the gratification of the senses,...the men whom we are supposing to exist when the earth shall refuse itself to a more extended population

will probably cease to propagate. The whole will be a people of men, and not of children. Generation will not succeed generation, nor truth have, in a certain degree, to recommence her career every thirty years.

In this anticipated future, "the term of human life may be prolonged [simply] by the immediate operation of the intellect beyond any limits which we are able to assign."

In Malthus's opinion, these vistas were no more than "a beautiful phantom of the imagination." He began his rebuttal with two "fixed laws of nature": "food is necessary to the existence of man" and "the passion between the sexes is necessary and will remain nearly in its present state [into the indefinite future]." However, there is a discrepancy between these two potentials; the "power" of population to increase is "indefinitely greater" than the "power" of the earth to provide food.

Population, when unchecked, increases in a geometrical ratio. Subsistence increases only in an arithmetical ratio. This disparity between potential growth in numbers and potential food supply, Malthus argued, pervades the "animal and vegetable kingdoms," throughout which nature spreads seeds profusely and nourishment more sparingly. Man cannot wholly escape a law that applies to all of nature. However, with humans the check on population growth is "more complicated" than with the rest of animate beings.

Impelled to the increase of his species by a powerful instinct, reason interrupts and asks [man] whether he may not bring beings into the world for whom he cannot provide the means of subsistence.... Will he not lower his rank in life?... May he not see his offspring in rags and misery, and clamoring for bread that he cannot give them?... These considerations...prevent a very great number in all civilized nations from pursuing the dictate of nature in an early attachment to one woman. Yet...a constant effort towards an increase of population...tends to subject the lower classes of the society to distress and to prevent any great permanent amelioration of their condition.

In the Second Essay (as the 1803 and subsequent editions are called) the principal preventive check is "moral restraint," or the chaste postponement of marriage. To follow Malthus's illustrative example, if the number of people increased faster than the amount of food, then on the average each person would get less to eat. Because of the consequent distress among the poor, more of them would put off getting married. With the fall in the wage rate resulting from the oversupply of laborers, farmers would hire more hands to improve agricultural land and turn up fresh soil, until the food available was again sufficient to supply everyone adequately. In the new turn of the cycle there would be a greater amount of food grown, so that the return to a people-food balance would (or could) be at a higher level, stimulated also by the aspirations of workers as reflected in the wages they demanded.

How valid is this picture of the determinants of marriage? In a famous paper, the British demographer John Hajnal described what he called "the European marriage pattern," which combined a high age at marriage with a large proportion who never married. As late as 1900, the percentages of Western European males still single at ages 45-49 ranged from 9 in Denmark and Germany to 16 in Belgium and Switzerland and 20 in Ireland. Even after the spread of modern contraception was well under way, throughout Western Europe one person in seven or eight remained single during the whole of his or her fecund years. As against cultures in which virtually everyone married, most girls at or very shortly after puberty, the West European system represented an enormous check on the potential increase in population.

Like today's analysts, Malthus separated the world between what we term developed and less developed countries, in which fertility is and is not under adequate control. The structure of the Essay emphasizes his division between eras or places with a high mortality and those with a low fertility. Book I is on checks "in the less civilized parts of the world and in past times," Book II on those "in different states of modern Europe." After a mainly economic miscellany in Book III, the final chapters of the work deal with "future prospects," which he judged with a degree of optimism.

Interpretations of Malthus

If we adopt the cynical definition of a classic, a work that everyone cites and no one reads, then the *Essay on the Principle of Population* must be designated a superclassic—written by a man whose name has entered all Western languages but whose central ideas are often not accurately known even by some professional demographers. The persistent inaccuracies infest accounts not only of his ideas but also of the man.

Malthus was born on February 13, 1776 and baptized the following day. His date of birth is given as February 14 on the memorial tablet that the Royal Economic Society placed in Bath Abbey, and as February 17 by Leslie Stephen in the *Dictionary of National Biogra-*

phy. Others who cited the 14th could not resist adding a witticism about St. Valentine's Day. Peter Donaldson, president of the Population Reference Bureau, and Amy Ong Tsui, a professor at the University of North Carolina at Chapel Hill and deputy director of its Carolina Population Center, inform us in their joint essay in *Beyond the Numbers: A Reader on Population, Consumption, and the Environment* (1994) that Malthus wrote in the seventeenth century.

His full name was Thomas Robert Malthus, but the "Thomas" was never used; to designate him as "Thomas Malthus" is not formally incorrect, no more an error than calling the twenty-eighth president of the United States "Thomas Wilson." Even a privately printed monograph on the Malthus family mentions Robert's older brother Sydenham but only one of his five sisters.

Many commentators label the man "Parson Malthus" or "Rev. T. R. Malthus," but during his lifetime this pious layman was denounced as an atheist and, presumably in an attempt to defend himself against such attacks, only then began to preface his name with "Rev." According to Marx, Malthus "had taken the monastic vow of celibacy," while the introduction of an early Everyman edition of the *Essay* informed the reader that the author "practiced the principle of population to the extent of eleven girls." In fact, he was married and the father of three children.

In a recent book prophetically titled *An Incomplete Education* (1995), the American economist Alan Webber summed up his professional knowledge about Malthus in the following few lines:

> A clergyman who punctured the Utopianism of his day by cheerfully predicting that population growth would always exceed food production, leading, inevitably, to famine, pestilence, and war. This "natural inequality of the two powers" formed, as he put it, "the great difficulty that to me appears insurmountable in the way to perfectability of society." Malthus's good news: Periodic catastrophes, human perversity, and general wretchedness, coupled with the possibility of self-imposed restraint in the sexual arena, would prevent us from breeding ourselves into extinction.

As is typical even in professional writings, the author ignored the theory of the mature Malthus, basing his comments on an inaccurate paraphrase of the preliminary version. Malthus did not "predict" that population would always exceed food production; he presented a model in which that might take place.

Malthus the Man

As a student at Jesus College, Malthus devoted most attention to the study of mathematics, and he won prizes in Latin and in English declamation. After his graduation he became first a curate and then a professor at a new college in Haileybury that the East India Company had established in England to train personnel for its expanding operations in India. The college's curriculum included considerable training in Indian languages, beginning with Sanskrit, then Persian and usually Hindustani, with other languages as optional supplements to this minimum. Students also studied classical languages, mathematics, and the other standard British subjects, as well as the English legal system, general history, and—a discipline not yet recognized at Oxford and Cambridge—political economy. It was this last subject that Professor Malthus taught.

At the two established universities, the stipulated duties might be only to deliver four lectures a year and to publish one of them. At Haileybury, in contrast, the professors put in a solid workweek. It also represented a partial break with the biases routine at Cambridge and Oxford; students of any religion were accepted from any kind of school in England, Scotland, and Ireland. Its unabashedly secular purpose set it apart from a higher education closely linked to the Anglican Church, and in politics it was something of a utilitarian stronghold. The works of Jeremy Bentham were used as texts; in London James Mill acted as an examiner.

At Haileybury Malthus led a seemingly uneventful life, engaged in teaching and guiding his students. He was, however, also an important political figure, involved in disputes over a number of national issues. Most significantly, he wrote two books that still today reverberate among those concerned about people and the environment—the *Essay* and *Principles of Political Economy*.

After his death, Malthus's library was donated to Jesus College by his nephew, and I was delighted with what I saw as a chance to explore his mind by examining the books that he had owned. Setting aside several days in December 1976 for what I anticipated would be a profitable and pleasant bit of research, I made an appointment and traveled to Cambridge. One of the librarians took me through several locked doors along a corridor to the end of one building's wing, where in a cold and gloomy room there were stored, uncatalogued, the literary remains of one of the college's most distinguished graduates. A few small light bulbs hung from the ceiling, and to read the title of a book taken at random from the shelves, I had to carry it over to one of those skimpy lights. It was impossible even to reach the top shelves. Bundled up in my overcoat, I asked the librarian how one could work under such conditions, and she suggested that I might return on a pleasant summer day. The anecdote is worth recalling as an indication of how little Malthus was then honored even by his alma mater. I should add that the books I could not examine have since been cataloged, and Pergamon Press published *The Malthus Library Catalogue* (1983).

During the past several decades, after more than a century of denigration and misunderstanding, there has been a remarkable and widespread revival of interest in Malthus and his works. Once the principal source about his personal life had been a memoir by William Otter, a good friend whose daughter married Malthus's son; and over the next century there was only one significant book-length study of Malthus's ideas, the already cited one by James Bonar, published in 1885 and in a second edition in 1924. Indeed, there were popular writings and journal articles galore, but many of these misrepresented seriously both the character of the man and the substance of his writings. Then, quite suddenly, a breakthrough started when the late Patricia James edited Malthus's travel diaries. This was followed shortly by two complementary books, Mrs. James's splendid biography and my own attempt to counter the long vilification of Malthus and state his views accurately. Subsequently the most impressive recognition of Malthus's renewed importance was a 1980 Paris conference arranged by the Société de Démographie Historique; more than 500 participants from 61 countries listened to and discussed 164 papers. In 1984 the British Society for Population Studies sponsored a conference to go "forward from Malthus" in the further development of population theory. As a culmination, an elegant edition of Malthus's works was published in eight volumes, a long overdue tribute to an important nineteenth-century economist and the father of modern demography.

The Malthusian Heritage

Malthus today is frequently judged to have been a political reactionary. In fact, the social reforms he advocated included universal free schooling, an extension of the suffrage, free medical care for the poor, state assistance to emigrants, and even direct relief to casual laborers or families with more than six children. Similarly, he opposed child labor in factories and free trade when it benefited the traders but not the public. Apart from such details, he was an honest and beneficent reformer, committed throughout his life to the goal that he shared with every liberal of his day—the betterment of society and of all the people in it.

Malthus had a complex mind. He was a pious Anglican who saw man not merely as a spiritual being but as a member of *Homo sapiens*, ultimately hardly more independent of biological instincts and needs than any other species. Of the various dualities to be found in his writings, the most significant is that between nature and nurture, between man as an animal and as cultural being. The two naturalists who hit upon the theory of evolution and, exceptionally, agreed to share the consequent honor both acknowledged that the crucial catalyst that brought their vast data into meaningful order was Malthus's *Essay*. "Here," Charles Darwin wrote in his *Autobiography*, "I had at last got a theory by which to work." "I became convinced," Alfred Russel Wallace noted in *My Life*, "that I had at length found the long sought for law of nature that solved the problem of the origin of species."

From the facts that all species have the power to increase their number many times over, and that the number of surviving individuals of each species typically remains almost stationary, the two biologists deduced that there is a struggle for existence. In an ever changing environment, those fittest to survive among the varied offspring in each generation set the future mold of the species. In short, the principle of population was the scaffolding on which Darwin and Wallace hung their data, the base from which they advanced the most revolutionary theory in biology.

It is axiomatic among democratic humanists of the West that the most fundamental reform of a less developed country, the one from which much else will flow, is the establishment of universal literacy. In the Britain of Malthus's day, the best national system of mass education was in Presbyterian Scotland, which generated also such manifestations of high culture as excellent universities and the *Edinburgh Review*.

Adam Smith, a product of that environment, advocated tax-supported public schooling, but in England few welcomed his proposals. The main political argument against mass education was that, if the common people were able to read such writers as Thomas Paine, this would increase the tendency toward discontent and rebellion.

On the contrary, Malthus argued; "an instructed and well informed people would be much less likely to be led away by inflammatory writings," since they could better judge the "false declamation of ambitious demagogues."

Malthus's support of universal education was part of his program to solve the dilemma posed by the principle of population. When wages rise, Malthus held, the workers will acquire a taste for the conveniences and comforts they were enabled to purchase, and their habits will be changed accordingly. That is to say, workers who move into the middle-class income range would come to aspire to a middle-class style of life. As Gertrude Himmelfarb wrote in the Introduction to the Modern Library edition of the *Essay:*

> The initiation [of the lower classes] into the middle classes was, in effect, the defeat of the principle of population. If Malthus had to abandon the latter (at least implicitly), he was more than recompensed by the former, for the embourgeoisement of the lower classes did prove to be, as he hoped, both their deliverance and society's salvation. In this, even more than his predictions about population, he was truly the prophet of our times.

The rise in workers' standard of living, Malthus wrote, could be greatly facilitated by an appropriate political setting:

> Of all the causes which tend to generate prudential habits among the lower classes of society, the most essential is unquestionably civil liberty. No people can be much accustomed to form plans for the future who do not feel assured that their industrious exertions...will be allowed free scope....[Moreover,] civil liberty cannot be permanently secured without political liberty,...[which] teach[es] the lower classes of society to respect themselves by obliging the higher classes to respect them.

If anyone had polled the English population in 1800 on the number of children they desired, presumably a substantial proportion would have replied, "It is up to God." Malthus was attacked by conventional Christians because, in effect, he asserted, "No, it is up to you!" And, on the other hand, Malthus is attacked by modern liberals because when they assert that it is up to the state to care for its subjects, he would have countered, "No, it is up to the people themselves!" To hold every person responsible for his behavior, denying him the escape of blaming either Providence or Society, is a moral rather than an empirical stance—a moral stance that fitted in with neither the liberal nor the conservative ideology of the first decades of the nineteenth century.

5

Marx and Early Marxists

No adequate review of the debates on population questions during the past century and more can pass over the various Marxist positions. In spite of the manifest lack of interest in the matter of both Marx and most early Marxists, there has been a steady flow of exegesis and explication. Virtually every issue of the bibliographic journal *Population Index* includes a reference to at least one such work. Whether of past or more recent vintage, such writings are generally based on a zealous opposition to the postulates of standard political economy, and their typically sharp polemical tone does not help in the interpretation of their arguments.

A review of how early Marxists viewed population, both in itself and in relation to economic growth, can consist of no more than a recapitulation of fragments or even of silences. In the usually tangential treatment first by Marx and Engels and then by their immediate followers, population was pictured less as a significant ingredient of the historical process than as an epiphenomenon. Indeed, a few writers who call themselves Marxists have combined their interpretation of the doctrine with standard demographic theories, but I do not find their amalgam worth discussing.

First Formulations on Population

The Condition of the Working Class in England, which Engels wrote in 1845, is in sharp contrast to the treatment of population in later Marxist writings. The advent of the machine, Engels wrote, brought unemployment, as well as "want, wretchedness, and crime." Industrial areas underwent a "gigantic expansion" of population for the reasons given in Malthus's principle of population, which had "a good deal of truth in it under existing circumstances." "The whole of the economy was affected by this expansion" in the number of people. With manufacturers fiercely competing for growing but still limited markets, there would be a business cycle of some 5 to 6 years, with each recession deeper than the preceding one. The population surge needed at the height of each boom resulted in unemployment at all other times. "The number of those who are starving increases," and some of those in the "surplus population" may not survive.

In *The German Ideology* (1845–46), Marx and Engels represented population growth as one basic determinant of long-term change in the productive system:

> [Men] begin to distinguish themselves from animals as soon as they begin to produce their means of subsistence,...[by which they are] indirectly producing their actual material life....This production only makes its appearance with the increase of population.

The last important element in the Marxist theory of population was a "history" of human progress from its beginnings. Working from notes that Marx had left when he died, Engels wrote *The Origin of the Family, Private Property, and the State* (1884), which in some respects was a notable throwback to the early socialists' fascination with communitarian life. The argument was based largely on the work of the American anthropologist Lewis Henry Morgan (1818–1881), whose theories most of today's anthropologists would hardly rate as plausible. There were three main stages in this Marxist schema of history: savagery, barbarism, and civilization. The matriarchal gens or clan had existed everywhere before it was supplanted by its patriarchal counterpart, and this "overthrow of mother right was the world historical defeat of the female sex." The status of women declined disastrously under capitalism, and a fully free marriage could come only with the advent of socialism. Recently some feminists have based their radical proposals on a revival of this Marxist reconstruction of human history.

Population and the Economy

According to Marxist economic theory, competition under capitalism drives all entrepreneurs to increase their efficiency to the utmost by installing more and more machinery. As Marx wrote in *Capital*, "Accumulate, accumulate! This is the Moses and the prophets!" The growing stock of capital goods that results gradually displaces some of the workers who had been employed with the earlier, less efficient technology. "The laboring population therefore produces, along with the accumulation of capital produced by it, the means by which [it] itself is made relatively superfluous, is turned into a relative surplus population; and it does this to an always increasing extent." Moreover, the composition of the employed force steadily deteriorates; the capitalist "progressively replaces skilled laborers by less skilled, mature labor power by immature, male by female, that of adults by that of younger persons or children." If they are to remain in business, employers have to respond to the state of the market and cannot afford to adjust their production also to the supply of laborers. In the long term no amelioration is possible under capitalism, which depends on this "industrial reserve army" of the technologically unemployed.

This line of reasoning can hardly be regarded as a successful prophecy. The effects of technological advance on the size and composition of the work force are considerably more complex than in this depiction, and the long-term consequences of the greater efficiency were, in fact, a higher level of living, a shorter workweek, and the development of tertiary services. In presently less developed countries, where the surplus agrarian population is often large, the consequent very low wage ordinarily does not stimulate but seriously impedes the nation's accumulation of capital.

Even if Marx's main point is granted—that with increasing mechanization there is a trend toward an ever larger number of unemployed—it still does not follow that this trend would run "independently of the limits of actual increase of population." Given the state of the market, the proportion of the work force able to find employment depends in part on the number of new workers seeking jobs; indeed, in another context Marx himself noted that "the demand for laborers may exceed the supply and, therefore, wages may rise." If the number of people were to decline at the same rate as machines displace workers (taking Marx's dogma as valid), then there would be no "industrial reserve army," no "immiseration," no Marxist model at all. Marx built his system on the unstated and unexamined postulate that the rapid population growth in nineteenth-century Europe would continue indefinitely.

Marx versus Malthus

According to Malthus's principle of population, the natural force of sexual attraction tends to raise the population beyond the number that can be fed. Socialists of every denomination—among others, Charles Hall, Robert Owen, P. J. Proudhon, Charles Fourier—all but unanimously repudiated this theory (as already noted, the young Engels was an exception). Marx rejected Malthus and his theory in language especially vitriolic even by his standards. "The contemptible Malthus," "a plagiarist," was a "shameless sycophant of the ruling classes" who perpetrated a "sin against science," "this libel on the human race." In light of his belief in the scientific inevitability of socialism, Marx's opposition to Malthus is not surprising. As he wrote in *Critique of the Gotha Program* (1875):

> If Malthus's theory of population is correct, then I can not abolish this [iron law of wages] even if I abolish wage labor a hundred times, because this law is paramount not only over the system of wage labor but also over every social system. Stepping straight from this, the economists proved fifty years ago or more that socialism cannot abolish poverty, which is based on nature, but only *communalize* it, distribute it equally over the whole surface of society.

The "iron law of wages" means the tendency of population always to increase up to the limit set by the subsistence available to it. Thus, a virtually unlimited supply of labor can always be hired at a fixed wage. The relation, given its designation by the German socialist Ferdinand Lassalle, was analyzed most fully by Malthus's contemporary, David Ricardo. For him, as for Marx, the rigidity of wages was a consequence of Malthus's principle of population, but Malthus himself rejected the link. As he wrote repeatedly in both the *Essay on the Principle of Population* and *Principles of Political Economy*, a rise in wages tends to generate a taste for a higher level of living, which the worker will endeavor to preserve, among other ways, by reducing the size of his family. Among socialists who have discussed the matter, two English Fabians were distinguished by their correct appreciation of Malthus's social philosophy. As Sidney and Beatrice Webb wrote in *Industrial Democracy* (1919):

> The ordinary middle-class view that the "principle of population" renders nugatory all attempts to raise wages otherwise than in the slow course of generations was, in fact, based on sheer ignorance not only of the facts of working-class life, but even of the opinions of the very economists from whom it was supposed to be derived.

Moreover, according to Marx, the principle of population was merely a biological generalization, supposedly valid irrespective of the society's class relations. On the contrary, he wrote:

> Every special historical mode of production has its own special laws of population, historically valid within its limits alone. An abstract law of population exists for plants and animals only, and only in so far as man has not interfered with them.

As with many key assertions in Marx, this one is subject to widely differing interpretations. It may mean that population growth in a capitalist society is no reliable forecast of what the future holds under socialism. Or, alternatively, the contrast between the human species and all other forms of life suggests that Marx was claiming that humans can transgress their biological limitations; and this utopian vista was later adopted by some Soviet spokesmen, as we shall illustrate later.

From Marx, however, it was a strange dictum. In the view of Marx and Engels, it was only the men they termed "utopian socialists" who held that with a good social system man could escape some of his physiological limits. Summing up the essentials of his friend's work at his graveside, Engels held that "Marx discovered the law of evolution in human history: the simple fact, previously hidden under ideological growths, that human beings must first of all eat, drink, shelter and clothe themselves before they can turn their attention to politics, science, art, and religion." This, of course, was not the first expression of this simplistic version of materialism. Among earlier statements one need look no farther than Ludwig Feuerbach's delightful play on words: *"Der Mensch ist, was er isst"* (Man is what he eats); and later Communist paraphrases include Bertold Brecht's *"Erst kommt das Fressen, dann die Moral"* (First comes stuffing one's face, then morality).

Marx had little or nothing to say about what governed the population growth of primitive, feudal, or socialist societies, the types that he and Engels used to project history into the future. And his remarks about the fourth type, capitalist societies, pertained mainly not to population but to the work force. There is also a fifth type, omitted from the four-stage classification enshrined by Engels's *Origin of the Family* but elsewhere discussed by both him and Marx. This "Oriental despotism" or "Asiatic mode of production" proved to be an embarrassment and eventually disappeared from Marxist writings; it has been analyzed most fully in Karl Wittfogel, *Oriental Despotism* (1957) and Shlomo Avineri, *Karl Marx on Colonialism and Modernization* (1968). Marx discussed such societies mainly in his articles on India, but the societal type also included China, Russia, and some other countries. The distinctive attribute of Oriental despotism is that it lacks the social progress built into the four Western stages. According to Marx, "India has no history," only "successive invaders who founded their empires on the passive basis of that unresisting and unchanging society." Because there was no internal dynamism of its own, only an external force—that is, European colonial expansion—could establish the capitalist economy that in the Marxist schema was the necessary preparation for socialism.

In the Marxist model, each of the Western types of society has its specific ruling class—the slaveholders in antiquity, the nobility in feudal society, and the bourgeoisie in modern capitalist society—a ruling class that controlled the means of production and extracted the "surplus" created, respectively, by slaves, serfs, and workers. Marx ridiculed antagonists who avoided a social-class analysis and, as he put it, "reified" such concepts as commodity and the state. However, he pointedly refrained from identifying the bureaucracy as the ruling class of Oriental despotism, as it would also be in Communist countries; it was the "state" that controlled a society based on the Asiatic mode of production. After Marx and Engels eliminated Oriental despotism from their list of societal types, other Marxists incorporated examples of it into Western "feudalism."

If Marx can be said to have had a theory of population, it passed over those portions of the globe that have become a main focus of present-day demographers. If countries like India and China are outside the central Marxist schema (or are returned to it in a manner that ignores their distinctive social history), then the theorizing based on Marx has no direct bearing on the population problems of less developed countries. Neither such direct descendants of Marx as "Maoists" nor such more remote offshoots as "African socialists" have grappled with the issue of what Oriental despotism implies concerning the population of their countries.

Theories of Crisis and Adjustment

According to Marx, because the "value" of any commodity is based on the human labor expended in producing it, as the ratio of capital to labor increases in any society, the value of its total social product tends to decrease and the rate of profit tends to fall toward zero. Because all entrepreneurs are driven to accumulate capital goods, which generally result in a higher productivity, there is a long-term propensity for the supply of commodities to outstrip the demand for them. The capitalist system will therefore come to an end unless its life is saved by one of the following means, each of which was advocated by economists of various schools:

- As Eduard Bernstein, the principal Revisionist theorist of Marxism, pointed out, by "organizing the market" *cartels* had eliminated waste and cut-throat competition—as well as setting artificially high prices and customs barriers. Although not a permanent solutions, such "manufacturers' associations" could long postpone the self-destruction that Marx had decreed as inevitable.

- Malthus's solution was a class of *unproductive consumers* to match the underconsuming producers. Marx held the supposed solution to be ineffective, for the first reaction to every crisis is to cut outlays for such luxuries as servants. Moreover, he found it politically reprehensible to be "unconcerned with the fate of the agents of production, whether they be capitalists [!] or workers," and troubled only about that of "parasites and self-indulgent drones, in part masters and in part servants, who appropriate gratuitously a considerable quantity of wealth,...paying for commodities produced by [the capitalist class] with money they have taken from the capitalists themselves."

- The expansion of investment opportunities by the establishment of *new industries* was of considerable importance in the early years of capitalism, but according to the exposition of Marxist theory by the American economist Paul Sweezy in *The Theory of Capitalist Development* (1970), in a mature economy the influence of innovations is bound to decline. The establishment of new industries counteracts the tendency to underconsumption "roughly in proportion to the relative share of total investment for which it is responsible." He found it difficult even to imagine a series of new industries with "a *relative* importance comparable to that of the textile, mining, metallurgical and transportation industries in the eighteenth and nineteenth centuries." Others might challenge this statement with references to the exploitation of such fields as electronics and the computer, developments from the laser, or space exploration. According to John Doerr, a venture capitalist in California's Silicon Valley, the introduction of the personal computer resulted in the largest creation of wealth in world history.

- Improvement of the population's *well-being* was well under way during the lifetimes of Marx and particularly Engels, both of whom speculated that socialism might be established by peaceful means in England, the United States, and one or two other countries. More typical was Marx's sarcastic comment about the concept of effective demand—that is, demand for goods backed by the ability to pay for them. "It is sheer tautology to say that crises are caused by the scarcity of effective consumption," for under capitalism there is no other kind. The tautology could be given "the semblance of a profounder justification by saying that the working class receives too small a portion of its own product and the evil would be remedied as soon as it receives a larger share of it." That last phrase—that underconsumption would be "remedied" once the working class got "a larger share" of the goods the society produced—was prophetic in a sense Marx did not intend, for that is precisely what happened in Western nations.

- It is remarkable how little attention Marxists have paid to an *increase in population*, for it would mitigate the effects of underconsumption—at least until the children were old enough to enter the work force. In a paper on a related topic, one of a series he wrote on "Problems of Socialism," Eduard Bernstein noted that a rise in population size and density would result in a greater division of labor, "leading to greater responsibilities of the state administration as it takes over more kinds of enterprise and converts them into public services." In other words, population increase would reinforce the trend toward socialism rather than the reverse. In Rosa Luxemburg's main work, *The Accumulation of Capital* (1913), she remarked that the supposition that more consumers would solve the capitalist dilemma of underconsumption was not well founded: according to Marx's schema, any increase in the number of persons would mean either more capitalists or more workers—or also possibly more unproductive consumers. For reasons both Marx and Luxemburg had noted in their comments on underconsumption, however, none of these social classes could remedy the overproduction.

An extended exposition of underconsumption appeared (so far as I know for the first time in Marxist writings) in Sweezy's book, which was written after the publication of Keynes's *General Theory* had stimulated an active exchange of views on the issue in a non-Marxist context. From a distantly related passage in Marx's *Theorien über den Mehrwert*, Sweezy wrote, a "general principle may be deduced":

> The strength of the tendency to underconsumption stands in inverse relation to the rapidity of population growth....Over the last four centuries, the population factor has been extremely favorable to rapid and uninhibited expansion of capitalism,...a most important factor in counteracting the tendency to underconsumption....[However,] the well known downward trend in the rate of population growth, which is characteristic of all highly developed capitalist countries,...is in no sense accidental.... Resistance to underconsumption is steadily diminishing.

- If the demand for goods does not grow enough in the home country to counter overproduction, the remedy can be sought by expanding the market to other countries. First expounded in 1902 by the English radical liberal J. A. Hobson, the thesis concerning *imperialism* was developed by a whole series of Marxists—Otto Bauer (1907), Rudolf Hilferding (1910), Rosa Luxemburg (1913), Nikolai Bukharin (1918), Fritz Sternberg (1926), and Henryk Grossman (1929). In particular, the version by Lenin (1916) had a massive political impact, as great as any of his other writings. For revolutionaries, it became axiomatic that capitalism would inevitably lead not only to its own destruction but in the process to wars of new intensity.

Socialists on Birth Control

If underconsumption can be a recurrent problem of a capitalist economy, and if in the past a significant growth of population was one effective counterforce, then the determinants of the fertility rate would obviously be a relevant topic for would-be analysts of the system. Strangely, the typical position of socialists, the advocates of a planned society, was hostility to family planning. The stance was evident from the founding of modern socialism.

The Second International was Marxist only in a loose sense. As Bertram Wolfe pointed out in an essay included in *Russian and Soviet History* (1963), representatives from the twenty countries who in 1889 attended its inaugural congress in Paris ranged from such Marxist pioneers as August Bebel and Wilhelm Liebknecht (of Germany) to such an unconventional designer, craftsman, and poet as William Morris (of England). No control was exercised over diverse or contradictory positions. A permanent body, the International Socialist Bureau, was established only in 1900, and it was no more than a center for exchanging information. Even within each of the parties represented, wide and principled differences divided opposed wings, as between the orthodox Germans led by Karl Kautsky and the Revisionists who followed Eduard Bernstein or, in the French party, between those who wanted to support Alfred Dreyfus's fight for justice and those who held that disputes among sectors of the ruling class were no business of socialists. Which of those more or less socialist commentators and organizations one designated as "Marxist" was to some degree a matter of interpretation, as it remains today.

The largest and most influential unit of the Second International, the German Social Democratic Party, was also the most direct descendant of Marx. In Bebel's *Woman and Socialism* (1883), that exemplar of German Social Democratic orthodoxy maintained that "socialism is better able to preserve the equilibrium between population and means of subsistence than any other form of community," for in a socialist society man will for the first time "consciously direct his entire development in accordance with natural law." In any event, population control was not urgent, for the world had "a su-

perabundance of land capable of cultivation, awaiting the labor of
fresh hundreds of millions."

The principal theorist of the German party, Karl Kautsky, wrote
two books on population, neither of which has ever been translated
into English. The first, *The Influence of Population Increase on Social Progress* (1880), represented an all but unique attempt to strike
a compromise between Marx and Malthus. Malthus was wrong,
Kautsky wrote, in his main thesis, that population always tends to
increase faster than the supply of food on which it must subsist.
(This is not, of course, an accurate representation of Malthus's mature position.) But Malthus was right in his assertion that every improvement in the condition of the lower classes is accompanied by
an increase in their numbers. (Although this remains a common interpretation of Malthus's theory, his final stand was precisely the
opposite: workers who raised themselves into middle-class circumstances generally have adopted the smaller families typical of the
middle class.) For the young Kautsky the crucial question was how
to reduce the number of births:

> The question can no longer be *whether* birth control should be used, but
> only *when* it should be used....The sterile rejection of population theory, at
> least on the part of socialism, is definitely out of place, for the two are not in
> principle incompatible. ...Only a transformation of society can extirpate the
> misery and vice that today damn nine-tenths of the world to a lamentable
> existence; but only a regulation of population growth by the most moral
> means possible, probably the use of contraceptives, can forestall the recur-
> rence of this evil.

Within a few months Engels sent Kautsky an often quoted letter
commenting on his anomalous point of view. "Professional socialists," Engels wrote, had persistently demanded that "we proletarian
socialists" should solve the problem of possible overpopulation in
the future socialist society, but Engels saw no reason to accommodate them. Moreover, it was hardly a burning issue:

> If at some stage communist society finds itself obliged to regulate the pro-
> duction of human beings,... it will be precisely this society, and this society
> alone, which can carry out this without difficulty.... It is for the people in the
> communist society themselves to decide whether, when, and how this is to
> be done, and what means they wish to employ for the purpose.

The critique followed the general Marxist position that it was only
utopian socialists who attempted to describe the workings of the
ideal society of the future.

Kautsky adjusted his view to Engels's orthodoxy. In his second book on population, *Propagation and Development in Nature and Society* (1921), he wrote that the collectivized agriculture of a socialist society would be able to expand food production much faster than any possible growth of population "for at least a century." True, mortality would fall "enormously," but fertility would also decline as women took an interest in "the possibility of enjoyment and creativity in nature, art, and science." In fact, with so many distractions from family life, one might suppose that the consequence might be depopulation; but this fear was also groundless. In short, socialist society would be self-regulating, for whenever population growth deviated from the optimum rate, "public opinion and individuals' consciences will make women's duties clear."

When some pre-1914 socialists called for a birth strike in order to deprive capitalists of the cannon fodder they needed to conduct their wars, it might have seemed that the anomalous thesis of the young Kautsky had been widely adopted. However, the slogan soon acquired a somewhat archaic ring. In the United States the Socialist Party, never a significant factor among workers, generally supported the nascent birth-control leagues, but in Europe the usual relation between the two movements was antagonistic. At its Berlin congress in 1913, as an important example, such luminaries of the Second International as Rosa Luxemburg and Klara Zetkin opposed propaganda for birth control as a capitulation to reformism.

Why should so many of those committed to establishing a planned society have opposed the planning of families? One reason was a conventional Victorian prudishness. Like the respectable workers and lower middle-class employees who made up their membership, Europe's socialist parties were generally squeamish about any issue related to sex, and in particular they judged it politically essential to distinguish themselves sharply from the libertarian or quasi-anarchist advocates of free love.

A second reason for the hostility was the almost accidental association of birth control with Malthus. So far as I know, Marx never commented on the neo-Malthusian movement active in England, particularly from the first trial of the birth-control pioneers Charles Bradlaugh and Annie Besant (1876) to his death (1883). According to such Marxist classics as *The Communist Manifesto* and *The Origin of the Family*, in the future socialist society women would be emancipated from household drudgery, but whether also from bear-

ing many children was left in abeyance; and Marx's socialist followers were free to transfer to neo-Malthusianism his malevolence toward Malthus. This antagonism was not merely the doctrinal stand
of party intellectuals. According to an informed appraisal in
Schmollers Jahrbuch (1922), members of the German party opposed
birth control "almost without exception"; the whole membership was
represented, for instance, in a 1913 mass meeting "against the birth
strike."

In any discussion of the decline of Western fertility, a principal
example must be France, whose birth rate began its fall probably
before the 1789 revolution and by the 1850s was well below that of
the rest of Western Europe and still falling. The widespread control
of births had been effected with no organizational stimulus—mainly,
it would seem, by the practice of withdrawal backed up by (illegal)
abortions. After France's defeat in the 1870–71 war with Prussia,
French statesmen and scholars devoted much effort to trying to formulate a policy that would halt—or, better, reverse—the downward
path.

From the Franco-Prussian war to the present time, a strong
pronatalist sentiment prevailed throughout France, and the marginal
neo-Malthusian propaganda had little influence. A League for Human Regeneration and an associated periodical, *Régénération*, were
founded by Paul Robin, a one-time friend of Marx who was dis-
missed from his post as a boarding-school director for having es-
poused the use of contraceptives. Later, Eugène and Jeanne Humbert,
who published a series of birth-control magazines, were supported
mainly by anarchists. The two principal parties of the Left, the Socialists and the Communists, were either indifferent or hostile. In the
1950s, when Jacques Derogy, a Communist author, wrote *Children
in Spite of Ourselves* to oppose the law limiting access to contraceptives, the head of the Communist Party, Maurice Thorez, and his
feminist wife, Jeannette Vermeersch, denounced him in the name of
Marxist orthodoxy. Their argument was soon complemented by a
book following the party line, *L'Épouvantail malthusien*—"The
Malthusian Scarecrow."

Opposition between the doctrines of socialism and neo-Malthusianism was strongly reinforced also by the birth-control activists'
hostility to socialism. In England one of the most important figures
of the neo-Malthusian movement was George Drysdale, founder of
the original Malthusian League and author of *The Elements of So-*

cial Science (1905), a book of some 600 pages that went through thirty-five English editions and was translated into at least ten other languages. Drysdale's sympathetic exposition of classical economic theory bound his movement not only to Malthus but to the whole school of thought that socialists opposed. Neo-Malthusianism, the especial bête noire of the socialists, land reformers, and other advocates of redistribution and democratic control, was allegedly disliked by the laboring classes. The reason for this, as the family-planning pioneer Marie Stopes remarked in her *Early Days of Birth Control* (1923), was that "the intense antisocialism of the Malthusian League antagonized the great mass of the working people." Partisan accounts of neo-Malthusians and socialists each laid blame on the other, but they agreed that in England the two movements were adversaries who on both sides conducted a war with intolerant fervor.

As late as 1925 the British Labor Party took an ambivalent stand toward planned parenthood. When the Department of Health banned birth-control information from its clinics, a party conference refused to protest, as reported in G. D. H. Cole, *A History of the Labour Party from 1914* (1948). "The subject of birth control," the party statement asserted, "is in its nature not one which should be made a political party issue, but should remain a matter on which members of the Party should be free to hold and promote their individual convictions." One reason for this neutral position, of course, was that the leaders did not want to affront the many Catholic members, but another was that socialist tradition suggested that this stand on the government's policy should be adopted.

Class differences in European fertility, ordinarily explained in part by the greater religious or cultural traditionalism of the lower classes, may well have been the consequence also of the fact that socialism, the main antitraditionalist ideology of the working classes (especially in Germany), opposed contraception either implicitly or explicitly.

6

Lenin and His Successors

Marxist population theory, to the extent that it existed, was maintained and supplemented in the Russian Marxist parties. But however much Lenin deemed himself to be a Marxist, in crucial respects he deviated from orthodoxy. Most important, of course, was his supposition on how socialism would be brought into being; for Marx the causal factor was the force of History, but for Lenin it was the action of a party of professional revolutionaries. Neither man was much interested in population, but whatever guidance Lenin provided on the issue was to some extent realized in the state that he and his party founded.

The Early Bolsheviks

The loose and diverse movement that the Russian economist Peter Struve labeled *Narodniki* (or Populists) was for the several decades ending the nineteenth century the dominant element in Russia's radical politics. Their unifying theme was a veneration of the *obshchina*, or village commune; and in a famous letter that Marx wrote to the Russian revolutionary Vera Zasulich in 1881 (first published in Russia in 1924), he asserted that if it was cleansed of its deleterious characteristics and allowed to develop spontaneously, the village commune would be "the pivot of Russia's social regeneration." Even so, Russian Marxism evolved in a running debate with Populism, a debate concerned largely with the relevance of agrarian communes to national politics.

Lenin's first works, in part analyses of agriculture, were in greater part political tracts to demonstrate that, contrary to Marx's expectations, the *obshchina* could not serve as the nucleus of a larger cooperative society. Both inside and outside the village commune, Lenin argued, agriculture was developing in a capitalist framework. Instead of the unitary communes that Populists wrote about, Lenin saw peasantry split into three subclasses: "rich," "middle," and "poor," which were parallel to the class structure of the industrial population. Migration out of agriculture, mainly of middle peasants, had dealt "an enormous impetus to the disintegration of the peasantry." The Narodnik program to impede such movements would not only deny the individual migrant the advantages he was seeking but also retard a progressive social phenomenon. Proper policy, Lenin contended, would be to remove all obstacles to migration and facilitate it "in every way possible."

Although Lenin wrote prodigiously not only on agriculture but on many other subjects (the fifth Russian edition of his works appeared in fifty-four volumes), he had little to say specifically on population theory. In a remark by a scholar quoted in John Besemeres, *Soviet Population Policies* (1980), his writings on population were characterized as "merely a few pedestrian details of economic and social statistics." Like Marx before him, Lenin opposed what he represented as Malthusianism. In the best known statement on the issue, an article in *Pravda* (June 16, 1913), titled "The working class and neo-Malthusianism," he attacked those who would justify legalized abortion in order to avoid the suffering of future offspring and contrasted such a petty bourgeois pessimism with the life-affirming vigor of the proletariat:

> Why not have children so that they may fight better,,,than we against the living conditions which are deforming and destroying our generation?...We are already laying the foundation of the new building and our children will finish its construction. That is why—and that is the *only* reason—we are unconditional enemies of neo-Malthusianism, which is a trend proper to the petty bourgeois couple, hardened and egotistical....
> It stands to reason that such an approach does not in any way prevent us from demanding repeal of all laws prosecuting abortion or laws against the distribution of medical works on contraceptive measures and so on....These laws do not cure the ills of capitalism but simply turn them into especially malignant and cruel diseases for the oppressed masses.

The notion that excess fertility can be a cause of working-class misery was in Lenin's view "reactionary and impoverished." Moreover, if only the capitalist classes practiced birth control, the restriction of their numbers would hasten their defeat.

Lenin's stand on contraception was echoed in his position on "free love," a topic much discussed in revolutionary circles during the first years of the Soviet regime. His most detailed statement was a comment on a pamphlet that Inessa Armand was proposing to publish on "the woman question." The demand for free love, he wrote her, is "really not a proletarian but a bourgeois demand," for the public will understand the term to mean freedom from serious relations and from childbirth, the freedom to commit adultery. Armand might well have resented the last point; as Robert Service spelled out in *Lenin: A Biography* (2000), she was (or would soon become) Lenin's mistress who for many years lived with him and his wife in a *ménage à trois*. Some of the early Bolsheviks were puritanical in judging sexual transgressions, but in this as in other matters Lenin was above his comrades' assessment.

Joseph Stalin, who succeeded Lenin as leader of the Communist Party of the Soviet Union and of world Communism, was an expert in all fields. Concerning the relation between population and the economy, while following the standard Marxist line that the organization of society is decisive, he commented only incidentally on growth in numbers as a factor in social progress. In demography his interest centered on ethnic composition, and after his accession to full power, *Marxism and the National Question*, a work he had written in 1912, became the definitive text on the subject. As noted in Bertram Wolfe, *An Ideology in Power* (1969), an interesting extension of Stalin's thesis on how the ethnic units of the Soviet Union should be integrated is found in a 1920 letter to Lenin, later expunged from Stalin's collected works. Stalin noted with remarkable prescience that a transitional form of annexation must be provided for states that had never been in the tsarist empire and, like the later People's Democracies, were not yet part of the USSR.

The few writings that the early Bolsheviks composed on population were essentially paraphrases of Marx's thin dicta. Whatever influence there may have been on population policies was overwhelmed by the effects of the First World War and the overlapping civil war, of famines and epidemics, and of terror on a new scale.

Agriculture in the Soviet Economy

The development of the Soviet economy and society from the revolution to its demise was erratic, with a counterpart to the business cycle of capitalist economies setting alternating stages of greater repression and relative relaxation. During each upswing the Party drove the country at breakneck speed toward the future it had planned for the masses; then the clogged economy and resistant population forced the leaders to slacken the pace during an ensuing downswing. When this looser control encouraged a threat to its power, the Party enforced its sole domination again and renewed its forward thrust. Generally these abrupt turns in policies took place through factional disputes within the Party, with recurrent purges of the losing side. Dramatic shifts occurred in every element of the society from the family to the arts, from central-provincial relations to the pace of industrialization.

The relation of the state to the peasantry greatly affected agricultural production; it was both a significant trend in itself and the one most relevant to the balance between food and population. In pre-1917 debates within the Party, it was axiomatic that the key to taking and holding power in an overwhelmingly agricultural country was a so-called *smychka*, or union of the urban proletariat with the peasantry. Thus, the Bolsheviks borrowed some key elements of the Populists' program, especially their demand that large estates be divided among those who worked the land. For Lenin and his comrades, however, such a rural-urban coalition never evolved beyond its use as propaganda.

After the Bolsheviks took power in the main cities and while they were still fighting to establish control over the rest of the country, they tried to institute an instantaneous full communism. The sale or purchase of commodities was prohibited, but no alternative distribution system was established. Peasant women were arrested for selling a few heads of cabbage on the street. Cities could be fed only by sending armies into the countryside to confiscate peasants' food, including often their seed grain.

Terror and counterterror killed thousands, civil strife hundreds of thousands. Epidemics spread by the constant movement of hungry hordes; typhus alone killed more than 1.5 million in 1919–20. According to official figures of the Soviet Central Statistical Bureau, 5,053,000 lives were lost in the famine of 1921–22. As Frank Lorimer wrote in his classic work, *The Population of the Soviet Union* (1946), a reasonable estimate of total losses from the First World War, the civil war, and the attempt to establish a Communist economy makes sober reading. By comparing figures from the censuses of 1897 and 1928, he calculated that there were 2 million military and 14 million civilian deaths, a net emigration of 2 million, and 10 million fewer births than would have occurred had fertility continued at its prior level; the total deficit of 28 million, he thought, is probably correct to the nearest million. "During the years 1915–23 the Russian people underwent the most cataclysmic changes since the Mongol invasion in the early thirteenth century."

Under the New Economic Policy (NEP) that Lenin proclaimed in March 1921, its two principal goals were to return to the smychka and, in Lenin's words, "to increase at all cost the quantity of output" in agriculture. Both goals were sought by granting peasants a relatively free use of their land and whatever they produced on it. Private enterprise was authorized also in trade and petty industry, while the Party retained control of the "commanding heights" of large-scale industry, banking, and foreign trade. In spite of a remarkable economic revival, most Communists opposed the establishment of a mixed economy that Lenin himself termed "state capitalism."

With the high cost of manufactured goods, peasants found it pointless to produce for the market and gradually shifted to subsistence farming. But the industrialization beginning in the mid-1920s needed both food for the urban work force and raw materials. Stalin sought a solution in an all-out forced collectivization of agriculture. He used Lenin's three-way classification of the peasantry to try to break down the peasants' collective opposition to his policy. The Party tried to exacerbate antagonisms between "rich" and "poor" peasants and ousted from the land the most efficient among the former, the so-called "kulaks." As Stalin put it, this confiscation was "an integral part of the formation and development of the collective farms. That is why it is ridiculous and fatuous to expatiate today on the expropriation of the kulaks. You do not lament the loss of the hair of one who had been beheaded."

The collectivization of agriculture by terror has often been characterized as a prime instance of Stalin's deviation from Marxism. However, in the *Communist Manifesto* Marx and Engels had ridiculed those who would preserve the "hard-won, self-acquired, self-earned" property of the small peasant, which "the development of industry has to a great extent destroyed and is still destroying daily." By increasing the proportion of the population living in cities, the bourgeoisie had rescued many agriculturists from "the idiocy of rural life." Stalin's program was also laid out in the *Manifesto*: first, "expropriation of the land and use of the rent for state needs"; then, "armies of laborers" cultivating the land according to "a common plan."

The "rich" peasants were not permitted to join the collective farms being established out of their land. In the words of an American Communist, Anna Louise Strong, who was in the Soviet countryside during the expropriation, "a million families suddenly found themselves pariahs, without any rights which need be respected, and without any knowledge as to what they might do to be saved." Deprived of their means of existence, they lost also their ration cards and the right to purchase in the cooperative stores; their children were expelled from school, and their sick were excluded from medical treatment. Whole groups of villages were starved out. As Robert Conquest described in detail in *The Harvest of Sorrow* (1986), the remaining resistance of Ukrainian peasants was broken by a deliberately planned famine that killed millions. In this and in the more general famine brought about by the chaos in agriculture, the number of deaths was greater than twelve years earlier, but the regime not only sought no relief from abroad but refused to accept it when it was offered. Since it could not be admitted that a socialist society could ever be short of nourishment, the head of an international relief organization was permitted to send in only a few parcels. The ousted peasants formed one principal element of the developing forced-labor camps, which furnished the industrialization programs with such raw materials as timber and minerals, as well as fish from the northern seas.

The brutality of the forced collectivization broke opposition to it, but it also destroyed Soviet agriculture. Every Soviet leader over the following decades tried to repair the damage, and none succeeded. A full generation after the terror in the countryside, the core of Mikhail Gorbachev's proposed reforms was in agriculture. Tiny private plots regained legitimacy; though they totaled some 3 percent of the country's farmland, at least a quarter of the total farm yield was produced on them, varying in proportion from one commodity to another. Those private plots stood as highly visible symbols of the gross inefficiency of the socialist system. As measured by the Soviet Union's food production, one of the two superpowers was part of the Third World.

Soviet Views on the Control of Fertility

It was part of Communist dogma that collectivized agriculture would bring greatly increased harvests to the world. As noted in the previous chapter, no less an authority on Marxist thought than Karl Kautsky had proclaimed that, "for at least a century," the enhanced food production would outpace any conceivable increase in the number to be fed. In a socialist country there could be no Malthusian problem and therefore there need be no bar to maximum fertility.

According to two of the best known Soviet demographers, B. TS. Urlanis and D. I. Valentei, in capitalist countries private ownership resulted in an excessive decline in fertility, but the Soviet Union was immune from that social disease and the consequent economic disorganization. In some expressions of this creed, unlimited human reproduction was advocated even in other types of society. In 1947, when for the first time representatives of opposed ideologies formally met in the UN Population Commission to debate the problems of world population, the Ukrainian delegate (supported by the other Soviet delegate) recited the canon with breathtaking abandon:

> I would consider it barbaric for the Commission to contemplate a limitation of marriages or of legitimate births, and this for any country whatsoever, at any period whatsoever. With an adequate social organization it is possible to face any increase in population.

And the Yugoslav delegate added: "Cruelly, you [Western demographers] intend to adjust the population to the economy, while we Communists want to adjust the economy to the population."

This contrast became a standard element of Soviet propaganda. The principal Soviet delegate to the 1954 World Population Conference in Rome, T. V. Riabushkin, concentrated his report on birth control, which he labeled the dominant issue that divided the East from the West—"the struggle between two trends in the underlying questions of theory and practice of population statistics: the reactionary one, connected with neo-Malthusian ideas, and the progressive one, led by the delegates of the Soviet Union and the People's Democracies." In 1959, when the UN Population Commission was listing terms to be included in a demographic dictionary, Riabushkin objected to "Malthusianism" and "birth control" on the basis that "such mistaken concepts should not find a place in an official dictionary." In such international bodies as agencies of the United Nations, there was a bizarre cooperation between Communist and Catholic spokesmen, uncomfortable for both and, for proponents of planned parenthood, a constant source of hilarity.

As earlier in the dispute between socialists and neo-Malthusians, whatever rational substance existed on either side of the argument was often buried under rabid rhetoric. Even one familiar with the language of Bolshevik polemics must find the distortions and bizarre associations of the Stalinist period something of a new departure. According to these effusions, Bertrand Russell, because he supported birth control, called for "immediate atomic bombing of the peace-loving peoples and advise[d] the rulers to see to it that 'the death rate is high.'" He preached "the raving fascist idea of breeding a special stock of people especially adapted to atomic warfare." "The American racist Margaret Sanger" argued that there should be compulsory reduction of Japan's population. "Masquerading as scientists and philanthropists, lackeys of American monopolies openly advocate cannibalism and try to justify the demoniacal plans for the mass extermination of peoples." The "progressive forces" said to be struggling against this "Malthusian obscurantism" were also a curious array, including Friedrich Burgdörfer, a leading population official of Nazi Germany; Josué Castro, a Brazilian physician who had revived August Bebel's theory that a large intake of food reduces fecundity; Lucas, "a British ichthyologist"; such Communist luminaries as J. D. Bernal, R. Palme Dutt, and Maurice Thorez, head of the French Communist Party. A. IA. Popov, a philosopher and journalist, wrote a longer work, *Modern-Day Malthusianism: A Misanthropic Ideology for the Imperialists* (1953). Like Popov, most of those in the front line against family-planning advocates had little or no training in demography. Exceptions were likely to be such demographers or statisticians as B. IA. Smulevich, who was German-trained and prominent abroad, and therefore suspect. He was under arrest or in internal exile from 1937 to 1946, and after his rehabilitation he became one of the crudest defenders of orthodoxy. Smulevich's thesis was countered by Wilhelm Billig, a Polish physicist and demographer who several years later retired, or was forced to retire, possibly because of his Jewish origin.

As chronicled by James Brackett in *Demography* (1968), it took about ten years from Stalin's death in 1953 for the Stalinist line in population theory and policy to begin to erode. Very low birth rates in Eastern Europe, particularly in Hungary, suggested that in spite of the contrary expectation, a socialist economy provides no guarantee against a declining birth rate or even depopulation. When the small-family system spread to portions of the Soviet population, V. I. Perevedentsev, a social scientist who had begun his career with analyses of internal migration, became a prolific advocate of pronatalist policies, and his exhortations to raise Soviet fertility were usually interpreted abroad as expressions of official views. V. P. Piskunov of the Ukrainian Academy of Sciences wrote papers on the same theme— frequently with his wife, V. S. Steshenko—as well as a book on the general theory of population reproduction. For several years, however, the revised orientation that such intimations in the mid-1960s seemed to presage did not develop fully. Rather, differences continued not only among those writing on population policy but also, one can presume, among top members of the Party. Even the use of the opprobrious term "birth control" (*kontrol' nad rozhdaemost'iu*) could be indicative, for in Russian the word *kontrol'* suggests bureaucrats or indeed policemen stationed by the bedroom door. Genady Gesarimov, a prominent journalist, suggested that the term "birth control" be replaced by "guidance of the birth rate" or the avoidance of "deliberate motherhood."

As Soviet demographers repeatedly pointed out, the work of females outside the home was a prime factor in the country's low fertility, for it was especially difficult in the Soviet Union for a woman to combine the roles of mother and worker/employee. With the concentration on accumulating capital goods and weaponry, it had not been possible to improve housing conditions significantly or to provide the consumer goods that would have made a homemaker's tasks less burdensome. Yet the contributions of female workers could not easily be forgone; the sex ratio had been badly skewed by massive losses of adult males in the successive Stalinist purges and the Second World War, and then aggravated by increased conscription into the armed forces.

Sizable differences in fertility by nationality also presented a dilemma to policymakers. Russians (including those with other forebears who chose to declare themselves Russian), who according to the 1979 census constituted only slightly over half of the population, had small families and a population structure with relatively few in the peak reproductive ages. The same was true of the two other major Slavic nationalities, Ukrainians and Belorussians, and of the three Baltic peoples, the Georgians, and the Moldavians. The Muslim nationalities, on the contrary, had grown by a quarter or even a third over the prior intercensal period, and if the trend continued they might become able to express their demographic weight in politics. This contrast, disastrous in the Russians' view, was repeatedly analyzed with public opinion polls, census data, and vital statistics.

As director of the Center for the Study of Population at Moscow University, Dmitri Valentei was the most prominent demographer to suggest that the state vary family allowances regionally in order to stimulate the fertility of Slavs but not of Muslims. As opponents of this proposal pointed out, however, a differentiated allowance would give more aid to the relatively well-to-do families in the Baltic states than to the poorer ones in Central Asia (the examples, as was typical of such suggestions, avoided any mention of either Russians or other Slavic peoples), and such an allocation would contradict the "policy of raising the welfare of all members of the socialist society."

A gradual shift took place in Soviet attitudes toward population growth also in less developed countries. Some abatement of the shrill denunciations of the birth-control movement in Soviet journals in the late 1960s seemed to express a nascent concern about population pressure. In 1965 two articles on the world's population appeared in the *Literaturnaia Gazeta:* the first, by one Cheprakov, continued to prescribe social and economic reforms that would bring into play the "unlimited" capacity of science; and in the second the demographer Boris Urlanis in effect responded to Cheprakov and, without yet calling for a program to limit births, spelled out how serious the problem was becoming.

A most remarkable fact about the sharp reversal from pronatalist to antinatalist policy was how little discussion ensued on the tacit turnabout also in population theory. It was no longer axiomatic that a socialist economy would protect a society against the small families supposedly endemic under capitalism. And Soviet demographers continued to exercise prudence in challenging too openly the older doctrines that, in empirical work or policy recommendations, they implicitly rejected. The very limited glasnost in discussions on population did not break through to full acceptance of demographic realities until after the fall of the Soviet regime.

Conclusion

Karl Marx died over a hundred years ago, and one might have expected him to have receded into a comfortable chapter in histories of Western thought, the counterpart of, say, Adam Smith or John Locke. Why have movements more or less based on his writings continued to flourish, to some degree even after the implosion of the principal society ostensibly based on Marxist principles? In his book *The Unfinished Revolution* the American political scientist Adam Ulam traced nineteenth-century radical schools of thought against the background of the attitudes generated by industrialization and the rise of concurrent social and political movements. One wing—anarchists, guild socialists, Russian Populists—sought utopia in the reconstitution of a preindustrial gemeinschaft; the other wing—Saint-Simon or the Fabians—projected the rise of industry and science by a quite different route to a remarkably similar ideal world. Only the Marxists squared the circle and successfully combined the appeals of the revolutionary élan of a Mikhail Bakunin with the practicality of a Sidney Webb. The Bolshevik victory in Russia contradicted fundamentally the Marxist timetable, but it also produced a bureaucracy that was inclined to label any rebellious movement as Marxist or, if that term had to be stretched even beyond the wide expanse of Marx's interests, as neo-Marxist.

For both author and reader, an essay on Marxist theories of population and their projection in Soviet society is a frustrating encounter. This is a drama in which most of the characters have but few lines, speak them haltingly, and hurriedly leave the stage to seek roles more to their taste. In Marx's few relevant passages he either denied the importance of population growth in human affairs or, more frequently, denounced Malthus for his contrary view. Even such deviants from orthodoxy as Eduard Bernstein offered no striking or original observations on the interdependence of population and resources. The one major exception, the young Kautsky, reversed himself as a mature theorist. In this large desert one might have anticipated at least one oasis, for the question of how population growth affects underconsumption is closely tied to the Marxist interpretation of the capitalist system. The only Marxist scholar to address this question at length, the American economist Paul Sweezy, could do no better than to suppose that if Marx had lived to develop fully the thesis that he found implicit in Marx's works, he would have written as Sweezy himself did.

Non-Marxist infidels, for whom population is a necessary and central component of any rounded analysis of how a society or an economy operates, have been puzzled that Marx and virtually all who deemed themselves Marxists more or less passed over this factor in their theoretical and practical work. Moreover, they did not so much overlook the topic as willfully bypass it, and on occasion they said why. Within capitalism, they believed, the resources on which a population depends, the food that people need to live, set limits; but wherever it was established, the socialist world would flourish unimpeded by these encumbrances. Marx and Engels criticized Saint-Simon, Fourier, Owen, and others as utopians. But does it evade utopianism in one's analyses to ignore crucial demographic factors that impede the transformation to socialism? By its denial of even the existence of the population factor, Marxism defined itself as one of the most utopian of all the socialist denominations.

7

Parents versus the State

For the past century there has been a war between prospective parents and state bureaucracies over who shall decide on the size of families. First in Europe, then in the third world, fierce battles have been fought, and the state won rather few of them.

Like all other species, humans are profligate in the supply of their reproductive matter. Males produce millions of spermatazoa, only one of which can fertilize each receptive egg. At the start of her fecund years, each female has some 200,000 to 400,000 oocytes, as immature ova are called. Most of these potential eggs, however, decompose at an early stage, and during her reproductive life perhaps as few as 400 will be ovulated, and of the fertilized ova perhaps only one in five will implant itself in the wall of the uterus, an early step in the formation of a fetus. The number of potential offspring from a single mother, thus, provides a very wide margin for the frequent mishaps.

Given this physiological framework, what is the maximum number of children that a population can produce? The largest recorded families have been in an Anabaptist sect called Hutterites, after their sixteenth-century founder, Jakob Hutter. From their original home in Moravia, they moved to Russia and then, in the late nineteenth century, to South Dakota, with eventual daughter colonies elsewhere in the United States and Canada. With an average of more than ten children in every completed family, Hutterites have been taken as the measure of "man's capacity to reproduce," the title of a pioneering work on their reproductive system. Though conversions have been few (fewer even than the tiny number of defections), in a bit more than a century their population in the United States rose from 443 persons in 1880 to more than fifty times that number.

Ansley Coale, an economics professor at Princeton, devised an elegant measure of family size based on this anomalous population.

If a woman marries at age 15 and, throughout her fecund period, has the same number of children that Hutterites do in each age interval, she will bear an average of 12.6 children during her lifetime. If we take this to be a population's maximum potential (exceptional individual families have, of course, been larger), the reproduction of less prolific peoples can be related to this base by what Coale termed the index of overall fertility.

From Fecundity to Fertility

What is it, then, that in all societies cuts down the actual family size below this potential? Everywhere the typical age at marriage fluctuates about a figure set by more or less stable cultural imperatives. In the already discussed "European pattern" of family formation, its distinctive features have been an advanced age at marriage and a large proportion of adults who remain single. Seemingly the Western standard that a marriage should be founded on the ability to care for the resultant family is contradicted by the usual inverse relation between social class and fertility: in the modern West those better able materially to care for children have generally had fewer of them. To understand this relation, one must place it in the context of upward mobility.

One of the best studies of the matter is a book titled *Prosperity and Parenthood* (1954) by the English sociologist J. A. Banks. During the nineteenth century, when Britain became the world's wealthiest nation, it was possible for many to climb into high social strata. To succeed in this effort, however, aspirants had to set and maintain an appropriate style of life, with a minimum of one full-time servant, a carriage, and an annual holiday away from home. Outlays for children, especially the cost of the socially stipulated boarding school, rose steadily, and reducing family expenditures could be accomplished mainly by postponing the formation of families. Among the clergymen, doctors, lawyers, aristocrats, merchants, bankers, manufacturers, and other Englishmen of the gentleman class who married between 1840 and 1870, the average age was a shade under thirty years. Not only in Britain but also in other Western countries, the decline in fertility began in the rising middle class and from there gradually spread to the rest of society.

Banks's study suggests that reproduction must be perceived not merely as "natural," with all that that word connotes, but also in a rational perspective, legitimately subject to human control. The social structure should preferably be open; in the words of Norman Himes in his classic history of the birth-control movement, "The widespread desire for self-advancement economically, which is such an outstanding characteristic of capitalist civilization, is fundamental." The crucial element is aspiration: as affluence rises, the desire for a still finer style of living declines very slowly, if at all. When middle-class parents say they cannot afford another child while those with much lower incomes can and do, the difference does not derive from the costs of living.

One or two generations ago demographers often hypothesized that until the first steps toward modern birth control started in the first decades of the nineteenth century, there was no conscious regulation of fertility. In his early survey of tribal societies, the English social scientist Alexander Carr-Saunders concluded that without exception these cultures restrict the increase of population by such practices as abstention from marriage, delayed marriage, periodic abstinence from intercourse, coitus interruptus, prolonged lactation, contraception of various types, abortion, and infanticide.

Or, as another example, consider the "familial society"—as it is often termed in Western texts—of classical China. It is true that the ideal was a large family to guarantee continuity in the male line. But if peasants had many children, most of them died in infancy; and the gentry had to consider the consequence, given the absence of primogeniture, of a repeated division of family-owned land. Perhaps the best historical account of the Chinese upper class was by the American sinologist Chung-li Chang, and he estimated that the gentry family averaged just under three children. Marital coitus was regarded as unlucky or dangerous on the 1st, 7th, 15th, 21st, 28th, and 29th days of each lunar month; on the 16th day of the 5th month; when there is an earthquake, rain, thunder and lightning, great heat, or great cold; after washing the hair, a long trip, heavy drinking or eating; when the man is tired, very excited, too old; during the woman's menstruation and for one month following the birth of a child; during 27 months following the death of a parent; permanently after the woman has reached age 40 or after the birth of a grandchild. Books and astrological calendars denoting auspicious and inauspicious days still circulate in Taiwan (and possibly also in mainland China). If all the rules are observed, intercourse is permitted on only about a hundred days per year in order to achieve the family's primary goal, to bring forth healthy and lucky sons.

The small library about the English pioneers of neo-Malthusian-ism is almost entirely laudatory, yet their direct effect was probably far less than is often supposed. Most of the noisy advocates of birth control were all-round dissidents. Charles Bradlaugh was a notori-ous atheist, a lonely voice in a religious age. Annie Besant, his code-fendant in the two famous trials for distributing a pamphlet on con-traception, also began as an atheist and then championed the hardly more popular causes of theosophy and Indian nationalism. The re-spectable barristers and businessmen who were actually producing fewer children would not have been attracted to their writings. Though the neo-Malthusian movement probably affected behavior far less than is generally supposed, it did set the image of birth limitation by its enormous emphasis on the means rather than the end, on contra-ception as contrasted with family responsibility.

In the United States, Frederick Hollick's *The Marriage Guide*, first published in 1850, went through more than 300 printings, with a total sale of almost a million copies. The methods of contraception he described included a rhythm method (based on a false timing of ovulation), intercourse without ejaculation, condoms, "womb veils" (that is, diaphragms), a sponge, douche, and abortion. Also recom-mended were such chemicals and extracts as ergot, cotton root, al-oes, savin (a type of juniper berry), tansy, opium, iodine, lemon juice, vinegar, prussic or sulfuric acid, and Lysol. Only quacks pre-scribed the more startling items in this list, but in even the best medi-cal circles knowledge of the physiology of reproduction was slight and often faulty.

Sponsored Births

Fertility in France probably began to fall before the 1789 revolu-tion, and by 1800 it was an estimated tenth below the earlier tradi-tional level. As has been noted already, one could ascribe the fall in France's birth rate to a neo-Malthusian movement even less than in Britain. The two main parties of the Left, the Socialists and the Com-munists, were either indifferent or hostile to antinatalist propaganda, and in the middle classes the tiny movement had virtually no sup-port.

The French state was the first in modern times to intervene in an attempt to raise the country's fertility, not merely with pronatalist broadsides but with various positive and negative inducements. Fam-ily allowances were given successively to mailmen and telegraph operators (1900), the army (1913), civil servants (1916), and private employees with dependents (1932). Laws forbidding abortion and the disssemination of contraceptives culminated in a broad family code, enacted in mid-1939 and put into effect under the Nazi occupation. It increased family subsidies and provided for other types of family assistance, strengthened the prohibition of abortion, introduced measures designed to reduce infant and maternal mortality, and prescribed education on population matters. In 1945, within a few months of the end of the Second World War, the French government established the National Institute of Demographic Studies (INED) and charged it with providing an accurate factual base for a continuing population policy.

Similar programs were adopted in most European countries, both democratic and totalitarian. Fascist Italy had a full range, from the discouragement of celibacy and the subsidizing of marriage to special awards for large families and the inhibition of emigration. Two Swedish socialists, Gunnar and Alva Myrdal, together wrote a work in Swedish that stimulated a lively discussion culminating in the enactment of extensive pronatalist measures. When the same arguments were presented in English in Alva Myrdal's *Nation and Family* (1940), it became probably the most influential pronatalist tract of the period.

In the United States, the decline in family size during the depression of the 1930s stimulated many intellectuals to sound an alarm. In a famous presidential address to the American Economic Association, Alvin Hansen spelled out the dire consequences of zero population growth. Louis Dublin, chief demographer of the Metropolitan Life Insurance Company, traveled to one women's club after another personally imploring the members to have more children. The state itself, however, did not intervene with pronatalist measures. American tax laws have penalized the married state, and the deductions from taxable income for dependent children have been, by European standards, ridiculously small.

Perhaps the most important work of David Glass, who until his death was the dean of British demographers, was *Population Policy and Movements in Europe* (1967). Glass's critical review of the pronatalist measures instituted in several West European countries concluded that, with the possible exception of the rigorous ban on abortion in Nazi Germany, they had all been failures. It had proved to be well-nigh impossible to build a bridge between potential parents' decisions whether to have children and the need that the national governments perceived for more citizens or subjects.

One reason was that in a democracy prohibitions were difficult to enforce. In France, nominally illegal abortions were readily available, at least in the major cities and probably also in most of the countryside. For a time when it was forbidden to sell condoms to be used as contraceptives, the same devices could be bought everywhere as prophylactics. The inhibition of birth controls of any kind was fully enforceable only in a totalitarian framework, and even the degree of regimentation instituted in Fascist Italy did not suffice.

Nor was the attempt to bribe potential parents generally any more successful. According to a number of papers by Thomas Espenshade, in 1960–61 the money spent to raise three American children from birth to age 18 amounted to 59.1 percent of a lower-class family's income, 47.4 percent in the middle stratum, and 38.8 percent in the upper class. From 1977 to 1980 the cost rose by a third, to a possible maximum of $85,000 per child. The U.S. Department of Agriculture estimated that in 2000 the average cost of rearing a child in a middle-income family was between $8,740 and $9,860 per year, or a total from birth to age 17 of $165,000. Whatever the comparable figures have been in other countries, in none of them did the state attempt to subsidize the full cost of child rearing. So far from stimulating fertility, an official emphasis on monetary outlays may well have helped undermine the traditional underpinning of large families, which functioned—when it did—with little regard to cost.

As economists use the word "cost," it includes what are called opportunity costs, or the value of alternatives that have to be forgone in order to make a particular purchase or follow a chosen course of action. Thus, one of the main costs of having a child may be that, at least for a period, the woman stops working outside the home or that she fails to seek a job or even to train adequately for one. Though such factors cannot be measured precisely, potential parents who calculate their choices certainly weigh both the direct and the opportunity costs of each child.

Birth Control in Poor Countries

Eventually the main emphasis of the campaign for zero population growth shifted to Asia, Africa, and Latin America. In the countries that were gaining their independence after the Second World War, intellectuals were often opposed, at least initially, to any effort to cut the rate of population growth. Nationalist, Marxist, and Catholic spokesmen, whatever their differences on other issues, were all generally hostile to birth-control programs. Eventually, however, most of the governments of less developed countries became involved in efforts to reduce the rate of population growth, using various means of birth control.

The rationale behind state-sponsored family policy over the past century or so can be summarized in a few bald statements. There is a crisis, which demands official intervention by the state. The principal means of achieving the goal is to deny (or furnish) potential parents the contraceptives they might use.

There is a crisis. A diagnosis of "underpopulation" or "overpopulation" implies that there is a norm toward which policy is directed. The first formal specification of an "optimum population" came as late as 1928, when the English economist Edwin Cannan defined it as the number of inhabitants of a country that results in the highest per capita economic return. From this pioneer effort there ensued not a consensus but a continuous scramble to redefine the concept. Successive economists proposed criteria that became more and more esoteric, ranging from the population that results in the largest total production per head to the point at which the marginal and average product per laborer are equal. As still more complications were added, a reaction resulted in utter simplification: the optimum is "the number socially desirable." However, even the notion that there is one optimum population is dubious, for the number of persons able to produce the maximum income per capita, for instance, is usually considerably smaller than that best able to carry out the equally legitimate purpose of defending the country.

In the early 1970s, when the American Association for the Advancement of Science posed the question, "Is there an optimum size of population," to 31 presumably knowledgeable persons, 13 responded Yes, 7 responded No, and 11 had no answer. Still today, this is an accurate reflection of the state of the concept. In other words, those involved in implementing population policies were seeking the better without being able to define the good.

Nevertheless, according to the policymakers' thesis, there is a crisis. Even if we cannot stipulate precisely the best population, the disparity between the ever growing number of people and the ever smaller resources on which they depend obviously demands a remedy from the government. Those who are inclined to accept on faith such cries of woe should read some of the key works of the late American economist Julian Simon. His book *Population Matters* (1990), for instance, gave solid evidence for his argument, which he summed up as follows:

> Raw materials and energy are getting less scarce. The world's food supply is improving. Pollution in the United States has been decreasing. Population growth has long-term benefits, though added people are a burden in the short run.

Pronatalist measures in Europe, based ostensibly on reasonably accurate data, actually were derived from population extrapolations. Some projections proved to be more or less accurate for a period; but the virtually universal prediction in the 1930s that the size of Western families would remain small or, more probably, continue to decline was blown to smithereens by the baby boom. In works on less developed countries, similar projections have been made with a typical lack of reliable data. Nicholas Eberstadt of the American Enterprise Institute called the figures "guesses dignified with decimal points" as concocted by ideologues masking as scientists.

What is to be done? The crucial factor in fertility, the Australian demographer John Caldwell believes, is whether on balance wealth flows up from children to parents or down from parents to children. In the third world, children start working at a very early age and, moreover, they are expected to care for their elderly parents. Under capitalist production, on the contrary, wealth generally flows in the opposite direction, with an inevitable tendency to reduce family size. One important factor in facilitating such a transition is mass education, for educated children cost their parents much more and generally contribute far less.

To the degree that Caldwell is correct, furnishing the world's peasants with contraceptives can do no more than perhaps quicken a transition under way. If wealth flows from children to parents, no control of births will be effective unless, as in China, it is forced on the parents.

8

Efforts to Reduce the Fertility of
Less Developed Countries

As briefly noted in the previous chapter, during the 1960s and 1970s both private American agencies and officials of the United States government tried to cut the rate of population growth in various parts of the third world. The consequence was that population policies in less developed countries were remarkably similar in spite of the wide divergence in such key variables as the countries' population size and density, their family types, the cultural practices affecting their fertility, and the level and rate of growth of their economies. For the programs did not develop separately within each national context but were introduced, sponsored, and largely financed by Western or international institutions, which set a relatively unitary perspective on the problem.

The view dominant in the United States on how to cut the fertility of less-developed countries was challenged by a few dissidents, of whom Kingsley Davis and Edwin Driver were the most prominent. Generally, however, the perspective of government and foundation officials was echoed in academics' papers. The "great debate on population policy," which for Bernard Berelson was an "instructive entertainment," has passed its high point. But it is still relevant to ask whether it is true, as Donald Bogue asserted in a presidential address to the Population Association of America, that the American birth controllers really had hit upon the "necessary and sufficient conditions" to achieve success anywhere in the world. Any effort to appraise the effectiveness of the programs is hindered by their underlying methodological principle. In what was termed "action-research" the effort to obtain information was combined with proselytizing, and this blend of "is" and "ought" did not produce a wholesome dish. The desire of the world's population for contraception that the birth controllers imagined was projected onto the programs' subjects, and the supposedly factual data were often contaminated by wish fulfillment.

The Theory of Family Planning

What picture of the world did the persons hold who were responsible for the family-planning programs that Americans sponsored and financed in less developed countries? The theory at least implicit in these projects was not one that could have been derived from a detailed knowledge either of cultures of particular countries or of the history of how fertility had declined in the West. It can be summed up in a series of propositions:

- The population growth both of the world as a whole and of almost every country in it is too rapid. Under almost any conditions, to reduce fertility immediately would bring mainly, or only, benefits to everyone.

The debate over this issue was not new. Neither the position of, for example, the Catholic Church nor such antinatalist works as *The Limits of Growth* and *The Population Bomb* reflected much of a change from earlier decades. Apart from these two polar positions, recommendations concerning the population of the United States went through an extraordinary cycle.

During the 1930s, when American fertility was at a low level, almost the entire scholarly community saw this as economically deleterious, if not disastrous. However, in the subsequent campaign to effect zero population growth, a paradoxical counterpoint to the decline of American birth rates to their lowest levels in the country's history, most of its proponents ignored the seemingly established wisdom of the prior decades. According to the 1972 *Report* of the quasi-official Commission on Population Growth and the American Future, "it does not appear, for several reasons, that a lower population growth rate will cause serious problems for any industry or its employees." While it may indeed have been that disruptions from a lower growth rate would be balanced by equal or greater benefits to other sectors of the economy, only ideologues would assert that there would be no serious disruption to "any" unit of the economy.

- The most important reason for the over-rapid population growth of less developed countries, given the reduction in mortality, was the lack of physical, moral, and financial access to contraceptives.

The proposition was based on the notion that contraception, almost like antibiotics, had been an invention of modern Western technology, and thus that other peoples could control their fertility only through the beneficent intervention of those disseminating these materials. It is true that less developed countries have varied greatly in both the traditional means and the effectiveness of their control of fertility. But the premodern culture of no single one of them has lacked impediments to unrestrained procreation. Even so pronatalist a country as Hindu India forbade the remarriage of widows, many of whom had been betrothed in infancy or early childhood and were thus totally excluded from procreation. In Confucian China it was crucial to have sons but no less important to avoid conceiving them at inauspicious times. When the Confucian ethic was transferred to Japan, it was adapted marvelously to the more straitened circumstances: the emphasis on continuity of the lineage was undiminished, but the same end was achieved by stressing quality rather than quantity in the male offspring. Tokugawa Japan, artificially isolated for several centuries from the outside world, could be designated the very acme of traditionalism, but its population remained more or less static. "The necessary conclusion from the Japanese experience," Irene Taeuber remarked in her definitive *The Population of Japan* (1958), "is that the role of family limitation in premodern societies may have been underestimated and the motivating factors oversimplified."

One cannot even say that modern technology has brought about an overall improvement in efficacy; as a means of controlling the number of one's offspring, nothing works better than either celibacy or infanticide. The decline of the fertility of France and the United States, the two Western countries where natality fell first and fastest, was well under way before the creation of any means more effective than withdrawal, douche, or sponge. The subsequent innovation of the birth-control movement, in France under continuous and effective attack and in the United States not organized until well into the twentieth century, was not a decisive factor. What these two countries had in common was a democratic ideology, with revolutionary slogans repeated so often that they spread from narrowly political issues to the family.

> • Since the fertility of industrial societies is far lower than that of most less developed ones, any shift from traditional to modernist culture is likely to bring about a lower fertility.

This notion was a corollary of the false postulate that no traditional society had its own bars to maximum procreation. Since, on the contrary, these bars were often embedded in religious or superstitious beliefs, the first effect of assimilation to Western secular norms was likely to be their dissipation. The smaller family size we associate with industrial societies came late in their development. Neither proposition is plausible, neither that every underdeveloped country will be industrialized nor that the end products will be similar to the present developed societies. But even if these propositions were accepted, during the several generations of the transition the effect of modernization on natality was likely to be questionable at best.

Why should the pronatalist view, so obviously wrong according to Western standards, have been fostered by so many Westernized statesmen and intellectuals in less developed counties? One recurrent charge by nationalist leaders seeking independence, that the imperial rule was inefficient, had instigated the typical response that the population was growing so fast that no administration could keep up with it. Nehru, Nasser, and their equivalents elsewhere came to power convinced that the difficulties supposedly associated with high fertility were nothing more than an excuse for imperialists' maladministration, and this nationalist canon was reinforced by Marxist doctrine. Birth-control programs in less developed countries were infused not only with bureaucratic sloth and corruption, but also with some persistent doubts about their necessity or urgency.

- The birth-control programs in less developed countries are most effective if administered by state agencies or at least under government auspices.

This premise hardly derives from the history of the West where, without exception, efforts of private groups to disseminate contraception were fought by officialdom. The postulate is rather a corollary of the previous one: if modernization connoted a turn toward the control of fertility, and if the states of less developed countries generally were the chief modernizers, then birth control should also be the province of the government.

- Societies generally comprise a mass of undifferentiated individuals among whom ideas and attitudes flow freely, and the benefits that everyone would derive from a smaller progeny are so great that each potential parent needs only a minimum stimulus to curb his or her procreation.

In the West fertility declined first among the middle classes and then, partly because the lower classes followed this lead and partly because the benefits of the small-family system were indeed general, it spread throughout society. When Donald Bogue advocated the use of "influentials" or J. Mayone Stycos of "elites" to disseminate the process known as KAP (for knowledge-attitude-practice), this was a large-scale imitation of Planned Parenthood. Proposing that Westernized elites, as alien to the mass of the population as Westerners themselves, be used as missionaries passed over the typical rigid structure by castes (as in India), tribes (as in Africa), or widely divergent social classes (as in all nonindustrial countries). Such impediments to diffusion were seldom considered in analyses of how antinatalist practices might spread.

It was typically supposed that declarations about general welfare could motivate individuals to change their norms concerning childbearing. The most successful birth-control programs in the West, on the contrary, had been those that tried to motivate prospective clients by emphasizing such personal factors as the woman's health. In England, for example, the societal rationale of the Neo-Malthusian League under the Drysdale family proved to be very much less appealing than the medical and personal advocacy started by Marie Stopes. In less developed countries some programs were associated with medical clinics, where advice was offered in terms of individual needs, but this was far from the general pattern.

- Typical prospective parents behave rationally, weighing the advantages of having another child against the disadvantages.

This improbable thesis became a key to American economists' reentry into demography. Gary Becker's notion that prospective parents consider whether their children will have separate bedrooms, nursery schools and private colleges, dance or music lessons, and so forth was manifestly drawn from a rather small sector of a well-to-do country. A more pertinent guide to attitudes of most of the third-world populations is the thesis that the poor in Western countries are enmeshed in frustration; they have not succeeded in the past, and they wait for the future with no stimulus to plan for it.

That this thesis received so little attention is in one sense amazing, for it applied both the sector of the American population whose high fertility sometimes generated serious social problems and also, by extension, to a large proportion of the masses in less developed countries. Understandably, would-be policymakers found it to be an unattractive theorem, for except in an outright dictatorship it allows them no leverage. Paradoxically, wholly passive people are difficult to move, since they do not conduct their lives on the basis of any sort of utilitarian calculus. When someone knows that life brings only misery and that nothing can alter that truth, what incentive can be offered to make the overprolific change their behavior?

The "Success" of Family Planning

The social theories on which family-planning programs were based were dubious or false; the agencies that distributed the contraceptives were often inappropriate; the belief that the world's peoples lacked only IUDs in order to have fewer children was frivolous. Yet, ostensibly, almost all programs succeeded. Obviously, if the listed postulates approximate the premises on which the programs were based, the criteria of success were inappropriate.

In a 1976 publication of the Population Crisis Committee, various data or suppositions were used to show that programs' aims had been achieved, and these illustrate the criteria that had become standard. In Indonesia, we read, "a record high of 1.5 million new acceptors were recorded in 1974." In Bangladesh, "over a six-month period 16 percent of all eligible couples in four test villages were brought into the program." In Colombia, "Profamilia together with the Coffee Growers Association using local volunteers reached 20 percent of all eligible couples." In Egypt, "over a five-month period several rural pilot projects recruited an average 30 percent of the eligible couples." In Brazil, "within six months a community-based project in the Northeast region recruited 12 percent of the fertile couples."

One of the commonest measures of progress was the number of "acceptors" or even, as in the Colombian example, the number who had been "reached." The distributors of contraceptives were the missionaries of our secular age, intent for personal as well as ideological reasons on building up a good record of conversions. Villagers who resisted their blandishments were characterized as ignorant and prejudiced; those who accepted them were bathed in approval. In what may have been the most significant independent replication of a major study, Mahmood Mamdani quoted one of the respondents to the prior zealots as follows:

[The program's field workers] were so nice, you know. And they came from distant lands to be with us.... All they wanted was that we accept the [foam] tablets. I lost nothing and probably received their prayers. And they, they must have gotten some promotion.

On being reinterviewed, some of the "acceptors" admitted that, as in one instance, they had piled up the boxes with the foam tablets still inside as a decoration to their home.

If some actually used the contraceptives they accepted, they did not necessarily contribute to a reduction in fertility. Some merely shifted from less convenient or more expensive methods to the means furnished by Western taxpayers; others soon lapsed into recurrent childbearing. In the best case, the acceptors were never typical of the target population. They were the cream skimmed off the top, those most receptive to birth-control propaganda. The implicit snowballing from encouraging beginnings was the opposite of the extrapolation that should have been assumed.

Just as sectors of particular populations were used to indicate the rate of acceptance of whole countries, so those countries in which fertility had declined were used to indicate the supposed trend of the whole world. Consider, for example, *Population: Dynamics, Ethics and Policy* (published in 1974 by the American Association for the Advancement of Science), in which a chart was reproduced from an article by R. T. Ravenholt and John Chao, employees, respectively, of the U.S. Agency for International Development (AID) and the U.S. Bureau of the Census. The statistics thus circulated were not only misleading but also—it is impossible to avoid concluding— deliberately so. They included only the eighty-two countries "with good vital statistics," and in seventy-two of them the crude birth rate had declined over the period from 1960 to 1972—by a full 50 percent in Greenland down to only 0.8 percent in St. Lucia. The rather exotic flavor of these two countries was characteristic of the whole table. It included, for example, Gibraltar, St. Kitts-Nevis, Cook Island, the Isle of Man, and the Faroe Islands—whose combined population was well under that of the District of Columbia. It also included the United States, the United Kingdom, both Germanies, the USSR, Australia, New Zealand, and so on through all developed countries. Omitted were only less developed countries like China, India, Pakistan, Bangladesh, Nigeria—or more than half of the estimated population of the world.

The senior author was an officer of AID, which distributed the contributions of American taxpayers to antinatalist organizations throughout the world. Apart from Thailand and South Korea, none of the top ten recipients of U.S. family-planning funding showed a declining rate of population growth from 1965-70 to 1975-78. Two (Tunisia and Ghana) had a recorded marked rise in fertility, and the rest reflected only the fact that no one could know what the trend in their fertility was. According to Dr. Ravenholt:

> These fertility patterns document a widespread and substantial though by no means uniform decrease in fertility during the 1960s in many countries of the world.... But a much more powerful and concerted worldwide effort is needed during this decade [of the 1970s] to insure that every person of reproductive age has the information and means for effective fertility control....When that goal is achieved, world fertility will surely decrease rapidly with accelerating improvement in socio-economic development and individual well-being.

In other words, since the vast sums spent by AID have been used effectively, kindly increase its budget.

A surmise that less developed countries did show a downward trend in fertility might be tested, first of all, against the datum that even in the United States the proportion of contraceptive failures was far higher than most persons would suppose:

With one year of exposure:
      Failure to prevent a pregnancy   14 percent
      Failure to postpone a pregnancy   26
Failure to prevent a pregnancy with five years of exposure:
      Youngest age category   56
      Oldest age category   16
      All respondents   44

These figures were derived from a 1970 National Fertility Study, which reflected an improved control over an earlier survey. More than half of this greater efficacy in both preventing and postponing pregnancies was attributed to the fact that the pill had largely re-placed other contraceptives; but hardly any oral contraceptives were available in most less developed countries.

In order to determine the trend of even the crude birth rate, one must have as a minimum reasonably plausible figures at two points in time for the number of births and the size of the population. If only some sectors of a society had good statistics, it was highly im-probable that these were typical in any of their other characteristics;

it was quite misleading to extrapolate from advanced regions or social classes or villages to the remainder of the population. If there were censuses but no vital statistics, then one had to face the fact that the greatest gap in the census data was likely to be the number of children aged under five years, which with the number of women in the fecund ages comprises the child-woman ratio.

The efforts of some of the West's best demographers to derive plausible projections from incomplete data, using the method first devised by William Brass (Brass et al., *The Demography of Tropical Africa*, 1968) and later developed in collaboration with Ansley Coale, can be exemplified by a work on the population of tropical Africa. As in many other less developed areas, the civil unrest during the postcolonial period inhibited the collection of data, so that sometimes there was a deterioration from even the poor and incomplete coverage of earlier years. The summary appraisal by Étienne van de Walle was realistic:

> The very size of [Nigeria's] population is uncertain after the last censuses, its mortality is unknown, and its fertility can only be guessed.... No sophisticated procedure upon which we would base even a mere guess about what this population would be in 10, 15, or 25 years ahead is justified. Unfortunately this is still true of a large part of Africa.

If, however, acceptable data did show a definite downward trend in fertility, there was no necessity that such a decline resulted from the government's purposive action rather than any of a dozen factors that typically influence natality. If fertility rose, the contraceptive program may have been successful—in preventing its more rapid rise. If fertility fell, the program may have been a total failure—by impeding its more rapid decline. In other words, in order to evaluate the reasons for a particular trend in fertility one needed much more than bare data on births and population. A successful policy constitutes more than planned change that is congruent with actual change; the analytic question is, can one reasonably substitute "the determinant of" for "congruent with"?

Taiwan

Of all non-Western countries with official efforts to reduce fertility, Taiwan was the subject of the most analysis. For a period it became a showpiece to demonstrate the efficacy of the contraceptive program there and, by implication, elsewhere. Even the first half of this appraisal was not really warranted. The island had better statistics than some fully industrial countries, and they did not show a clear relation between antinatalist efforts and the decline in fertility. As the American demographer Wen Li pointed out in a paper in *Population Studies* (1973), from 1962 to 1970, while the total fertility rate fell by an average of 182 units in all of Taiwan, by 211 in small towns, and by 156 in major cities, in Taichung, where the program was initially concentrated, it fell by only 154 units—less than in any of the other categories. One need not conclude that the special effort in Taichung inhibited the decline that was going on with no official encouragement, but one can hardly ascribe to it any reinforcement of that downward trend. The same conclusion came from a temporal analysis: not only did the downward trend in fertility begin well before the program got under way, but it also continued thereafter at the same slope.

More generally, the less developed countries with the earliest demonstrable declines in fertility were mainly in what Parker Mauldin and Bernard Berelson termed "islands and peninsulas": Hong Kong, Taiwan, Thailand, Mauritius, Costa Rica, Puerto Rico, Trinidad, and so on (*Studies in Family Planning*, 1978). These were relatively small countries whose social problems were slight compared to the infinite complexity of an India, partly because these were typically developing areas rather than less developed ones. The paper by Mauldin and Berelson was a conscientious and useful summary of a large number of studies, and it avoided the most obvious flaws of some earlier analyses. With an engaging frankness, the authors noted that the initial letters of the "best available data" they used spell out BAD. But is a joke, even a good one, sufficient to cover the deficiencies in the data from ninety-four countries ranging from Afghanistan to Bangladesh, from Ethiopia to Laos, from the People's Republic of Yemen to the People's Republic of China? No caveats could cover the irresponsibility of citing crude birth rates in 1965 and 1975 from such an array.

Figures on natality from such sources were correlated with seven other variables, of which we can take Gross National Product per capita as representative. For seven countries in the list this was given as less than $100 a year, ranging down to $84 for Mali and $80 for Bhutan. That it is probably impossible to subsist at such a level did not seem to disturb the two analysts. They apparently did not realize that a systematic error was built into the data. Gross National Product is measured ordinarily from commercial operations, and in countries where much of the countrymen's produce is not marketed but consumed directly, as with the work of housewives in advanced economies, much of the country's production is either excluded from the GNP by definition or is brought in by the wildest of guesses. Since the extension of the market economy means precisely that a larger and larger proportion of this household production is shifted to cash crops or paid work, a recorded increase in GNP can reflect either that transformation of the distribution system or a higher overall production, or both in an unknowable ratio. As Oskar Morgenstern put it in *On the Accuracy of Economic Measurement*, rates of growth in GNP are "worthless in view of the exacting uses to which they are being put"; that is, they provide a loose suggestion of broad distinctions but not an acceptable basis for exact differentiation.

As Mauldin and Berelson pointed out, only four of the twenty-four studies they summarized included a consideration of the availability of contraceptive services, and all four were "done with the participation of donor agencies directly concerned with policy issues." It is no reflection on the honesty of every businessman that we expect his books to be audited by someone other than his own bookkeeper, and it is not because we find every scientific researcher suspect that the canon has been enshrined that findings are to be checked independently. In every type of study, the many judgmental decisions one has to make can shift the reported results decisively.

Most self-appraisals were positive. In the famous Khanna study, however, the six target villages were compared with six control villages. The temporary decline in the birth rate began before the program got under way, continued at the same rate for a certain period among both the test and control population, and was due to a rise in the age at marriage rather than the increased use of contraception. But this honest admission of failure was highly exceptional.

Statements about what has happened to the world's fertility depend largely on guesses about countries of which we know least. What can be reasonably averred concerning the trend in the world's two most populous countries, China and India? Of the United Nations' guesstimated population of the world in 1978, 4,365 million, Communist China supposedly had 1,004 million and India 657 million. Between them, thus, they made up almost 35 percent of the whole, hardly a lacuna any researcher could accept comfortably. Bits and pieces about the traditional mores pertaining to population in the two countries have been mentioned earlier; here a focused account brings together data about a period when overt policies were presumably guiding the growth of population.

Communist China

What could be said about the world's most populous country, Communist China? It had had precisely one officially released census, in 1953, when the count was almost 583 million. There was a declared net underenumeration of only 0.116 percent, thus making this the most accurate large-scale census in world history! Though we can reject this judgment as pure bombast, the figure was the best datum available.

From 1949 to the mid-1950s China followed the standard Marxist line that with its planned economy and socialist society the country could cope with any growth in numbers. After the unexpectedly large number counted in the census, the country's constitution was revised to include a new canon: "The State advocates and encourages birth control." Laws raised the minimum ages at marriage, and any who married earlier were to be forcibly separated. Urban couples who pledged to hold their family size to a single offspring could apply for a "one-child certificate," which entitled them to a monthly stipend until the child reached 14 years, preferential treatment in his or her schooling, and, for themselves, in housing, jobs, and pensions. This first antinatalist policy was initiated in a curious fashion: the state continued the traditional Marxist opposition to birth control while inducing couples, ostensibly for their personal welfare rather than for societal reasons, to put off getting married. But twice during that short period of Communist China—during the Great Leap Forward and again during the Cultural Revolution—the Party reverted to the earlier orthodoxy and abandoned its intermittent antinatalist stance.

Western experts were inclined, however, to believe that over the long term the Party was committed to the "planned-birth program," which combined postponement of marriage with contraception. The farther the time moved from 1953, the wider was the range of population estimates, whether by officials of the government or by knowledgeable outsiders. The government's figure of 800 million was repeated year after year together with statements that the population was growing annually by 1.5 percent or 2.0 percent or whatever.

Three journalists associated with the London *Economist* traveled around China in 1977 and wrote three independent reports, which in sum were a fascinating picture of every facet of that society. They were not demographers or sinologists, but intelligent and generally well informed Westerners, somewhat more skeptical of propagandistic reports than some experts in the U.S. State Department. In his contribution to this survey, Norman MacRae remarked:

> The director general of the agricultural ministry in Peking rather crossly assured us that the population of China was only 800 million; the day before a member of the Politburo told us the population was really 900 million; and the week after a specialist research team on population growth had been told it was 950 million.

The difference of 150 million amounted to a sixth of China's supposed population, or almost 4 percent of all humankind.

All three journalists were inclined to accept the claim that life expectancy had been raised from around 30 years in 1949 to around 60 years. Middle-aged Chinese, according to Brian Beedham's report, "unlike their fathers and grandfathers, are in no danger of dying of starvation in a ditch; [and] they are in reach of at least some rudimentary medical help if a sudden pain grips their insides."

China's principal means of reducing the rate of population growth was a more or less forced abortion. Steven Mosher, a young American then living in China, wrote the first extensive report on this campaign in his *Broken Earth: The Rural Chinese* (1983). When the Communist government complained to Stanford University about his detailed account of forced abortions, his doctoral committee ousted him from its program. Subsequently, Mosher wrote another book on the subject, *A Mother's Ordeal: One Woman's Fight against China's One-Child Policy* (1991), based on a narrative by a reformed one-time abortionist. Remarkably, many Americans advocate setting trade policy with China as a means of combating that country's persecution of dissidents, but the more prevalent persecution of prospective parents is almost never mentioned. The one-child policy cut the average Chinese family, according to the usual account, from six to somewhat more than two children. The estimated population in 1996 was 1,210 million, projected to rise to 1,413 million in 2020. How realistic are these figures?

The same pressures that induced production cadres to exaggerate, falsify, and fabricate their reports on industry or agriculture have been evident also in pronouncements on family size. Details in abundance have been given by John Aird, an American demographer who has concentrated his scholarly work on China. His several papers were summed up in *Slaughter of the Innocents: Coercive Birth Control in China* (1990).

Almost everyone in Chinese cities was paid according to a system setting rates from one to eight, or one to ten in the countryside. Though in general the rating was based on productivity, and less on political attitude than when the practice had been started, such relative leniency apparently was not carried over to behavior flouting the Party's line on family size. "One senior official said that in his province a girl who had an illegitimate baby after being refused permission to marry below the stipulated minimum age of 24–25 would have her work points cut." A girl could protect herself against such penalties only by claiming that she was raped, and the penalty for rape was death. Mothers of three children were sometimes threatened that a fourth child would get no ration book. The control of labor, of rates of pay, of the distribution of food, meant that it may well have been possible both to raise the legal age at marriage with little premarital dalliance and to restrict sharply the number of children per family.

In all likelihood no one in China knew what its fertility was, but during the course of any policy official pronouncements proclaim its success almost automatically. Curiously, one of the few exceptions one could cite pertained to this question. At the end of 1978 an official radio broadcast noted that the number of births in Kwantung province would be some 100,000 in excess of the planned figure. Since this was the first time such a failure was admitted, analysts in Hong Kong interpreted the statement as a truthful indication of official concern. The change in policy during 1978 increasing the income to peasant families that did more work apparently had had the unintended effect of stimulating procreation. Yet from both anecdotal evidence and more detailed reports by Western scholars, one could reasonably suppose that overall fertility had been cut considerably.

But even if we assume that all figures are cooked and that in any case the cooking was with ingredients not too precise to start with, there is no doubt that in record time China's forceful measures have effected a very significant decline in population growth. Like the Soviet Union, Communist China had a totalitarian counterpart of the business cycle: full adherence to dogma was maintained until it choked the economy and supplanted any initiative with fear, and then a relaxation was permitted until its continuation seemed to threaten the

Party's full and absolute control. The crucial element, the totalitarian control of people's lives, was neither easily diffused nor welcome. China's antinatalist program, like the pronatalist policy of Nazi Germany, suggests that totalitarian controls may be needed to bring about, independently of the individual couples' desires, a significant rise or fall in average family size.

India

How difficult is it to apply authoritarian methods in a nontotalitarian state was exemplified by the experience of India, the world's second most populous country. During the quarter century 1951–76, its population increased by an estimated 68 percent, from 361 million to 607 million. In the mid-1990s it was estimated at 866 million, and a set of projections based on three alternative trends in mortality and six in fertility forecast one of about 900 million by the end of the century.

Though India reportedly began its antinatalist effort earlier and more energetically than other less developed countries, in fact it started slowly and reluctantly, during Nehru's lifetime never achieving even a minimal success. Nehru's first minister of health was a devoted disciple of Gandhi, and his project to implement the rhythm method by distributing colored beads became an international joke. By the end of the second Five-Year Plan in 1961, India was still engaged in what the director of the census termed "a pilot experimentation." When the census of that year recorded a total larger than had been anticipated, efforts to generate a full program really began. In the subsequent period control was partly decentralized and experiments were effected with various types of motivation and distribution systems, but essentially the administrators engaged in a continual search for the contraceptive means. The large-scale program based on IUDs was more or less abandoned when it became evident that an excessively large proportion of women either expelled the device or removed it because of bleeding or pain, and that other prospective users were being frightened off.

Disappointing results with contraceptives, which have to be constantly renewed, induced Indian administrators to move toward sterilization as the favored method of contraception. But according to an analysis of vasectomies in *Population Studies* (1963), the 3,465 men who had been sterilized averaged 39 to 40 years in age, with an average of 5.33 living children. The author saw "no possibility of vasectomy camps having a significant effect on the birth rate,...[but] they have no doubt helped to create a climate favorable for popularizing family planning." Even though those sterilized were mainly fathers of more children than the birth controllers had set as their upper limit, when Sripati Chandrasekhar became minister of health and family planning in 1967, he continued to emphasize male sterilization. It was, he said, "of all the methods tried so far the only one that has yielded significant results." According to a 1974 report in the periodical of the International Planned Parenthood Association:

> Funds earmarked for drought relief, road building, and Harijan welfare are believed to have been used to mobilize respondents. When villagers applied for loans to buy seeds or fertilizers they were ordered first to undergo a vasectomy. . . . Even Nirman Bhawan [of Indira Gandhi's health and family planning ministry] cautiously admits that some of the camps may have been counterproductive, leaving family-planning workers little time to propagate conventional contraceptive methods.

In part as a result of such irregularities, the budget for family-planning programs was cut from $101 million in 1972–73 originally to $50 million and then, after a partial restoration, to $68 million for 1974. Ostensibly, this deduction was motivated by the general financial pressure, but it also reflected doubts about both the wisdom and the effectiveness of the government's program. The targets in the fourth Five-Year Plan (1969–74) were 15 million sterilizations (contrasted with 10 million performed), 6.6 million IUD acceptors (2.4 million actual), and 10 million users of conventional contraceptives (4.1 million actual). Instead of a cumulative total of 28 million couples with one means or another of birth control, there were only 19 million. The announced goal of reducing the birth rate to 25 per thousand in 1978-79 was put off until 1984—symbolically hardly the most propitious year.

According to Karan Singh, minister for health and family planning in the 1970s, "Clearly, only the fringe of the problem has so far been touched." The minimum age at marriage, he declared, would be raised to 18 for women and 21 for men. The compensation would be increased for undergoing a sterilization (either male or female). Medical facilities for sterilization and what was termed MTP (medical termination of pregnancy) were being extended to rural areas. "Suitable group incentives" would be introduced for the medical profession, district and block councils, teachers at various levels, cooperative societies, and labor organizations, in order to "make family planning a mass movement with greater community involvement." Sanjay Gandhi, the Prime Minister's son, took on birth control as his special province and, with no official position, attacked the problem with his characteristic combination of enthusiasm and corruption. India's seventeen states were informed that, contrary to the constitution, increases in population would no longer bring them more representatives in Parliament or a larger share of federal revenues. Bounty hunters began to offer their services, charging a fee for each subject found. According to Karan Singh, India might have to "think the unthinkable"—to impose a limit on family size through what was termed "compulsuation," an amalgam of COMPULsion and perSUASION. Civil servants were denied raises or transfers or sometimes even salaries until they had convinced a specified number of potential fathers to undergo sterilization. Officials withheld the licenses from hotels, theaters, banks, airlines, and other businesses until the firms induced their employees with three or more children to have the operation. Opposition was exacerbated by charges (quite valid, according to Ved Mehta's *The New India*, 1978) that the Hindu majority was using the program to reduce the proportion of Untouchables and particularly of Muslims. A Muslim slum was cleared of its inhabitants at gun point and then razed. When the people were allowed back to where their homes had been, they were given ration cards, which would be renewed only if the men underwent an operation forbidden by their religion. Police and family planners were killed, and in one ugly incident, according to seven opposition members of Parliament, several dozen protesters were shot down and 150 wounded in sterilization riots. As Prime Minister Gandhi was forced to admit, "Some deaths have taken place due to firing." Even a flawed democracy like India under Mrs. Gandhi could not use totalitarian methods without stimulating a backlash that partly erased whatever reduction in fertility had been effected.

After her government fell, the new minister of health and family planning, Raj Narain, recommended abstention from sex as the best means of birth control. "Instead of the barbarous methods of compulsion employed by Mrs. Gandhi, we will draw inspiration from our old epics and traditions of celibacy, self-control, yoga, and self-discipline." The number of sterilizations per month fell from an estimated 1 million to about 40,000, the lowest rate in a decade. True, the Desai government remained committed to reducing India's fertility, but even its reduced goal could hardly be met under the program it initiated.

Conclusions

With whatever embellishments one can find here and there, the American efforts to cut the fertility of less-developed countries have been based essentially on offering contraceptives to the masses, usually with inducements of some sort to use them. These so-called Malthusian programs have been attacked by such neo-Marxists as Mahmood Mamdani, author of *The Myth of Population Control* (1972), as not merely inefficient in detail but also unsound fundamentally. According to his analysis, the reluctance of most lower-class Indians to accept contraception was due not to ignorance or irrelevant tradition, but to a rational choice between correctly judged alternatives. If each of the smallholders or landless workers (in sum, the vast majority of the Indian population) rationally chooses to have a large family, the composite of these correct individual decisions builds up to a disaster for the whole country. When the societal consequences of population growth are contrasted with the effect of offering contraceptive services to individuals, the dispute has often been interpreted as a continuation of the controversy between Malthus and Marx. No less a theorist than Alfred Sauvy entitled one chapter of his best known work, "Les pays sous-developés: Marx ou Malthus?" A compilation of Marx's own writings on Malthus was introduced with the opinion that "if the social struggles of the early nineteenth century were essentially summed up in the controversy between Malthus and Ricardo, those of our times are perhaps not unfairly summed up in that between Malthusians and Marxists." This recurrent label, however convenient many have found it, is a strange commentary on the actual theories of both historic figures.

9

A State in the Desert

Frederick Jackson Turner, an American historian associated with the University of Wisconsin, is remembered mainly for a single article, "The Significance of the Frontier in American History." This was an address delivered at the 1893 meeting of the American Historical Association, and it set off a decades-long debate about "the Turner thesis." He argued that American culture did not derive mainly from Europe, as was generally assumed, but rather from successive colonizing of an advancing "West." From a continuous contact with the "frontier," he averred, there developed such American characteristics as individualism and the love of liberty.

From the point of view of a demographer, the main question is what are the characteristics of the typical frontier population? Generally, most of the early settlers are male, and with the scarcity of females, there are few wives and many prostitutes. Thus, the family life that in an established area is seen as the universal norm is largely supplanted by a rugged and crude male-dominated culture.

How this hypothesis worked out in the United States can be exemplified best in such originally uninviting regions as the Rockies and the desert just east of them. Nevada typifies the thesis, and a closer examination of that state is a convenient way to elaborate on the theme.

Nevada as a Frontier

Nevada is part of what the Bureau of the Census calls the Mountain Division, and of those eight states it may have had the least appeal to potential early migrants. In the whole of its almost 111,000 square miles, the Indian population before whites arrived numbered only about 15,000. In the eighteenth century Spanish explorers, having reached what is now the state's southern border, saw no reason to proceed farther, and it was not until the 1820s that a beginning penetration was undertaken. The famous John C. Frémont crossed and recrossed the region, but even that hardy individual saw little prospect of any sort of development in the Great Basin.

The first white settlement was in 1851, an offshoot of the 70,000 wagons that passed annually on the way to the gold rush in California. In 1859 Nevada's Comstock Lode was discovered, and the silver miners who flooded in founded Virginia City. As in many similar sites, it was this mining that occasioned the initial growth of population. Nevada became a territory and then a state not because of a developing economy and a growing population, but rather by an entanglement with the national dispute over slavery. In 1861, only ten years after settlers there applied for Washington's formal recognition, a bill was signed to grant "the people in the region of the Washoe silver mines" a territorial government that would permanently bar slavery. The secretary of the new territory was one Orion Clemens, who was accompanied to his new post by his brother Samuel, a journalist and eventually, under the name Mark Twain, a novelist. In one of America's literary classics, *Roughing It*, Twain described his trek through an almost unpeopled land and how he and his companions lived, how they joined in the wild search for silver.

Only three years later, only thirteen years after the first white settlement, Nevada was admitted as the 36th state, again because of national politics. President Lincoln feared that the Thirteenth Amendment, which prohibited slavery, would not be approved by the three-quarters of the states that the Constitution required, and the recognition of Nevada was rushed through to provide one more antislavery vote.

In the single year between the two censuses of Nevada Territory, in 1860 and 1861, the population grew from 6,857 to 16,374. At the latter date more than half the males were in their twenties, and of females more than half were under twenty. A third of the population were foreign-born, especially Irish and German. Half of the men were miners, the other half laborers, merchants, teamsters, carpenters and masons, farmers and ranchers. There were nineteen doctors and no preacher.

Virginia City was a lusty place. In the late 1870s, when Eliot Lord, an employee of the U.S. Geologic Survey, surveyed the town, he found about 18,000 people, 100 saloons, almost as many gambling houses, 39 groceries, and 1 library. Punning on the name of one of the mining companies, a San Francisco clergyman dubbed it "a city of Ophir holes, gopher holes, and loafer holes." During the twelve months ending June 1, 1870, according to the census of that year, only 132 persons had been convicted of a crime and only 99 were in prison—figures that, compared with the population, might suggest an astoundingly law-abiding spot. In fact, law-enforcement agents were too few, too weak, and sometimes too corrupt to protect citizens even against murder.

Some of the inhabitants would have liked a more efficient government, but a transient and predominantly male population cannot easily be converted into a stable community. However, the town eventually had a water pipeline to the Sierras that cost about $2 million, municipal gas, four daily and four weekly newspapers, schools, churches, hospitals, and many substantial homes. The more genteel half of Virginia City was like towns of comparable size in the East, for there was enough cash to build overnight what had elsewhere taken decades to develop.

Over the following decades the state's population grew erratically. Three intercensal periods showed a loss in population, 1880-90, 1890-1900, and 1910-20. The settlements that popped up when new mines were opened disappeared soon after the veins were exhausted; the state is now the site of more than 2,000 ghost towns. As is generally the case, agriculture was based on a very low population density. In the first decades of the twentieth century, when an effort was made to use Lake Tahoe as a huge reservoir and thus to stimulate farming, Nevada advertised itself as "last in population and wealth, first in virgin opportunities." But the ambitious scheme never materialized.

It is a commonplace that a frontier population has a "young population," but for most of this pioneering period the median age of both sexes was higher than that of the country as a whole. The reason, of course, was that while the place attracted many young migrants it had almost no children. For any area at the frontier the median age of the whole population is a less suitable measure than the proportion of the population in the age sector on which both children and the old depend for support. In 1900 among all the states and territories Nevada ranked fourth from highest in the percentage of the population aged 15–59.

Post-Frontier Nevada

The construction of the Hoover Dam was perhaps the most important demarcation between the period of the frontier and the more recent past. One of the world's largest dams, it was built across the Colorado River in the years 1931–36, providing irrigation and hydroelectric power to portions of three states. The project was more than an engineering marvel. According to a history of the dam's construction, edited by William Gates:

> When the United States government began the construction of the Hoover Dam, it was decided to build a city where workers and their families...might live in comfort and safety, where churches, schools, and peaceful homes would be provided in place of a frontier camp life. Boulder City...was planned on paper in its entirety before any ground had been broken.... Needless to say, there are no gambling permits,...redlight district,...speakeasies. [It is a] moral utopia.

The strong influence of Washington continued during the Second World War, and the number of federal employees in the state more than doubled between 1939 and 1961.

A more significant impetus to the rise of modern Nevada was its entrepreneurs in legal sin. In the early 1930s, when the population had fallen to 91,000 and the state government was on the brink of bankruptcy, Nevada began to offer services that in most other states were prohibited: "gaming," quickie divorces and marriages, legal brothels, and an ostensibly illegal complement of drugs.

The law was changed to define a "resident" of the state as anyone who had lived there for at least six months (later, six weeks), after which the person could take advantage of the very lax divorce law. In the common phrase, tourists from around the country came to be Renovated. They were all well-to-do, and their brief stopover in the state benefited not only lawyers and hotels but also merchants offering all sorts of luxury goods and services. Perhaps one can assume that permanent residents divorced more often than other Americans and that, therefore, one should compare the rate in Nevada with, say, twice the national rate. Even so, of the roughly 9,000 that, at the height of the mill's operation, of the divorces that Nevada courts granted annually, some 7,800 were to persons who had come to the state for that purpose.

Each state sets the conditions for marriage within its borders—whether a waiting period is required, whether the bride and groom must take tests for venereal diseases, whether interracial marriage is permitted, and so on. While in the United States these restrictions have generally been less exacting than those pertaining to divorce, any couple bothered by any of them can, with no legal complications, be wed in another state. In 1927 California set a three-day waiting period, and in 1939 it required a premarital blood test. After the enactment of both laws many Californians chose to marry in Nevada. While migratory marriage initially depended on such restrictive laws in other states, once the pattern was set it tended to continue, eventually culminating in drive-through wedding chapels. Moreover, a couple that visited the state to become man and wife often stayed also for the conventional honeymoon, so that the legal fees were only a start of the cash inflow to the state.

Gambling was part of the frontier culture, which Nevadans seeking a new image wanted to eliminate. In 1910 all games of chance were prohibited, and many commentators compared the casual enforcement and consequent corruption with the similarly farcical national Prohibition. In 1931, partly as a response to the depression, a relegalization was begun; and in 1945 all games of chance were placed under the control of a State Gaming Commission, which issued licenses and collected taxes. By the early 1960s the state's income from gambling was almost $10 million out of a total general revenue from all sources of $70.5 million.

The effects of legal gambling were broad. As one example, the innovation of female dealers in order to attract more female players became a general pattern, and as a consequence the proportion of women in the labor force rose to almost double that in the country as a whole. Over most of the period prostitution was neither lawful nor criminal, just accepted and prevalent. The main consequence, however, was that gambling acted as an entryway, and as a catalyst, to every type of illegal and quasilegal activity. The shelf of books about the rise of Las Vegas has become largely superfluous by the more complete analysis in the latest one, *The Money and the Power: The Making of Las Vegas and Its Hold on America, 1947-2000*, by Sally Denton and Roger Morris, published in 2001. Its theme is essentially that a civic entity that uses half-legal enterprises to finance its operations is likely to become an auxiliary of genuinely illegal mobsters.

Las Vegas (Spanish for "the fertile plains"!) is now the state's largest metropolis, and still growing. Nevada has two congressional districts, Las Vegas with its environs and the rest of the state. Each year more than 50 million tourists come; "only Mecca inspires as many visitors." Las Vegas has more rooms for visitors than any other American city, twice as many as in New York, Chicago, or Los Angeles. The Flamingo, the first of the mammoth hotels along "the strip," was built by Bugsy Siegel, a hit man for the mob, and most of the casinos have been owned by other mobsters. Meyer Lansky invested heavily in gambling and did much to build Las Vegas into its present kitschy splendor. In a family-friendly environment, members of the middle class came to watch and listen to nationally famous performers, to soak up sun, and—to gamble. Even the Southern Baptists have held their convention in Las Vegas.

This bizarre combination of mobsters with respectable persons and official institutions extended to Washington. Two federal agencies, the FBI and the Federal Bureau of Narcotics, entered into a symbiotic relation with the notorious gangster, Meyer Lansky, who cooperated in arranging for the arrest of a notorious drug trafficker, "Lepke" Buchalter, an important business rival who was thus removed. At the beginning of the Second World War, U.S. Naval Intelligence and the Office of Strategic Services were faced with the urgent task of ridding New York docks of left-wing unions and mobsters: Lansky's thugs prevented sabotage and helped keep the flow of goods to war-torn Europe. Later in the war, the invasion of Sicily by American troops was aided by the notorious gangster "Lucky" Luciano, who had ties to the Mafia; the invasion was successful, and the Mafia was resuscitated.

One of the chapters in *The Money and the Power* is about Pat McCarran. The son of Irish immigrants, he grew up on a sheep ranch and was brought into state politics by the political machine of his uncle, William Sharon. His rise through the ranks was boisterous, and he became the enemy not only of Republicans but of many of his Democratic fellows. In 1932, at age 56, he finally became a U.S. Senator, elected, as he said, by the state's "toilers and men in the mediocre walks of life." He managed to get on the most influential committees and as a somewhat maverick Democrat, an "unpredictable mustang," he became a powerful force in Washington and "the most formidable politician in the state's history." Under serious attack in 1944, he had black "voters" bused from Los Angeles to Las Vegas, and they provided the margin that saved him. He used a newly formed Senate Internal Security Subcommittee to conduct investigations similar to those for which Senator McCarthy became notorious—for instance, denouncing the Supreme Court as "an instrument of Communist global conquest." In such bouts against windmills,

McCarran sometimes cooperated with real culprits, for instance by procuring scarce construction materials so that gangster Meyer Lansky could build a luxury casino in Las Vegas. The corruption endemic in Nevada politics also invaded Washington. In the last night of the twentieth century, television networks of several countries communicated the celebrations in the world's great cities, Paris, London, New York—and Las Vegas. From a bare hamlet, Las Vegas had become a global capital. The strip is lined with new resorts, featuring accommodations at $400 a night, world-famous chefs, internationally celebrated boutiques, all presented to the wealthiest Americans and a sizable sample of hangers-on, ordinary people who come to get the feeling of being extraordinary. "However discreetly lit or adorned, electronically encased or programmed, the racket works as it always has, with the single ultimate purpose of taking the public's money in a manner no other industry in the world can match."

10

The Abortion Controversy

According to a number of polls and elections, in 2001 about 23 percent of American voters thought abortion should be legal in all cases, 13 percent that it should be prohibited in all cases. This division in public opinion, with more or less constant proportions, has persisted for decades, with no resolution in sight.

Indeed, a reconciliation between those at the two poles is hardly likely. On each side the most zealous proponents are willing even to commit murder—the prolifers who shoot physicians or bomb clinics, and the prochoicers who defend infanticide under the alias of partial-birth abortion. And many others in the two camps often argue for an all-or-nothing position, which makes compromise impossible. Some 60 percent of the American electorate, however, is somewhere between the antagonistic points of view, somewhat sympathetic to the seemingly reasonable arguments from both sides.

Perhaps a middle ground can be found by focusing not on the situation of the mother, as is usual in most of the polemics, but rather on the age of the fetus.

Maturation of a Fetus

Reproduction takes place in a series of stages, to which the medical profession gives distinctive names. If sexual intercourse takes place during the short period each month when fertilization is possible and an ovum is fertilized, it is called a zygote, which begins as a single cell and repeatedly divides into two. It is termed a blastocyst during the first six or seven days; an embryo until it has implanted itself in the lining of the uterus; then, until birth takes place, a fetus; and finally an infant after it is completely outside the mother's body.

Distinctions between these physiological stages have been reflected in traditional moral doctrine, which can be exemplified by the writings of Thomas Aquinas. In his *Summa Theologica* he divided the powers of the soul between "sensitive" and "vegetative." In the section of that work labeled Question 118, "Of the Production of Man from Man as to the Soul," he declared that the vegetative soul exists from the moment of conception, but the sensitive soul, which is not procreated but rather created anew with each person, cannot be transmitted with the semen. Following leads from Aristotle's concept of "mediate animation" and from similar precedents in Augustine, he maintained that at approximately the end of the first trimester, when the soul enters the fetus, the fertilized ovum first becomes a full human being.

This crucial shift from one stage to the next is marked, he held, by "quickening." Except in the phrase "the quick and the dead," the definition of "quick" as "alive" is archaic. Probably because of Aquinas's use of the term, however, "quicken" is current English, meaning "to make alive" or "to reach the stage of pregnancy when the fetus can be felt to move." Although in this work Aquinas did not mention abortion specifically, somewhat earlier, in a Commentary on Peter Lombard's *Sentences,* he wrote as follows:

> This sin, although grave and to be reckoned among misdeeds and against nature,...is something less than homicide.... Nor is such to be judged irregular unless one procures the abortion of an already formed fetus.

In the March 1970 issue of *Theological Issues,* Father J. Donceel, S.J., related how the Roman Catholic Church abandoned this proposition of Aquinas. It is a chronicle worth recalling. According to Donceel, Roman Catholics made a principled distinction between early and late abortion until well into the era of the Reformation and then, surprisingly, may have followed the lead of Protestant innovators. Luther had derived his physiology from Aristotle and Galen, holding that God "takes a drop from the blood of the father and creates a human being." And, following his understanding of Augustine, Luther adhered to what theologians term traducianism—that is, the doctrine that the soul is inherited from the parents along with the body. Thus, the fetus is fully human from conception. Somewhat similarly, Calvin's doctrine of predestination had led him to declare that the creation of the soul took place at the time of conception.

"It is just possible," Donceel concluded, that the doctrine of the two major Reformers influenced the Catholic Church to abandon Thomas's contrary view. Around the turn of the sixteenth century, statements by the Vatican and various Catholic medical authorities began to attest that the soul was infused into the body either at conception or within a few days after it. By the middle of the eighteenth century, this had become the dominant Catholic dogma.

The 1967 edition of the *New Catholic Encyclopedia* has several articles on abortion. According to Thomas Burch, a reputable demographer and a prominent lay Catholic, abortion is "the deliberate destruction of a fetus before viability." And in the following article, by Father Thomas Joseph O'Donnell, S.J., a professorial lecturer on medical ethics at the Georgetown Medical School, it is "the termination of any pregnancy before the fetus has attained viability." According to canon law at that time, as summarized in the same source, an abortion can take place only on a nonviable fetus: "Once the fetus is viable, the interruption of pregnancy before term is not abortion.... It may be murder." In short, as late as the 1960s officials of the Church still echoed the Thomist distinction between early and late abortion. This was so in spite of the more drastic shift in the concept reflected in a 1951 allocution of Pius XII to midwives. In this he defended the God-ordained dignity of the fetus from the moment of conception against any abortion, whatever the "medical, eugenic, social, economic, or moral 'indication.'"

That an element of Catholic dogma clearly associated with Thomas Aquinas should have been abandoned is remarkable, for there is hardly a person in the Church's history who has been more revered. According to an official recommendation in 1918, canon law should be constructed "according to the method, doctrine, and theological principles of the Angelic Doctor," the only person mentioned by name in the Church's legal code.

Abortion in Law

To some degree Thomas's view is reflected also in American law. In 1973, the Supreme Court's majority opinion in *Roe v. Wade*, one principal element of the country's current legal doctrine, was written by Justice Harry Blackmun. He was joined by six Justices, of whom three also filed concurring opinions. Only two, Justices Rehnquist and White, dissented. The decisions in *Roe* and in the series of subsequent cases concerning abortion are outstanding instances of the many occasions on which the Supreme Court assumed the power of the legislature. After Justice Blackmun flatly asserted that "the Constitution does not explicitly mention the right of privacy," he proceeded to list a number of prior decisions in which the Court had nevertheless found it. He continued with the assertion that this right of privacy that he and other justices had discovered "is broad enough to encompass a woman's decision whether or not to terminate a pregnancy." This less than obvious connection he demonstrated not by any sort of logical argument but by listing instances in which allowing the pregnancy to proceed to term would be inconvenient or worse. In short, to this non-lawyer the legal underpinning of the decision seems to be a bit dubious.

The circumstances underlying the case were widely publicized. "Jane Roe," a single woman living in Texas, was joined in her suit by her physician, and her appeal to the Supreme Court was consolidated with another one from the "Does," a married couple. The complexity of the legal reasoning underlying the decision is suggested by the fact that, while accepting *Roe*'s rationale, the Court rejected the appeals of both the physician and the Does.

However, those who believe that *Roe* grants unconditional discretion to the woman and her physician should read the text. Specifically following "the medical definitions of the developing young in the human uterus," Justice Blackmun argued that at some point in the pregnancy the woman's desire to end the pregnancy is no longer the sole factor in setting the legitimacy of abortion. In most states' tort law, he continued, damages for injury to a fetus can be collected only if the fetus is viable or at least quick; in either case, the age of the fetus is crucial. Prior to approximately the end of the first trimester, "the abortion decision and its effectuation must be left to the judgment of the pregnant woman's attending physician," but for the stage subsequent to viability, the state "may, if it chooses, regulate, and even proscribe, abortion...except to preserve the life or health of the mother."

Thus, according to the Court's ruling, pregnancy is not an event but rather a process. That the Court reviewed in full the history of this interpretation reflected its desire to demonstrate a continuity from that traditional guidance to its own ruling. True, while the Hippocratic Oath, to which every starting physician swears, includes a ban on abortion, the justices cited a reference claiming that this prohibition followed only the Pythagorean school, while "in no other stratum of Greek opinion were such views held or proposed in the same spirit of uncompromising austerity." According to the "undisputed" view of common law, the decision continued, abortion before quickening was "not an indictable offense," and English statutory law retained the distinction between before and after quickening. From the middle to the late nineteenth century, a prior differentiation in the law of most American states gradually eroded; but subsequently many jurisdictions restored it. At the date of the court's decision, thus, state laws were widely inconsistent. On the same day that *Roe* was decided, the Court also decided *Doe v. Bohen*, which struck down three restrictions on abortions in Georgia: that they had to be performed in an accredited hospital, that a hospital committee had to approve the procedure, and that two other doctors had to acquiesce in a positive decision. The three stipulations were declared unconstitutional because they were not medically necessary to protect the mother's health.

In the 1970s and early 1980s a series of state laws concerning the legitimacy of abortion came before the Court. Some of these laws had been written with the avowed purpose of negating the Court's earlier decisions by making the performance of an abortion as difficult as legally possible. These efforts were struck down, but with the changing personnel of the Court, the seven-to-two majority in *Roe* shrank in some instances to five-to-four.

In 1987 Justice Lewis Powell resigned, leaving the court divided four to four on any subsequent case involving abortion. President Reagan nominated Robert Bork, who was known not to recognize the constitutional right to privacy on which the legitimacy of abortion rested. After a bruising Senate hearing he was not confirmed. When the Senate approved in his stead Anthony Kennedy, whose views on abortion were not known, the usual five-to-four supporting the Court's prior record was restored. With this incident the insecurity of *Roe* as part of American law became evident to everyone, and several interest groups developed a far greater concern about who would be nominated as a new member of the Court.

One of the recurrent challenges to *Roe* was an important case decided in 1992, *Planned Parenthood v. Casey*. A Pennsylvania law was disputed that required counseling, parental consent for minors, a 24-hour waiting period, and spousal notification. The public was thoroughly engaged; there were eleven amicus briefs supporting the previously established right to abortion and twenty-three opposing it. Apparently the petitioners expected that the Court would use the occasion to reverse its decision in *Roe*, and what happened came as a surprise. The decision continued the constitutional protection announced earlier and declared that states may abridge that right only if their laws do not impose an "undue burden" on it. However, states could, if they so chose, impose such impediments as a 24-hour waiting period or a requirement that minors notify their parents. The decision was significant also in that it openly depicted the struggle the Court went through in its effort to balance pro and contra views.

The Morning-after Pill

In mid-2000 the Food and Drug Administration approved RU-486, the "abortion pill." Women using this contraceptive would all have abortions early in the first trimester. That seemingly significant fact, however, hardly abated the loud and uncompromising debate. The prochoicers claimed total victory; the prolifers were divided. One position was proclaimed in an unsigned editorial in the *National Review* (October 23, 2000), commenting on the contention that, so early in the pregnancy, the potential human being is "only a clump of cells":

> A curious phrase, that: All of us are clumps of cells. And while this clump is tiny, it is no tinier than all of us once were. Morally, size doesn't matter. At any stage of pregnancy and by whatever method, abortion is the intentional taking of a human life.

Consider, in contrast, the nuanced view of Andrew Sullivan in the *New Republic* (October 16, 2000). "It seems to me that RU-486 is indeed a sort of progress, if a kind fraught with moral danger. I say this as someone horrified by any abortion." But "good people in good conscience disagree," and in a free society "the power of government to regulate such a personal medical decision is rightly limited."

Sullivan also held that stages in the pregnancy should be central to the argumentation about whether ending it is legitimate. Not only did the Catholic view once reflect the distinction about quickening, he pointed out, but the opposition to partial-birth abortions was "rightly" especially strong because "it appeals to our moral sense that crushing the skull of a third-trimester fetus is more worrisome that terminating a cluster of cells a few weeks after conception."

If the law on abortion were to follow from the argument that the age of the fetus is a crucial factor, then that datum would become a critical element of legal reasoning. In an interesting paper in the *Journal of the American Medical Association* (August 26, 1998), the authors try to define some key terms, but with only partial success. Weeks of gestation are to be measured from the first day of the last menstrual period, a definition that achieves numerical precision but with some cost in biological accuracy. Viability does not exist before 20 weeks of gestation, and does after 27 weeks. "The time between 20 and 27 weeks is a 'gray zone' in which some fetuses may be viable and others not." In short, in any legal restrictions on late-term abortions, one would have to cope with the biological variability of human beings, including fetuses.

When Does Life Begin?

Much of argumentation on both sides has based its position on the allegation that life begins at conception or, on the contrary, at birth. In *Roe* the Court expressed the "strong support" it had found for the view that "life does not begin until live birth." Those who contend that life begins at conception have generally concluded that the absolute rights accorded to a "person" in the Fourteenth Amendment apply also to a fetus. When the lawyers defending a Texas statute offered this argument, the Court rejected it: "Neither in Texas nor in any other State are all abortions prohibited.... An abortion for the purpose of saving the life of the mother is typical [of allowable exceptions]." Moreover, in virtually all laws governing abortion the penalty is significantly less than the punishment that a convicted murderer receives.

Those who hold that each new life begins at conception often use this denotation to argue against the contention that the legitimacy of an abortion depends on the age of the fetus. But if early and late abortions are equally illegitimate, then they are also equally legitimate. When the Supreme Court's 2000 decision in *Stenberg v. Carhart* invalidated a Nebraska statute that prohibited partial-birth abortions, its rationale was that that law might "unduly burden" the general right to an abortion that the Court had established under previous rulings. The latest (to date) of the series of prerogatives that five members of the Court have successively discovered, thus, is the right under the Constitution to perform an operation that is hardly to be distinguished from infanticide. Justice Antonin Scalia, the most prominent member of the minority, avowed that this remarkable finding will one day "be assigned its rightful place in the history of this Court's jurisprudence beside *Korematsu* [validating the internment of Japanese Americans] and *Dred Scott* [supporting slavery]."

Since life begins both with conception and with birth, depending on how the antagonist chooses to define the term, a controversy with both sides resting the argument on how that choice is made seems to me to be utterly hollow. The choice of definition is typically teleological: depending on whether he is prochoice or prolife, he ascribes the start of life to fit the argument he will make. Because the process from fertilized ovum to infant represents a gradual development, a more reasonable position, it seems to me, is to fit one's moral position to that fact. This means that the Thomist point of view that distinguishes early from late abortions, if not necessarily inerrant, is at least in accord with the facts of biology.

On the Catholic Position

Of the several notable conflicts in modern times between the Catholic Church and many of its adherents, only a few pertained to any theological matter—for example, intrusions of animism in Africa or a rock-star ministry in Brazil. The subject has typically been sexuality, which in logic one might assume would be marginal.

In the late 1960s the legitimacy or illegitimacy of birth control was to be discussed by a special commission, but instead Pope Paul VI himself wrote the Church's ruling that natural law bans any obstruction to the transmission of life. For what has been designated the first time in the Church's history, many of the faithful decided on their own to remain adherents but to disobey this commandment. In 1999 a poll of American Catholics, replicating several earlier ones, found that 80 percent of laymen and even about 50 percent of priests approved of artificial contraception. This has made the Church a seemingly irresponsible opponent to any effort to restrict excessive population growth, with the consequence that with respect to a number of public policies it has lost some of its prior moral authority.

Similarly, the requirement that priests remain celibate, as Church administrators themselves recognize, has hampered greatly the effort to recruit new ones. By a large margin Catholics in both Europe and the United States have stated that the rule should be relaxed, particularly since the infractions of a small number of priests have been widely publicized. A book published in 1999, *The Changing Face of the Priesthood* by Donald Cozzens, offered plausible evidence that about half of the priests and seminarians in the United States were homosexuals; the reaction of the Vatican was to ignore it. In 2002, the public admission that a number of priests in Boston and elsewhere were pedophiles, and that Church authorities had both permitted the continuation of this evil and helped keep it secret, was startling. For a significant proportion of Catholic clergy, the denial of the natural sexuality imposed by celibacy seemingly led to unnatural practices.

In spite of the Church's history of distinguishing early from late abortions, its doctrine on this issue has been more rigid than on contraception or celibacy. In any discussion of public policy the most vehement opponents of any concession, any compromise, have generally been avowed Catholics, who seldom recall publicly that at one time the Church had a different view.

Part II

Ethnicity

11

Concepts of Ethnicity

The English language has often been enriched by the incorporation of more or less synonymous words from two or more sources. The many terms used in the analysis of ethnicity or nationalism, however, have not generally contributed to greater clarity. With so complex and contentious a topic, all designations have remained more or less ambiguous, and commentators are often unable to agree on the precise meaning of any of them. It might be useful in an authoritative piece to stipulate the "correct" meaning of each term; more realistically, the intent here is to trace the meanings assigned to each, beginning with its etymology and continuing through the connotations associated with it in various contexts.

Search for a Terminology

The word "ethnic" derives via Latin from the Greek *ethnikos,* the adjectival form of ethnos, a nation or race. As originally used in English, ethnic signified "not Christian or Jewish; pagan, heathen": for example, in *The Leviathan* Thomas Hobbes exhorted Christian converts to continue obeying their "ethnic" rulers. "Nation" comes from Latin via French; its ultimate source is *nasci,* "to be born," and the closer one is *natio,* meaning originally "birth," later one of the barbarian tribes outside the Roman world.

The physiological association suggested by these etymologies was long retained in English, as we can see especially from some currently obsolete or rare usages. Like dozens of other words (such as "barbarian," meaning "not Greek") both "ethnic" and "nation" were applied originally to outsiders as a class. With the lessening of what we now term ethnocentrism, the range of many such words was extended from alien peoples to any people, including that of the speaker. And from their original biological context, the meaning of both terms broadened to include cultural characteristics and political structures. But neither of these shifts has been consistent or uni-directional.

"Ethnic" is an adjective, and English never adopted a noun from the Greek *ethnos*. The lack of a convenient substantive form has induced writers to coin a number of makeshifts, all of which have their drawbacks. Of these, the commonest is "ethnic group." Unfortunately, users of this term too often forget the crucial distinction between a group, which by definition has some degree of coherence and solidarity, and a subpopulation, category, grouping, aggregate, bracket, or sector, which denote no more than a patterned differentiation. The connotation of ethnic "group" is that its members are at least aware of common interests. Despite the difficulty of determining at what point people become a group, that is, the point at which coherence is established, it is important to retain the fundamental distinction between a group and a category, because many of the processes analyzed in the study of ethnic relations consist of the interaction between the two. Assimilation, thus, can be defined as movement from group to category, the rise of nationalism as movement in the other direction.

As professional jargon, "minority group" is even less suitable, for both its elements are ill chosen. According to Louis Wirth, whose writings did much to popularize the term, it refers simply to victims of a subordination that he condemned; "the people whom we regard as a minority may actually, from a numerical standpoint, be a majority." But in most of history, as well as in most of the non-Western world today, the dominant social division has been between a small ruling elite and a vast ruled mass; what Tocqueville called "the tyranny of the majority" can arise only in the exceptional democratic society. Wirth's term merely muddies, and thus facilitates a manipulation to fit the political occasion: in the British Isles the Irish are a widely dispersed minority; in all of Ireland the Protestants are a minority; in Northern Ireland the Catholics are a minority. Simply by drawing the appropriate boundary and stressing the self-serving portion of an area's history, partisans can almost always find a way to picture themselves as a victimized minority group.

In other works I have suggested the term "subnation," denoting simply a unit smaller than a nation but otherwise similar to it. A nation is a people linked by common descent from a putative ancestor and by its common territory, history, language, religion, and/or way of life. Neither all nations nor all subnations conform to every element of this list, but the precise limits of subnations are often more difficult to fix because they are seldom directly associated with the counterpart of a boundary-protecting state.

The meanings of other derivatives from the word "nation" are also often ambiguous. Originally "nationality" meant "national quality or character," then "a nation, frequently a people potentially but not actually a nation." However, in the most common current usage in such multiethnic countries as the United States, it denotes a particular type of ethnic category. The words "nationalism" and "nationalist" can pertain to existent nations (in which case they are more or less equivalent to "patriotism" and "patriot"), but they are more likely to refer to ethnic sentiment with or without an implicit aspiration to establish an independent country: Polish nationalists wanted an independent Poland; Flemish nationalists want equal status with Walloons in a continuing Belgian state.

It is unfortunate that we use the same word to designate both "black nationalism," most of whose advocates do not demand independence from the United States, and Canada's "French nationalism," whose leaders have demanded that the province of Quebec become a separate state. The term is especially imprecise in describing a shift from one level of group consciousness to another. In multiethnic Austria-Hungary, for instance, the creators of a new Slav awareness first demanded no more than greater group rights within the empire; only later did some of the Slav proponents begin to insist on independence for what eventually emerged as Czechoslovakia and Yugoslavia. And in such areas as black Africa today, it is less an analytic than a political judgment whether the surviving "tribalism" (or, in India, "communalism") expresses dissent within an essentially unified entity or the strivings of real nations to throw off the dominance of alien rulers.

Interpretation is likely to falter also when words in other languages are translated as "ethnicity" or "nationalism." This is the case even among the closely related western European languages. The French word *nation* has the same double meaning as its English derivative, either a community based on common characteristics or a political unit. A biological linkage is likely to be expressed by *peuple*, "people," and a territorial or sentimental one by *patrie*, "fatherland." The word *état*, "state," has the convenient derivatives *étatisme* and *étatisation*, which are rendered far less appropriately in English by "nationalism" (as in "economic nationalism") and "nationalization."

Under the Nazi program to delete all foreign words, *Nation,* which in German had usually implied a cultural rather than a political unit, was largely supplanted by *Volk,* very roughly, "people," but in fact untranslatable. The adjective *völkisch* denoted the essential, organic character of Germans, usually including more than those who were then living in the Reich. Since 1945 both *Volk* and *völkisch* have been used less, for they are considered tarnished by Nazism. French has a similar term, *ethnie,* to denote those bound by racial, cultural, and sentimental ties regardless of national boundaries; *l'ethnie française* thus comprises the French-speaking sectors not only of France but also of Belgium, Switzerland, Italy, and so on. According to Guy Heraud's *L'Europe des ethnies,* however, "each such population always represents, either actually or potentially, an *ethnie* also in the subjective sense—a nationality."

Ethnie is a neologism not yet included in general French dictionaries, and it may be that English will solve its lack of a suitable term by adopting either *ethnie* or the Greek *ethnos* or, more probably, "ethnic" itself. In recent popular writing it has been used as a substantive, usually applied only to certain categories: "white ethnics" are Italians and Poles, for example, but usually not Scots and Norwegians. If the meaning of the noun became comprehensive, like that of the adjective, and if the usage did not remain substandard, "ethnic" might be the most suitable term.

Ethnos versus Race

Of the various criteria of ethnicity, race is in many respects the most significant; the characteristics of the body, that most palpable element of one's persona, have been used throughout history to define the most pervasive type of group identity. Since *ethnos* with its derivatives pertained originally to a biological grouping, it was close to our "race" (probably derived from *ratio,* which in medieval Latin was used to designate "species"). In its current usage a biological connotation sometimes adheres still to "ethnic," but not necessarily: some groupings are defined by their genetic heritage, others by their language or religion or some other cultural criterion. Apart from poetry or metaphor, "race" in English has referred consistently to a biological unit, but its size has varied from a family line (as in Tennyson's "We were two daughters of one race") to the entire species (as in "the human race"). Indeed, as physical anthropologists use the term, the size of a race depends on the purpose of the particular investigator: it denotes a subpopulation that differs significantly from others in the frequency of one or more genes, with "significantly" specified according to the context. Its cognates in other European languages—French race, German *Rasse,* and so on—are still used with a seeming indifference to either the range of the unit or the amount of difference between it and other subpopulations. English, however, has shown a trend toward what would be a useful distinction, reserving "race" for mankind's major biological divisions and using another designation for smaller groupings within one of them. Thus, many American writers now distinguish "racial" from "ethnic" minorities, the former being Negroes, Asians, and other "nonwhites," the latter the European nationalities.

The separation of the two terms has been hindered, however, by the confusion in real life between physiological and cultural criteria. Very often a racial group is set off from the rest of the population by cultural characteristics as well; conversely, if the endogamy enjoined or at least encouraged by most religious faiths and other cultural groups continues for enough generations, it is likely to result in a perceptible physical differentiation. In a Mexican census enumeration, following that country's usual perception of its ethnic pattern, an "Indian" is one who speaks an Indian language and wears Indian clothing; if he learns to speak Spanish and shifts from huaraches to shoes, he becomes a "mestizo." The stereotype that an Indian is unable to perform industrial tasks is not only true but a truism: a factory worker is no longer an Indian.

In the aftermath of the Nazi program of genocide, a number of anthropologists have argued that we should delete "race" from our languages, not only because it is associated with racism but fundamentally because it is a vague category with imprecise and shifting boundaries. The notion that only "pure" categories may be admitted to exist is bizarre; it follows from the theory of evolution itself that all biological divisions, from phylum through subspecies, are always in the process of change, so there is almost never a sharp and permanent boundary setting one off from the next. Whether the removal of a word would also eradicate group antipathies is doubtful; one suspects that with another classification Jews and Gypsies would have been murdered just as bestially. In any case, deleting the term does not remove the need for some designation. Ashley Montagu, who has argued the case most vociferously, suggested that "ethnic group" be substituted for "race," but the consequent confusion of biological and cultural characteristics, paradoxically, is the hallmark of racism.

Culturally Defined Groupings

If the demand for pure categories were to be extended to the indicators used in the social disciplines, acceding to it would bar most research. For the difference is also partly arbitrary, and thus more or less mutable, between rural and urban, employed and unemployed, literate and illiterate, and so on. As Abraham Kaplan put it in his classic *The Conduct of Inquiry:*

> It is the dogmatisms outside science that proliferate closed systems of meaning; the scientist is in no hurry for closure. Tolerance of ambiguity is as important for creativity in science as it is anywhere else.

The meaning of "language," probably the second most prevalent indicator of ethnicity, is as ambiguous as that of "race." Forms of speech known to be related constitute what is known as a "linguistic stock," made up of what are deemed to be languages and what are called dialects. But with the advance of knowledge, the Germanic stock, for example, was recognized as a subunit of Indo-European. As Edward Sapir put it in his standard work on linguistics, the terms dialect, language, branch, and stock are all only relative, convertible as our perspective widens or contracts.

Often linguistic characteristics matter less in determining the designation than the cultural or political status of the subpopulation that uses a particular speech. Flemish was once the "dialect" of Dutch spoken in Belgium, but now, after the successful effort of Flemish nationalists to establish it as such, Flemish or "Southern Dutch" is one of the country's two official "languages." Romansh, comprising several dialects spoken by tiny remnants of some Roman legions, was elevated in 1938 to become the fourth official language of Switzerland. Perhaps the strangest case is the recent acceptance of a second language, Landsmål, in Norway, a country with slightly more than 4 million inhabitants and one of the few in the world that until then had not manifested any significant ethnic differentiation.

The meaning of "region," another ethnic indicator, is also far from clear-cut. Sometimes it is based on what is termed a "natural area," that is, a physiographic unit delineated by its topography, soil type, climate, or similar features. Particularly among primitive peoples, who have relatively little control over their physical environment, a natural area may overlap with what anthropologists call a "culture area," which approaches what we ordinarily think of as a region.

In short, none of the group characteristics—whether cultural or physical—that are used to denote ethnicity generally set off any sub-populations sharply. A great contrast is likely only when several indexes overlap. In Canada, for example, the French-speaking sector resides mostly in the province of Quebec, is Catholic rather than Protestant like most other Canadians, and—to add a nonethnic factor—was until recently concentrated in the lower and lower-middle classes in contrast with the English-speaking employers and professionals in the province. The world-famous amity of the Swiss, on the other hand, has been partly based on the happy accident that the lines of ethnic division have cut across one another. The most sensitive issue in nineteenth-century Switzerland was religion; then it became nationality, with each of the three main language communities speaking a tongue in common with a contiguous foreign country. But both the German- and French-speaking Swiss are both Catholic and Protestant; opposed in one arena, they have always been aware that they would be allies in another. Moreover, the proportions who spoke German, French, and Italian were constant for more than a century, so that no one had to fear the day that a minority would reach the fateful 51 percent—when any modus vivendi that had been worked out would become obsolete.

Official Counts of Ethnic Groups

The vagaries of ethnic classification are especially apparent in the several United Nations comparisons of the criteria used in the world's censuses. According to the first of these compilations, in 1957, 39 countries divided their populations by a geographical-ethnic criterion, 10 by race, 8 by culture, 22 by a combination of race and culture, 11 by a combination of culture and geography, one or two by origin as indicated by the language of the respondent's father, and several by "mode of life." Even when the same term was used, the meaning sometimes was different. Replies to questions on matters reflecting social prestige were probably often false. And the enumerations have hardly improved since this initial comparison.

If the subnations of any society are classified only partly according to their objective characteristics, how are the nonobjective criteria set? Most obviously, they are chosen to fit the view that the politically dominant grouping has of the whole, and invariably one of the principal dimensions divides "insiders," variously defined, from "outsiders." In the United States, for example, "English American" has seldom been defined as one nationality among others even though the Bureau of the Census tabulates persons with English-born parents or grandparents as part of the "foreign stock." More generally, those with English forebears have been regarded as the core population to which others have assimilated. In American statistics whites are divided by nationality, but Americans of other races are considered single entities—though in a black community the distinction is just as significant between a Southern and a West Indian background, or in a Japanese community between origin in the main islands and in Okinawa. On the other hand, American Indians are enumerated by tribe, including even very small ones, and in Hawaii a count has been made of the perhaps 2 percent of the population listed as pure Polynesian, though most in that category are actually part-Hawaiians who claimed unmixed ancestry in order to gain special access to schooling, homesteads, certain occupations, and other benefits.

In the continuous interplay among groups, any answer to the question of how they shall be designated seldom remains fixed. The formal names of those low in an ethnic hierarchy, recurrently seen as derogatory, are repeatedly replaced with one synonym or another. a decision not to classify a population along a particular dimension, though it is typically justified by an assertion that the differentiation is unimportant, may be based rather on a reluctance to publicize significant ethnic-class or ethnic-political correlations. For example, when the U.S. Bureau of the Census suggested including a question on religious affiliation in the 1960 schedule, the opposition from Jewish organizations was so strong that the proposal was dropped.

An important influence on any classificatory system, finally, is the convenience of the administrative agency that makes the count. The census bureau is under heavy and often conflicting pressures, and the choice between monetary or other costs and its assessment of national utility has varied from time to time. Since 1890, the first year that an attempt was made to count all Indians, the inclusiveness of the definition has shifted from one census to the next, so that the enumeration has fluctuated as though the population had been continually bludgeoned by epidemics. The money-saving procedure of dividing printed tables into only two categories, "whites" and "nonwhites," makes sense for areas where nonwhite is virtually equivalent to black, but not in the Southwest or Hawaii, where substantial proportions are Chinese, Japanese, American Indian, or Polynesian. The trend from a *de jure* to a *de facto* definition of residence has also affected reported counts of particular areas. The decision, for instance, to include members of the armed forces and their dependents in the population of Hawaii—a choice no less arbitrary than to exclude them—altered not only the state's racial proportions but also the reported age structure, mortality, fertility, income level, and so on through the whole range of demographic and social data.

In sum, ethnic differentiation is typically both important and imprecise. Paradoxically, an impressionistic account of how one ethnic sector is set off from others can be more accurate than one based on sharp divisions. In law and demography, however, an absolute demarcation is almost inescapable. If members of certain minorities are given preferential access to colleges and jobs through "affirmative action," precise criteria for eligibility are necessary. And a census that reports the race or nationality of every individual in the society generally leaves no place for a miscellany, though in the 2000 enumeration the Bureau of the Census, in a belated concession to reality, permitted persons to designate forebears of several races. Like most other social indicators, ethnic ones are likely to transform the stupendous complexity of our world into a more comprehensible simplicity, and much of what we think we know about ethnicity derives from such statistics.

Processes of Assimilation

The shorthand denotation of the prevailing belief early in the twentieth century was that America is a "melting pot." In later attacks on this symbol of total assimilation, it was often forgotten that the slogan derived from a play written by the self-consciously Jewish writer Israel Zangwill, paying homage to "the great Alchemist [who] melts and fuses them with his purging flame—Celt and Latin, Slav and Teuton, Czech and Syrian," and, as represented in the play's hero and heroine, Jew and Gentile. Indeed, the melting pot was probably an accurate metaphor for many in the insecure first generation who aspired to disappear totally, to merge into indistinguishable sameness with "real" Americans.

At that time placing restrictions on immigration was a prominent political issue. If all immigrants were indeed developing into identical American citizens, then obviously the xenophobic demands of restrictionists were not well based. Academic leaders gave ideological support to this antirestrictionist argument. According to the person generally regarded as the most important social theorist of the 1920s, Robert E. Park of the University of Chicago, all interethnic relations go through an invariable and irreversible four-stage succession of contact, competition, accommodation, and assimilation. Progress along this line is inevitable—except when some factor interferes with it temporarily. Once its premises are accepted, the schema is unassailable; the many ethnic groups that have remained distinct for decades (or centuries) can always be explained by special circumstances, and the dogma that full amalgamation will be attained "eventually" remains intact. In two respects Park went beyond even Zangwill's extravagantly utopian view. He generalized the vista to all peoples; as he wrote, "the melting pot is the world." And in the United States, Park was mainly concerned not with European nationalities but with races, whose differences were etched in law and in seemingly strong and unchanging sentiment.

This view of race relations in the United States was adopted in Gunnar Myrdal's *An American Dilemma* (1944), still a major synthesis of beliefs and works on its topic. In a hundred contexts, Myrdal argued that all but the most superficial differences between whites and blacks derived from white prejudice and discriminatory institutions. As one example of a vicious circle leading to a pattern of mutually supporting elements, racially segregated schools derived from the whites' contention that blacks are genetically of inferior intelligence, and products of their poorer black schools often validated the thesis that on the average blacks are indeed more stupid. For the common phrase "vicious circle," Myrdal substituted his own term, the "principle of cumulation," for he wanted to emphasize that the process could work in either direction. If those who did not accept racist dogma demanded the desegregation of education (and the Supreme Court handed down the *Brown* decision only twelve years after *An American Dilemma* was published), then the blacks who consequently got a better schooling would erode the belief in genetic differences in intelligence, and gradually all significant distinctions between the races would disappear.

The view of acculturation in Milton Gordon's *Assimilation in American Life* (1964), which incorporated the thesis of "cultural pluralism" that had been developed by Horace Kallen, was more cautious than the academic version of the melting pot. Desegregation, Gordon held, need not "immediately" or "necessarily" lead to the integration of ethnic communities; thus, the fear of "die-hard segregationists" that the granting of civil rights would result in widespread intermarriage was baseless. To the "built-in tension between the goals of ethnic communality and desegregation," there seemed to be no solution except good will on the part of all.

With such works American sociologists gave an aura of verisimilitude to the vista of a future either without meaningful ethnicity or at least with little or no ethnic conflict. In spite of its now manifest faults, this American theory (as we might term it) has been influential in other countries whose history has been shaped by immigration, such as Australia. European analysts were more likely to be concerned about how to *prevent* assimilation—how language communities, for instance, could maintain their identity and *prevent* what the Nazis termed *Gleichschaltung* (which can be inadequately translated as "homogenization"). And social scientists everywhere have been influenced by Marx, reflecting both his lack of interest in nationalism/ethnicity and his certainty that these primordial sentiments, remnants of a past age, had survived beyond their term.

The Rise of Ethnicity

To most analysts of ethnic relations, the worldwide rise of racial, religious, linguistic, or nationalist sentiment came as a surprise. Why, contrary to almost every informed opinion, have recent years seen a reassertion of ethnicity?

First, one should note that almost all the earlier doctrines—whether the melting pot or Marxism—typically evolved as support for a political position rather than as a supposedly objective analysis of the trend in interethnic relations. Even as ethnic identity was becoming more significant in the United States, attempts were being made, in accordance with national policy, to disguise the very existence of racial differences. These procedures were all based on the premise that an official recognition of ethnic (and particularly racial) differentiation facilitated discrimination, but even in the context in which they were proposed they were inept. It was hardly possible to evaluate the status of blacks, for example, without data on race.

For several decades the actual assimilation of minority groups was sometimes exaggerated by a systematic effort to blur remaining differences. For if all significant ethnic variation was disappearing (in fact, had not disappeared only because of racists' last-ditch efforts to maintain it), then it was incumbent on every person of good will to move a bit ahead of the trend and act as though the distinctions had already become obsolete. As recently as 1950 an American academic who voiced a phrase like "the Jewish vote" or "the Negro vote" would have put himself beyond the pale, for in relation to federal elections American citizens were expected to act as individuals in an ethnically undifferentiated population.

The subsequent change to new imperatives came so quickly that universities, for example, were for a time simultaneously forbidden to record the race of their faculty and students and required to report what proportions of each were of specified minorities. One reason that rising ethnicity burst with such startling suddenness was the earlier effort to combat racism by omitting race, religion, and nationality from public records or indeed, if proponents of the policy had their way, from public awareness.

A parallel stance was common in the analysis of prejudice. Literally, "prejudice" means prejudgment, a judgment before knowledge. In Theodore Newcomb's *Social Psychology* (1950), then one of the dominant texts in the field, prejudice was defined as "an unfavorable attitude—a predisposition to perceive, act, think, and feel in ways that are 'against' rather than 'for' another person or group," contrasted with a "predisposition toward intimacy and helpfulness." In the authoritative *Handbook of Social Psychology* (1954), as another instance, the term was defined as "an ethnic attitude in which the reaction tendencies are predominantly negative,...simply an unfavorable ethnic attitude." This substitution of adverse judgment for prejudgment was itself a political stand.

The negativism included blocking out scholarly works with a different point of view. Paradoxically, America's first outstanding analysis of ethnicity, William Graham Sumner's *Folkways* (1906) was in some respects the most perceptive. Terms that Sumner introduced—"folkways" itself, "mores," "ethnocentrism," "in-group," "out-group," and so on—became common usage in subsequent works, but no trace remained of his belief that group differences, because they are based on distinctions seen to be more or less immutable, are likely to persist. One cannot change the mores, he wrote, "by any artifice or device, to a great extent, or suddenly, or in any essential element....Changes which are opposed to the mores require long and patient effort, if they are possible at all."

Moreover, the assumption that assimilation, however fast or slow, is a one-way process proved to be quite mistaken. Marcus Lee

Hansen's hypothesis of "third-generation nationalism" showed an unusually shrewd appreciation of assimilation by picturing it as a cycle with marked differences between immigrants, their children, and their grandchildren. The national churches, immigrant-aid societies, foreign-language newspapers, and other institutions that immigrants set up were not impediments to acculturation but generally the contrary. The manifest difficulties of the second generation derived from "the strange dualism into which they had been born," and they tried to solve it by escaping the stigma they saw attached to their alien lineage. Immigrants' sons "wanted to lose as many of the evidences of foreign origin as they could shuffle off." But what the son wanted to forget, the grandson wanted to remember. Approximately sixty years—that is, two generations—after the high point of each nationality's immigration, the ethnic group into which it had evolved typically celebrated its origins in a succession of amateur historical and genealogical societies, folklore associations, and other organized efforts to maintain or revive (or invent) specific elements of various overseas cultures. Hansen's thesis, as he remarked in one place in the essay, was "deliberately overdrawn," and subsequent scholars have challenged its application to particular nationalities, but it was actually not only as a largely valid analysis of acculturation but also as a special case of social change of any type.

In the transformation to a modernist, bureaucratic society, much is given up that eventually is regarded as valuable. Personal identity is very thin unless it is enmeshed with what Harold Isaacs calls the "idols of the tribe," the symbolic meanings given to group differences in body, name, language, history, religion, and nationality. It was hardly surprising, after all, that once more pressing demands had been met, many tried to escape the impersonality of metropolitan life and retrogressively to establish a fuller emotional environment for themselves. Of course, the cycle was not precisely three generations long in every case. Zangwill, whose play was a prominent symbol of the first step, became an ardent Zionist later in his life. But apart from such details, it seems to be generally true that attempts to acculturate to the dominant population arise at least in part from a widely diffused personal insecurity, and that from a later security there develops in turn a yearning to distinguish one's group from the mass.

Because of their special circumstances, American blacks took several generations more to reach the attitudes that Hansen associated with the grandchildren of immigrants. A generation or two ago, most blacks who succeeded in moving up the social ladder—painfully, step by step—imitated the life style of middle-class whites, moving both physically and spiritually as far from the black slums as possible. Having achieved a middle-range income, in short, the "black bourgeoisie" (as the Negro sociologist Franklin Frazier opprobriously labeled them) generally tried to consolidate their new status through acculturation to the norms of the white sector.

With the federal government's accelerated legal attack on discrimination during the 1960s, the exceptional advance of individuals became more general. Blacks who took full advantage of the expanded opportunities moved ever farther from those who, because of age, region, or family structure found it difficult or impossible to do so. If we control for these three factors, the income of whites and blacks was close to parity by the early 1970s. Nothing in the whole assimilationist doctrine, from Park's race-relations cycle to Myrdal's principle of cumulation, prepared Americans for what happened. The response to an improvement in the average economic and civic condition of blacks, greater than at any time since Reconstruction, was a massive resurgence of black nationalism, led sometimes by the very men who had moved up farthest and fastest.

It would be fanciful to suppose, however, that the rise of ethnicity in the United States and throughout the world was due solely to a postponed search for roots. Obviously more is at stake than sentiment.

Even when it was fashionable to deny the relevance of race, religion, and nationality in national politics, this myth could hardly be applied with even minimum plausibility to America's multiethnic cities. In their relation to the federal government, voters were supposed to act as ethnically undifferentiated Americans, for an openly double ethnic identity was seen as a sensitive issue in national politics. But in a metropolitan context voters unabashedly constituted ethnic units, in large part because by their functions local governments could distribute jobs, contracts, licenses, access to facilities, and so on. In order to get preferential treatment from a ward boss, a person had to join with others into a smaller, less blunt wedge than the heterogeneous political parties, and one obvious base for mustering such power lay in the already existent, quasipolitical, ethnically based clubs or churches.

With the New Deal there began a continuous transfer to Washington of multitudinous local or private functions, most of them associated with special favors to particular sectors of the population. With this version of the welfare state, the United States moved closer to the European norm. The worldwide rise of ethnicity is based, in other words, not only on what Robert Nisbet called the "quest for community" but also, and often more importantly, on the wider functions of the state and thus the greater impetus to organize in order to get what the state is distributing—and to prevent others from getting it.

The Origins of Ethnic Groups

Even if we postulate the only half-effective melting pot that critics of Zangwill's original formulation seem to have substituted, we must ask how (rather than why) it is that ethnicity has become a more and more important organizing principle. The conventional American view of ethnic relations is that subnations come into being mainly—or even only—through migration, but relative to the world's population, generally only small proportions have migrated. Let us consider ethnogenesis, the origins of ethnic groups and the process by which they emerge. The examples are drawn from American society except when the types can be illustrated only from other parts of the world.

Migration. In the long and often disputatious discussion of how immigrants relate to American culture, some interesting analytical points have been largely ignored. It is not true that one can judge the impact of Swedish immigrants, for example, by comparing the cultures of Sweden and the United States; migrants are almost never a random sample of the populations they leave and enter. In this instance, since most emigrants were neither urban nor upper class, they took with them not the general culture of Sweden but rather a peasant variant, expressed in local dialects and comprising regional customs. Free migrants, moreover, are generally already half-assimilated even before leaving home; before someone left to go to a Swedish-American settlement, he started his acculturation in an American-Swedish milieu, made up of New World letters, photographs, mementos, knickknacks—all stimuli to what was termed "America fever."

In order to understand fully the interaction between migrants and a host population, therefore, one should conduct research at both ends of the movement, but of the many scholars of migration to the United States, only two men in their generation manifestly satisfied this requirement—Marcus Lee Hansen for emigrants from North-west Europe and Melville Herskovits for the movement of slaves from West Africa.

One characteristic of immigration that American analysts often take for granted is that the receiving population is sufficiently large, powerful, and cultured to act as a "host" to newcomers. In contrast to this pattern, the Jewish population of Israel in the early 1970s included about half who had not been born in the country, and fewer than a tenth were natives with native-born fathers. During the decades following the establishment of the state in 1948, acculturation was thus not to a host population but rather to the ideology of Zionism. As another example, immigration accounted for 58 percent of the population growth of Argentina over the century 1841-1940, and immigrants became Argentina's modernizing force, the major constituent of both the urban proletariat (as in the United States) and the urban middle class. The complexities of Argentina's politics, reflecting the rapid and anomalous shifts in the social structure, are related to the only partial integration of an unprecedented high proportion of the well-to-do foreign-born in the country's population.

Consolidation. According to a compilation by the anthropologists Charles and Florence Voegelin, at the time of Columbus's voyages the Indians of North America spoke a total of 221 mutually unintelligible languages, not including some contiguous dialects that permitted some communication. Such other basic cultural elements as means of subsistence, religion, and family organization also varied greatly, and the differences were aggravated by a history of violent competition and institutionalized warfare. Not only the name "Indian" but also the concept of a single people were products of white contact. Indians might have become a single ethnic minority in the American population except for various federal policies, in particular the Indian Reorganization Act of 1934, that reinforced the atomized structure by giving tribal leaders a much enhanced power. Efforts to establish an intertribal movement have been fostered mostly by young men, alienated as much from tribal life as from the white middle class. Over the next generation or two, the aspirations of many, probably most, younger Indians to participate fully in the world beyond the reservation will probably be realized. The decline of tribal units is likely to promote the rise of a new ethnic group, based not only on cultural remnants that its members half recall but also, and more fundamentally, on the benefits obtainable through today's ethnic politics.

Inhabitants of the Appalachian Mountains provide another example of consolidation-in-process. Like the American Indians, their past relations with one another have been hostile; residents of each hamlet, huddled in its narrow valley, perceived those from over the mountain as unwelcome strangers. Also as with Indians, the isolated pockets of humanity were first defined as a single entity from the outside, especially by those in federal agencies that were trying to contend with the region's poverty. A wide range of organizations and institutions were founded to promote the subculture of "the Mountain People," and the consequent consolidation may have been assisted by increased contacts with outsiders and the greater awareness that those who live in the Appalachian region are indeed distinct. It is at least possible, as it is probable for Indians, that their further acculturation to the general society will be by the circuitous route of uniting into a firmer and more self-conscious subculture.

Promotion. As we have noted in the case of Norway, raising a dialect to the status of a language can shift a lower social class to parity on an ethnic scale. In the United States the rise of "black English" suggests a similar process, though at a far earlier stage. Afro-Americans have always constituted a distinct ethnic group, of course, but the usual academic position a generation ago was to ascribe their cultural differences almost entirely to their lower-class status. The later alternative interpretation was that blacks are immigrants with significant transfers from Africa and with the speech of lower-class blacks designated as a genuine dialect. It is said to have derived in part from the pidgin English developed along Africa's west coast (like Swahili along the east coast) for the greater convenience of slave traders. Some students of black English advocated that it be used in elementary grades as a bridge to learning English; others proposed that clergymen, for instance, become "bilingual," preaching in the parishioners' language and communicating with the broader community in standard English. In other words, the typically long process was collapsed: even before a lower-class argot has been generally recognized as a dialect, some have begun to insist that it is in fact a language.

Schism. In the alternation between sect and church—that is, between a small group espousing unadorned doctrine and the end product of its gradual embellishment with ritual and institutional form— there are repeated schisms. Sometimes the differentiation, though at first defined in religious terms, broadens to include a whole way of life, with the consequent formation of a new ethnic group. The Latter-day Saints, or Mormons, might be so regarded. In the nineteenth century dozens of new religious or secular communal settlements blossomed in New York, Pennsylvania, and Ohio, but almost all except the Mormons disappeared. The crucial difference may have been persecution, for nothing is so likely to nourish a new religion as the martyrdom of its leaders. The long journey to Utah (celebrated in partisan accounts as are the trek of the Boers in South Africa or the Chinese Communists' "Long March") eventually brought about the Mormons' partial isolation, though not an end to hostility. Under two acts of Congress, polygamy was prohibited, the church lost its corporate status with its property escheated to the nation, and men with more than one wife were disfranchised and imprisoned. What was seen as a renewed martyrdom reinforced the devotion of the faithful, and even after church abandoned polygamy in 1890, relations with "gentiles" did not improve greatly. Contrary to the constitutional principle of separation of powers, church and state for Mormons were joined in what outsiders saw as a theocracy. Suffrage in Utah meant that church members elected religious leaders, who also became the heads of civil government. Thus, even after the issue of polygamy was long past and even after the isolation of their desert home had been breached by greatly improved transportation, Mormons remained a distinct group, now set apart less by their religious doctrine than by the social-political organizations associated with the church.

Race Crossing. In many works on ethnicity what is termed "amalgamation" is denoted as one major route to the formation of new groups. American history challenges the validity of this thesis in at least some instances. Afro-Americans have a high proportion of white forebears, but apart from the few who have passed into the white population, the group as a whole has usually been defined in law and general perception as one race, regardless of the degree of admixture. As a second example, sociologists in Hawaii have retained the melting-pot theory as a guide to their thinking far longer than the rest of the country, and one reads again and again that a new composite race is developing on the islands. Even if this were so genetically, it is an unlikely social prognosis. The Chinese in Hawaii, for instance, have set up Chinese-language schools for their children and made other efforts to maintain their separate subculture, even though probably a majority carry a great many Polynesian or other non-Chinese genes.

The Cape Colored of South Africa, in contrast, do constitute a separate subnation that was brought into being by race crossing. They have no tribal homelands, they are not tribally organized, they speak mostly Afrikaans rather than a language of one of the black peoples. For many years they had a separate juridical status, different from that of both whites and blacks, and vestiges of their intermediate status remain in certain occupational or residential privileges. In other words, the Cape Colored became a separate ethnic group not by race crossing alone but by this combined with a number of sociopolitical institutions that set them apart.

By one or more of these processes—migration, consolidation, promotion, schism, and race crossing—new ethnic groups are continually coming into being. The development is generally through three stages—category, group, and community. A category consists of a subpopulation distinguished in a census count, say, but with no internal coherence. The Bureau of the Census classifies as a unit all persons born in any other country and resident in the United States; in many cases they have not organized themselves along ethnic lines and sometimes have little or no knowledge even of one another's existence. From such a base, however, an ethnic group can arise, particularly at a time when the self-awareness of others has led to preferential treatment of various kinds. Often there is considerable difficulty in defining a nascent group's precise dimensions. The "Spanish-speaking" or "Hispanic" grouping includes immigrants from Spain and some of their descendants—Mexican Americans, Puerto Ricans, Cuban refugees, and contingents from other Central and South American countries. Whether such a conglomerate will merge into a single, self-conscious group may depend on such extraneous factors as the quality of leadership, the advantages of corporate effort as against intercategory competition, and so on. But if a group coalesces and prospers, it often develops enough of an institutional structure to be deemed a community. Such a progression from category to group to community, however, can be blocked or reversed by the contrary process of assimilation. Neither differentiation nor its opposite is ordained, and we know too little even to say which is more likely under specified conditions. No one, however, will any longer challenge the generalization that ethnicity is here to stay for quite a number of years, and that, strangely, is a new datum.

12

Political Influences on Ethnicity

Age and sex, the two characteristics of a population about which almost every census or survey asks, exemplify so-called hard data. The interviewer does not even need a response to specify a person's sex. Age is frequently misstated, but whether or not the respondent gives it accurately, various techniques can be used to approximate the single true figure. Other attributes frequently included in census or survey schedules, however, are decidedly softer. As one example, the number and diversity of types of work recorded in statistics have lagged decades behind those in the real world, and in the United States definitions of occupations were so greatly altered in the 1980 census that a commission had to be instituted to align the new data with those of 1970. In collecting soft data, one must set certain conventions to define each such attribute, which is thus moved partway from the population to statisticians' concept of it.

Is Ethnicity Mensurable?

Where in the hard-soft dichotomy should one place ethnicity? According to some analysts, any imprecision or ambiguity is due to distortions brought about by political pressures; and the misclassification most often cited in recent criticisms of ethnic counts, the underenumeration of particular minorities, might be used to support this view. Selective undercounts, however, constitute only one of the faults of ethnic enumerations. The American census has helped create groups, moved persons from one group to another by a revised definition, and through new procedures changed the size of groups. Though some of the resultant anomalies have probably never been discerned, others were so patently clear that the census volumes themselves pointed them out. Race and ethnicity differ from age and sex not merely in degree of mensurability but in kind.

Any enumeration depends essentially on how members of the population regard the particular attribute and, second, on the methods used by the statistical agency:

Most subnations, as noted in the previous chapter, consist of a core population, an intermediate sector with some but less than full participation in the subculture, and a marginal sector that, depending on the criterion used, can be classified as either in or out of the group. Whether it is a census enumerator or, as currently in the United States, the respondent who specifies the identification, neither precision nor consistency can be assured. When either the same or matched persons were asked their ethnic origin in Current Population Surveys of successive years, one out of every three gave different responses from one survey to the next. According to Tom Smith of the National Opinion Research Center (NORC), both the Bureau of the Census and survey organizations, including NORC itself, have all found that only about half of the white population is able and willing to answer a question on national origin, which "of all the kinds of basic background variables about a person, is the most difficult of all to measure and to measure reliably."

A transition from category to group is usually pioneered by a small hand of intellectuals, who may propagandize for decades or perhaps generations before their arguments are accepted, if ever, by the sector of the population of which they have appointed themselves representatives. Very often such leaders, in fact, have spoken not for the whole of their supposed constituency but for one part of it, with other parts either represented by other leaders or unorganized. In the United States ethnic spokesmen have acquired their influence through wealth (Germans Jews in the nineteenth century), professional standing (black clergymen), or a place in general American politics (Irish in Eastern cities), and only occasionally through elections in an ethnic organization that is accepted by most members of the minority as truly representative (the Japanese American Citizens League in its heyday). That it is difficult to determine how many are following supposed leaders impedes the analysis of the subnations themselves, for it is mainly from the statements of alleged heads that the public can decide whether a category has become a group and, if so, what its aspirations are and how seriously its demands should be taken. Self-designated conductors always pretend that the whole of the orchestra is following their beat, even when the cacophony of divergent sections is plainly audible. The mass media and social scientists gave much more attention to such minuscule bands as the Black Panthers, to cite an egregious example, than to the Negro churches, whose totally different social programs were supported by the vast majority of the population both allegedly spoke for.

The Bureau of the Census may have helped quicken the formation of groups by granting their self-defined leaders more authority than they yet exercised in other arenas, as when it established nonprofessional advisory committees in an effort to improve coverage among members of minorities. Inevitably, these committees comprised mostly activists or militants, interested not in statistical procedure as such but in how to shape the census count in order to validate their own perception of social reality. For example, the especially active Census Advisory Committee on the Spanish-Origin Population for the 1980 census produced a large number of recommendations, some of which pertained to nomenclature and some to procedures. It recommended, for instance, that the question on ethnicity appear before that on race; many Mexican Americans might designate themselves as either Hispanic or Indian, and many Puerto Ricans as either Hispanic or black, and in both cases the choice might depend on the order of the questions. As another example, the committee recommended that if a person reported himself as part-Spanish he be classified either in one of the subordinate Spanish-origin categories or in the residual "Other Spanish." The Bureau rejected this recommendation and instead asked a respondent derived from several nationalities which of them best described his own origin. Such committees seemingly tried to raise to the maximum possible the number that would be classified as members of the grouping that they supposedly represented.

In his analysis of traditional Hindu India, M. N. Srinivas coined a term, sanskritization, to denote lower castes' conscious adoption of certain of the customs, associations, and beliefs of a higher caste; for by such a closer identification over a generation or two, they could sometimes raise their own level in the caste hierarchy. If we generalize this concept to mean a group's social mobility by the manipulation of symbols, the statistical reclassification of marginal populations can be denoted as one type of sanskritization. Upward mobility in terms of such "real" differences as occupational status or income may be easier after a group has been given a new designation. Several groups of Negro-Indian-white ancestry in the southern

Appalachians successfully demonstrated against their enumeration as "Negro" and were reclassified as "Indian." In Hawaii the "Portuguese" and "Spanish" virtually began their ascent into middle-class life by inducing local census officials to redefine them in 1940 as "Caucasian," for in local usage the two nationality tags were known to denote racially mixed populations.

Since the civil status of the several sectors of the Republic's founding population set a basic differentiation between "race" and "ethnicity," the Bureau of the Census and its predecessors have classified subnations by one or two principles. Those of European origin have been designated as the "foreign stock" if they or one or both of their parents were born abroad; but from the third generation on, whites of any nationality disappear statistically into the native population. For nonwhites, however, a separate category has been maintained irrespective of how many generations lived in this country. At the margin this difference between race and ethnicity has been blurred, particularly since the statistical agency never developed an adequate and consistent definition of either term.

From 1790 to 1869 no definitions were given of racial terms, and each enumerator determined the race of each person in his district. Later, Negroes (or sometimes subcategories within the race) were defined by their supposed quanta of blood, hardly a criterion that could be readily used in a census count. At all times classification of marginal persons undoubtedly reflected local opinion, which for those of mixed blood would depend in large part on the respondent's social position. Thus, the association between social class and race was sometimes set not by the generalization that blacks were typically in the lower class but, on the contrary, by the postulate that a person in the middle class generally was not black.

The country of birth of respondents has been asked in every United States census since 1850, and the countries of birth of the respondents' two parents in many counts from 1870. These are seemingly straightforward questions that would yield unambiguous and meaningful data, but in fact most of those statistics are not. Even when it was correctly reported, the country of birth has been a very poor indicator of the ethnicity of emigrants from the multilingual empires of Central and Eastern Europe, who comprised the majority of newcomers from the 1870s to the 1920s.

If we can assume that for certain periods data on various foreign stocks are adequate, that does not at all mean that each ethnic component reacts in the same way to the general American culture. Some minorities are highly concentrated in a Chinatown, for instance, where they make up a sharply distinguished group. At the other extreme, descendants of immigrants from England are diffused over the whole country, cannot be readily differentiated from the native population, have no important ethnic organizations, and probably in many cases are unaware of one another's existence. The distinction between the first "group" and the second "category," a sine qua non in the interpretation of ethnic data, cannot be made directly from census counts.

Special Characteristics of American Ethnicity

The populations of the thirteen colonies that evolved into the United States lacked the characteristics ordinarily associated with a nation. Their inhabitants were not all descended from a single putative ancestor, they spoke different languages, many had migrated in order to practice freely their separate religions. J. Hector de Crèvecoeur (1735-1813), a Frenchman who traveled widely and eventually settled in New York State, wrote a series of essays later assembled as *Letters from an American Farmer,* which became internationally popular as an authentic picture of America in the late eighteenth century. The American, he wrote, is "a European or the descendant of a European,...whose grandfather was an Englishman, whose wife was Dutch, whose son married a French woman, and whose present four sons now have four wives of different nations."

Yet these diverse elements not only fused into a single nation but, over the following two centuries, absorbed more immigrants than any other country. Though English became the language of the new country and such other institutions as English common law were incorporated into American civilization, the country was too diverse to become a "nation" in the conventional sense. Lacking a natural unity based on biology or a common history from some mythical past, Americans—in the words of George Bancroft (1800-1891)— "seized as their particular inheritance the tradition of liberty." A conglomerate population unified by civil rights and personal liberty was so novel a concept of a "nation," however, that it was difficult to bring the colonies together and overcome their jealousies.

The instrument of this unification was the Constitution, and the delegates who assembled in Philadelphia in 1787 to write it were among America's most distinguished men. The country that had been fashioned by the Articles of Confederation was on the point of collapse; Britain and Spain had troops at the borders, ready to absorb the pieces if it did fall apart. Whenever differences among the delegates threatened to disrupt the convention, they would remind one another of the urgency of their work. In the existing Confederation each state had equal power, but the delegates from larger states wanted to give equal weight to each person. The compromise effected was to balance power by establishing a bicameral Congress; in the Senate, with equal representation from each member of the Union, the less populous states had relatively more weight, and in the House, with representation proportionate to the population, those with more inhabitants dominated. To maintain this balance the number in the lower house had to be adjusted periodically to population growth, and the first link between politics and enumeration was thus inscribed in the Constitution itself.

The North and the South were divided on several issues but most sharply, of course, on slavery; several delegates from the North aggressively denounced the institution and especially the slave trade, but to have called for abolition would have brought the convention to an immediate end. In a second major compromise (and it is important to remember that it was a compromise, unsavory to many Northerners), apportionment was based on all free persons except Indians "not taxed" (that is, not living in the general population), plus three-fifths of "all other persons." For each 100 slaves in a congressional district, that is to say, it received representation equivalent to that for 60 free persons.

The enumeration in 1790 followed the constitutional provisions regarding the census. The population in each district set its representation in Congress, and the national total was printed in a pamphlet of fifty-six pages. In the fourth census, in 1820, a question was asked to determine the number of unnaturalized foreigners. The first five censuses, in sum, were limited mainly to a count of the population classified by age category, sex, and race (with blacks subdivided between slave and free).

In 1840 the first effort to go much beyond the classification in force since 1790 produced a result notably deficient in many of its details. As a consequence of "the manifest and palpable, not to say gross, errors" in the 1840 census, as a Senate bill put it, a central control was established to set uniform practices for the marshals who supervised the count in each district. In 1850 and 1860, six separate questionnaires were used to make a complete inventory of the nation, with items (in 1860) covering population, health, mortality, literacy, pauperism, occupation, income, wealth, agriculture, manufactures, mining, fisheries, commerce, banking, insurance, transportation, schools, libraries, newspapers, crime, taxes, and religion. So many data, compiled by marshals as one of their subsidiary duties and tallied by hand, were hardly useful. Much of the information was not published until it was well out of date, and census officials themselves testified to the many weaknesses in their operation. Yet it is remarkable how few items in that vast mass pertained to ethnicity (apart from race), which up to the mid-century had little or no place in American law or, thus, in the country's censuses.

America as a Melting Pot

The American theory of ethnicity evolved in the context of two debates on two policy issues: whether to restrict immigration and what the Negro's proper place was in American society. The questions were whether differences between immigrants and natives, and between blacks and whites, were more or less permanent and thus significant, or merely transitory and therefore to be discounted for the long run.

Apart from the two anomalies, Indians and blacks, the population was seen as unitary or, at worst, in the process of becoming homogeneous. The expectation that all whites would assimilate into a single new nation was countered by opposition, usually temporary, to the various European nationalities. During the middle decades of the nineteenth century prejudice was strong against Germans and especially Irish, but only for a time. Many of the immigrants' leaders tried to preserve their native languages in the new country, but over the longer term generally with little success. For long the dominant impetus from both sides was to foster acculturation, and this peculiar feature was a typical leitmotif of writings on American ethnicity. In the American context the problem was long seen as identifying and mitigating impediments to full assimilation, while in Central Europe it was, on the contrary, how minorities could maintain their own languages, religions, and ways of life.

Both ethnic leaders and the general community used to pressure alien groups to acculturate, and until very recently most whites that could be distinguished as different not only aspired to disappear into the broader population but, to a significant degree, actually did so. With the present emphasis on searching for one's roots, on bilingual education and multilingual ballots, on civil rights defined in racial or ethnic terms, on affirmative action to compensate for the prior deprivation of whole groups, it is easy to forget how recently this official encouragement of differentiation came into being. The procedure of counting various subpopulations can be interpreted adequately only against a background of this sharp reversal in public attitudes and expectations.

Assimilation was taking place while the country was debating whether "New Immigrants" from Southern and Eastern Europe should be allowed to come in such large numbers, for they were allegedly unassimilable into American society. Their exclusion was first sought indirectly, by banning the immigration of illiterates, and then in a series of new laws. Many in academia opposed the argument behind these statutes and argued that the melting pot was indeed working. According to a typical statement of the period, "Assimilation...goes on wherever contact and communication exist between groups....It is as inevitable as it is desirable. The process may be hastened or delayed, it cannot be stopped."

Censuses taken during the era of the melting pot reflected concern about newcomers' supposed rate of Americanization. In 1890 foreign-born males aged 21 or over were asked how many years they had resided in the United States, whether they were naturalized, and, if not, whether they had taken out naturalization papers. Also in that year the entire population was asked whether they were able to speak English and, if not, what language or dialect they spoke. After the restrictive immigration laws of the 1920s were passed, interest in ethnic composition waned somewhat, and from the depression decade of the 1930s onward censuses reflected the growing interest in economic well-being.

From Cultural Pluralism to Ethnic Competition

In one generation, as we can now see, spokesmen for European immigrants went from an ostensibly joyful anticipation of their disappearance into general American society to a demand for full corporate equality with the earliest settlers. Even insignificant remnants of minority cultures might encourage each ethnic population both to maintain a certain coherence and to continue its links to the home country, and the most abrasive charge against immigrants had typically been that their loyalty to the United States was compromised by enduring ties of any sort to the country of birth.

As cultural pluralism soon supplanted the melting pot as the typical symbol of social policy, the list of acceptable characteristics of the alien stock was repeatedly expanded. Indeed, it soon included the one attitude that, according to many scholars, had to disappear— a vestigial political (rather than merely cultural) adherence to another country. According to the often cited thesis of Samuel Lubell, both the "interventionists" who wanted the United States to support the Allies in the Second World War and the "isolationists" who wanted to stay out of Europe's troubles were expressing hidden nationalist sentiments. Since it was politically impossible to advocate directly that the United States back Germany, isolationist descendants of Germans in the Midwest voiced this wish indirectly. And when Britain's need was dire enough, New England Yankees voted to help her even though they were half a dozen generations removed from immigrant status. In scholarly circles Lubell's work helped establish a link between ethnic blocs and American foreign policy as a routine element of most analyses, and thus to carry out the promise of its title, predicting "the future of American politics."

During the same years the melting pot, to the degree that it ever applied to blacks, was also rejected by them. The Martiniquan poet Aimé Césaire coined the word "négritude," the essential quality of black people, and his work was extravagantly praised by such Paris intellectuals as Jean-Paul Sartre and André Breton. Césaire tried to resolve "the dilemma of a victim forced to free himself from the shackles of his oppressor by the use of those very shackles." That is, though reason and the technology of white civilization were to be exorcised and replaced by blacks' vitality and "soul," the advance of black people had to come about in part by making use of the very attributes that they were rejecting.

The ferment among black writers over négritude was broadened by the "search for the roots" popularized by the novelist Alex Haley, who claimed to have traced his ancestry through two centuries of slavery and oppression. For eight consecutive nights during January 1977 an estimated 80 million persons watched a television version of Haley's work. According to a check by two professional genealogists, the roots that Haley had claimed to uncover were largely fictional: some of his presumed ancestors did not exist, others were too young or too old to have contributed to the family tree, others lived in the wrong place. The cited records "contradict each and every pre-Civil War statement of Afro-American lineage in *Roots*."

This refutation, published in an obscure journal (*Virginia Magazine of History and Biography*, 1981), was generally ignored even by academic historians; certainly it did not disturb the extension of the search for roots to all minorities.

During these same decades the concept of "equality" was revised, with momentous effects on ethnic relations and thus on the significance of how ethnic groups are classified. The moral equality guaranteed in the Declaration of Independence, compromised by the Founders' half-acceptance of slavery, was given legal force in the Thirteenth, Fourteenth, and Fifteenth Amendments to the Constitution, which abolished slavery, guaranteed all citizens equal protection under the law, and safeguarded the right to vote from racial discrimination. As one can see from the debate in Congress on those amendments, those who framed them wanted to outlaw all legal distinctions based on race, but the U.S. Supreme Court ignored this intent. The separate-but-equal doctrine, which it laid down in 1896, was not reversed until 1954, in *Brown v. Board of Education*. During the following decades the Court consistently denounced racial distinctions as, in Chief Justice Harlan F. Stone's words, "by their very nature odious to a free people whose institutions are founded upon the doctrine of equality" (*Loving v. Virginia*, 388 U.S.1, 11, 1966).

Congress also repeatedly insisted that the government remain neutral with respect to race, enacting the Civil Rights Acts of 1957, 1960, and 1964, the Voting Rights Act of 1965, and the Civil Rights Act of 1968. That these laws were intended to establish a colorblind standard is clear not only from their language but, even more obviously, from the debates in Congress. Opponents of the Civil Rights Act of 1964 worried about the possible effects of Title VII: prohibiting discrimination in employment, they feared, might lead to new racially determined preferences. The bill's sponsors adamantly rejected this interpretation, and finally Senator Hubert Humphrey, who was shepherding the bill through the upper house, became so exasperated with the continued skepticism that he declared, "If...in Title VII...any language [can be found] which provides that an employer will have to hire on the basis of percentage or quota related to color, ...I will start eating the pages [of this bill] one after another." Similarly, Title IV of the same act plainly stated that "'desegregation' shall not mean the assignment of students to public schools in order to overcome racial imbalance," and that the act would not "empower any official or court of the United States to issue an order seeking to achieve a racial balance" in public schools. Those who abhor racial distinctions in employment or in access to other kinds of benefits happily joined what seemed to be a national consensus in, at long last, establishing in American law a colorblind society.

However clear the mandate of Congress, it was ignored by federal agencies and federal courts, which once again frustrated the will to establish laws that abolished differentiation by race or ethnic affinity. The attempt to equalize education moved from securing equivalent schooling to the peripheral issue of busing children away from their neighborhoods in order to balance the number of white and black pupils. Affirmative action in employment went from equal opportunity as a goal, to using quotas to test the efficacy of programs set up to achieve that goal, to many instances of reverse discrimination. As implemented, the laws were not what their proponents had intended them to be; on the contrary, in many cases nothing mattered so much about a person applying for various types of preferment as race or nationality or sex. Class-action suits helped the move toward a restructuring of American society, with previously private groupings given a new public identity. The size of ethnic groups thus acquired a new salience. It was no longer the native stock checking on whether immigrants were being assimilated on schedule but rather certain minorities making demands on the public purse in proportion to their numbers.

From Race to Ethnicity

That two categories, blacks and Indians, were counted differently from whites set the contrast among races as a fundamental ethnic characteristic in the censuses and eventually also in other works. One consequence was that in American statistics the various Asian peoples have also been classified differently from Europeans. Some critics of this taxonomy objected to the distinction made between race and ethnos. Thomas Sowell, a black economist, was obviously fascinated by the discrimination and humiliations long suffered by Irish immigrants; the many parallels that he pointed out cut across the race line. As a broader analysis of America's minorities transcended earlier filiopietism, works on ethnicity acquired a far wider hearing. Andrew Greeley, who began with Irish Americans in Chicago and then in the whole country, expanded his view to "the rediscovery of diversity" and the importance of ethnic identity in itself, not simply as a function of social class. "We know less about

Polish Americans," Greeley wrote, "than about some African tribes," and he joined others in trying to repair that gap.

The shift from race to ethnicity was stimulated not only by piety but also by politics. One of the most influential works in documenting, and thus fostering, this shift was Nathan Glazer and Daniel P. Moynihan's *Beyond the Melting Pot.* As a study of politics in New York City, it started with a milieu in which ethnic blocs were traditional, but the interpretation included the whole of American society. The "new ethnicity" of their analysis, however, was not readily accepted. One of the funding agencies withdrew its support of the study, and some critics objected especially to the fact that racial groups like blacks and Puerto Ricans were discussed precisely in the same way as ethnic groups like Jews, Italians, and Irish.

As more groups were given preference under affirmative action, those who watched from the outside wanted to be included as well. The nationalities once labeled the New Immigration have suffered, and in many instances still suffer, from discrimination. One symptom of their resentment was at hearings in 1982 before representatives of the Illinois Department of Human Rights on a bill concerning affirmative action and equal employment opportunities. According to Representative Robert Terzich, who had sponsored the bill in the Illinois legislature, its main purpose was to amend the laws prohibiting discrimination so as to give protection to those defined not by race but by national origin. Included were "umbrella groups" and multiple ethnic communities, such as Southeast Asians, Eastern Europeans, and persons from the Baltic states. Asked to define an ethnic group, Becir Tanovic of the United Yugoslavs noted that neither federal nor state legislation is very specific, but it is "common knowledge that the intent was to include primarily East European and South European groups because they have been discriminated [against] and that has been demonstrated well enough over many years." He listed the ones he meant: first of all Poles, well over 15 percent of the state's population, Ukrainians, Yugoslavs, Czechoslovaks, Hungarians, Greeks, and Italians. How discrimination would be proved was suggested by Roman Pucinski, local president of the Polish American Congress; he cited a recent survey showing that only an infinitesimal fraction of the executives of the 500 largest Chicago corporations were of Slavic origin.

That virtually all writers on ethnicity have accepted pluralism as the norm does not mean that there is a consensus. In a review of historians' writings on the subject, John Higham divided the analysts into two types. What he called the "soft pluralists" followed in the tradition of Horace Kallen, perceiving cultural differences as values to be cherished for their own sake. Others, the "hard pluralists," followed Herbert Gutman in linking ethnic groups with social classes, for in this view only ethnic unity enabled otherwise defenseless workers to resist oppression.

If group-based quotas were to be set for Slavs, Italians, and other nationalities not proportionately represented in high-level positions, the Bureau of the Census would be called on to furnish the data on which these new quotas would be based. Presumably the already complex schedule would become yet more intricate.

In the past several censuses respondents were asked to define themselves as one of the following: "white, black or Negro, Japanese, Chinese, Filipino, Korean, Vietnamese, Indian (Amer.), Asian Indian, Hawaiian, Guamanian, Samoan, Eskimo, Aleut, or other (specify)." The list does not follow elementary rules for constructing a taxonomy— that the classes be mutually exclusive, that all the classes add up to the whole, and that they be of roughly the same order of importance and magnitude. It should be noted, however, that this mishmash was not created by the Bureau of the Census. It was the Office of Federal Statistical Policy and Standards that designated the races and ethnic groups to be used in all federal statistics and reporting:

> These classifications [its directive warned]should not be interpreted as being scientific or anthropological in nature, nor should they be viewed as determinants of eligibility for participation in any federal program. They have been developed in response to needs expressed by both the executive branch and Congress to provide for the collection and use of compatible, nonduplicated, exchangeable racial and ethnic data by federal agencies.

Ira Lowry suggested the implicit defense of the Bureau of the Census in carrying out the procedure that this directive mandates:

> Ethnic identity cannot be established by objective criteria, at least in large-scale self-administered surveys. We therefore accept that an individual's ethnicity is whatever he says it is. The Bureau's job is to elicit self-identification and then to group the responses into recognizable categories that (a) are mandated for federal civil rights enforcement, (b) satisfy the more vocal ethnic lobbies, and (c) provide enough continuity with past census statistics to satisfy social scientists engaged in longitudinal analysis.

"However," Lowry concluded, "the Bureau's success in balancing the claims of constituencies was achieved at the expense of its fundamental mission: gathering valid and reliable information about the population of the United States."

Since the line between category and group is not sharp, no indicator can distinguish between them absolutely. To ignore the difference, however, means that the statistics will often be misinterpreted not only by the general public but also by professional social scientists. Similar difficulties have arisen with various types of survey data, and polling firms have established methods of trying to cope with them. Ira Lowry has suggested that once ethnic categories have been identified in the census by a gross characteristic, a sample of each category could be surveyed to determine the intensity of ethnic self-identification. Possible probes might include questions about family lineage, languages used, and interactions with others of the same ethnicity. Until something of the sort is done, virtually the entire body of ethnic data collected is ambiguous or, worse, misleading.

Differentiation among Blacks

In the past, when blacks were much more homogeneous with respect to most characteristics, census enumerations denoted subgroups within the Negro population. Until general emancipation slaves were distinguished from freed blacks, and Negroes from the West Indies, like all other immigrants, were listed separately. Though in many respects slavery was more callous in the islands than in the United States, slaves there were assigned land and time to raise their own food, and they could sell any surplus in the market to buy other things for themselves. Thus, when they were freed—a full generation before American slaves—they already had developed something of the self-reliance and resilience that their descendants later brought with them to the mainland. Though in 1980 West Indians numbered only about 1 percent of the black population, their concentration in the upper levels of the Harlem community made them important. Allegedly they differed not only in their occupations but in behavior patterns, being more frugal, hard-working, and entrepreneurial; they had smaller families and lower crime rates than other Americans, black or white.

In order to emphasize how important these two differentiations were, Thomas Sowell entitled an essay, "Three Black Histories." Most "free persons of color," who constituted 14 percent of the Negro population in the 1830s, lived not on large plantations in the black belt but in cities or small towns. In the District of Columbia half the

Negroes were free in 1830, more than three-quarters in 1860. There and elsewhere they established their own schools and reduced illiteracy sometimes to nil and always to well below that of even the most favored urban slaves. That those who escaped from slavery before the general emancipation had an enduring advantage is shown by the fact that they and their descendants were the principal leaders of the black community up to about the time of the First World War.

In five censuses between 1840 and 1910, an attempt was made to subclassify Negroes by skin color, usually between blacks and mulattoes, but in 1890 into blacks, mulattoes, quadroons, and octoroons. According to the census report itself, the four-way classification was "of little value" and possibly "misleading." It is usual to dismiss these attempts to construct a taxonomy by quanta of "blood" as no more than manifestations of the nineteenth-century obsession with biologically defined race. On the other hand, one could take the black-mulatto dichotomy as a rough substitute for the slave-free one, with which there was a certain overlap. In the free Negro population of 1850, there were 581 mulattos per 1,000 blacks, contrasted with only 83 in the slave population. Years of schooling and proportion of illiterate also differed considerably between the two subcategories.

Whatever the differences in the past between slaves and the free colored, or blacks and mulattos, or natives and West Indians, one might contend that so long as all Negroes were denigrated in law, suffrage, employment, and other major institutional settings, no distinction within the race mattered very much. It is paradoxical that, after formal segregation and discrimination have been banned, the earlier statistical subclassifications have no significant counterpart. True, there is a large and growing immigration of blacks, who are sometimes distinguished as a component of the foreign-born (though many of them may choose to list themselves as Hispanics). Current data on native blacks, however, are often misleading, for along virtually every dimension Negroes are divided into two contrasting subgroups.

In a book whose title proclaims its subject, *The Declining Significance of Race,* William Julius Wilson contrasted the widely divergent backgrounds of the two sectors of American blacks. On the one hand, as one symptom of the general condition of the black slum, he noted that the nonwhite-white ratio of unemployment rates for those aged 16–19 rose from 1.37 in 1954 to 2.35 in 1974—and it has since gone higher. On the other hand, the number of visits made by recruiters from corporations to predominantly black colleges and universities, which averaged only 4 in 1960, rose to 50 in 1965 and 297 in 1970. In every respect the contrast is sharp between the black unemployed, many of whom are unemployable at the minimum wage set by law, and the newly risen middle class.

If blacks were given a chance in surveys by the Bureau of the Census to classify themselves into separate subgroups, would they avail themselves of that opportunity, or is the sentiment of unity so strong that it would make any such procedure nugatory? No one can say with certainty, but the past transformations of blacks' social status and life chances did bring about fundamental changes in their self-identity. As slaves they had no say in any public matter. For many years after emancipation, when it was difficult to advance or, in the worst periods, even to maintain oneself, the occasional espe-cially talented or lucky individual who succeeded usually modeled himself on the white middle class. Once the barriers had been sig-nificantly lowered and large sectors of the race could advance in status, this widespread upward mobility was accompanied by a new emphasis on ethnic values. Elements of past history that once had been deliberately ignored or suppressed were revived to reinforce group solidarity, which it was hoped would result in a further group advance.

As one indication of the change in identity, one can note the suc-cession of official or quasi-official designations as summarized by W. Augustus Low and Virgil A. Clift in their *Encyclopedia of Black America*. For some decades after the Civil War the usual polite group name was "Colored," which avoided the connotations of both black-ness and African origin. Its use declined from the 1950s, and it prob-ably would have disappeared altogether except for its retention in the name of the NAACP (National Association for the Advancement of Colored People); the former Colored Methodist Episcopal Church, commonly known as the CME, changed the "Colored" to "Chris-tian." The designation "black" became taboo during the first de-cades of the twentieth century, but "negro" (which is Spanish for "black") and eventually "Negro" were coming into increasing use over the same period. During the 1960s usages began to diverge among group leaders. Roy Wilkins, long head of the NAACP, wrote in his syndicated column that he would continue to call himself a "Negro," but younger or more radical spokesmen insisted on being called "blacks" (or "Blacks"), reflecting their "black consciousness" and their desire for "black power." The substitution was widespread enough to induce the publishers of the *Negro Digest* to change the name of their magazine to *Black World*. During the same several decades the link to Africa, once regarded as especially offensive, began to be emphasized in such terms as "African American" or "Afro-American."

Each of such changes in designation was insisted on with great emotional fervor. When they were taboo, "negro" or "black" connoted, in Low and Clift's summary, "bad, ugly, inferior, bestial, or subhuman." Yet only a short time later many blacks and some whites used epithets just as strong to condemn those who did not immediately discard "colored" or "Negro" and substitute "black." If a person calls himself a "Negro" and refuses to be identified as a "black" or "Afro-American" (or vice versa), what is a statistical agency to do when it is trying to count all in the category irrespective of the current name? In several of the recent counts the Bureau of the Census offered a choice—black, Negro, African American—and then coalesced the responses into a single aggregate. When I suggested at an academic conference that it would have been preferable to accept these several group names as indicators of separate ethnicities, my proposal to adjust the standard criterion of race resulted in my being denounced as a racist.

Yet in every respect the contrast was sharp between the "black" underclass and the "Negro" middle class. When any attribute of the composite category is given by a median or average figure, this depicts the bottom of a U-shaped curve, where the fewest persons are located. There are many with low or very low incomes, for instance, and many also with middle-class incomes, but there are fewer between the two extremes. While the change in self-identification was in process, thus, it might have been possible to catch this distinction statistically by compiling two subcategories separately. It could have been an important measure in lessening the racism implicit in federal data if this distinction were recognized; but the self-appointed spokesmen for blacks, in their fervent opposition to racism, insist on maintaining a single racial category.

The group name that this minority preferred at various periods, a significant datum in itself, merely illustrates a much more general point that can be illustrated with other indicators. For example, in the 1950s the ideal Negro girl or woman had a light skin, thin lips, and "good" hair. The slogan "Black is beautiful," often repeated over the next decades, was intended to transform more than this perception of feminine beauty. During the "colored" period, some of those light enough to pass as white shifted their racial identity by more than a change of designation. Obviously any estimate of the number who moved into the white population can be taken as only a plausible guess, but apparently the phenomenon was once relatively common, more prevalent in the United States than in countries with an officially recognized intermediate sector of mixed ancestry.

Who is an Indian?

The Bureau of the Census can be faulted for adhering with remarkable persistence to a unitary classification of blacks in spite of wide differences in occupational status, income, family structure, way of life, and even language ("Black English" versus standard speech). In contrast, it was never able to decide from one enumeration to the next what portion of the potential subpopulation should be classified as American Indians, who of all minorities have been counted most erratically.

Since the beginning of the nineteenth century, federal policy with respect to Indians has gone through six major phases: a continuation of the attempt to reduce the threat of Indian attacks and, through education, to prepare Indians for acculturation to American society (up to about 1850); the establishment of reservations and the removal of Indians to them (1850-85); the conversion of individual Indians into landowners and farmers by allotting to them a prorated share of tribal property (1887-1930); the reestablishment of tribal authority under the New Deal and continuing through the Second World War (1935-50); "termination," or a renewed effort to end the special political status of the tribes and to integrate their members as individuals with the rest of the citizenry (1950-70); a composite of prior goals sometimes identified as "self-determination" (1970-). With each of these policies there was an appropriate definition of the "Indian," based essentially but only partly on whether the aim was to foster assimilation to American society or to preserve and revive tribal life.

Because of the complex relations with various jurisdictions, however, no federal policy determined a single category of "Indians." According to a 1981 brochure distributed by the U.S. Bureau of Indian Affairs:

There is no one Federal or tribal definition that establishes a person's identity as Indian. Government agencies use different criteria for determining who is an Indian. Similarly, tribal groups have varying requirements for determining tribal membership.

Each legal definition—enrollment in a tribe, tribal membership, adoption (for example, of a wholly white person)—has its own background of legislation and court decisions, which also varies from tribe to tribe.

The more Indians have been tied to their relatively unproductive economy, the more they have required outside assistance. The reservations, ostensibly places where Indians can develop their distinct cultures in their own setting, are maintained largely at public expense. Inevitably the complexity of the law has increased with the growing number of entitlement programs, which established many new relations between individuals and either tribal institutions or those of the general community. Successful claims against one or another government for alleged past wrongs have induced many Indians to re-identify themselves with the tribes, countering both the pan-Indian movement and the inclination especially of younger Indians to find a place in the American culture. According to a report in the *New York Times* (March 21, 1976), a presumably authentic Mohawk commented that one consequence of federal programs had been a large-scale production of "instant Indians."

On the other hand, some of the regulations have induced tribes, contrary to the general trend, to reduce the number of persons enrolled. In 1954 a bill was offered in Congress to abolish the reservation of the Flathead Indians in Montana, for members of the tribe had become almost fully integrated into the general society. The chieftains, however, were able to forestall this threat to their prerogatives by tightening the rules for membership, so that of the 7,100 who by the earlier criteria would have been members in 1970, only 5,500 were actually enrolled. In short, if widespread intermarriage threatened the continued existence of Indian tribes that had signed past treaties and thus the present validity of those agreements, the solution was to bar from membership those with less than a specified quantum of Indian blood. Even so, at that date no more than about 3 percent of the tribe's members were full-blooded Indians; one member in two lived off the reservation; and Indians living on it made up only a fifth of the total reservation population. More generally, as more Indians moved into American society, the preservation of treaty rights has retained special privileges for a smaller proportion of those once defined as "Indians."

As has been noted, because the Constitution specifically excluded Indians "not taxed" from the population on which the apportionment of the House of Representatives was based, they were omitted from all enumerations before that of 1890. The volume of that year's census, *Report on Indians Taxed and Indians Not Taxed in the United States (except Alaska),* is a mammoth ethnographic compendium to which data on population were almost incidental. No reason was given why, with no change in the constitutional provision, it was decided to try to institute a complete count, but one can suppose that it was because of new and more complex relations between Indians and whites had started with the end of the prior direct conflict.

The number of Indians had fallen drastically during the nineteenth century, mainly because of the ravages of infectious diseases spreading through a fresh population, but also because of wars, relocation, social disorganization, and reclassification. According to Russell Thornton, the nadir was reached in 1890, when the 600,000 estimated for 1800 was down by almost two-thirds. The year 1890 was also the time of the nativist movement associated with the Ghost Dance, which would revive the dead and unite them with the living in a regenerated land cleansed of white intruders. This new sect spread rapidly among the Plains Indians and, as Thornton showed, especially to those tribes that had undergone the greatest losses of population.

The indicated number of all Indians, 248,253 in 1890, fell to 237,196 in 1900 and then rose again to 265,683 in 1910. As early as 1910 only 56.5 percent of those enumerated were designated as full-bloods, and the race mixture was interpreted as a symptom that tribal life was coming to an end. The 1910 enumeration was seen as a last chance to make a full count. According to a volume issued by the Census Bureau:

> In 1910 a special effort was made to secure a complete enumeration of persons with any perceptible amount of Indian ancestry. This probably resulted in the enumeration as Indian of a considerable number of persons who would have been reported as white in earlier censuses. There were no special efforts in 1920, and the returns showed a much smaller number of Indians than in 1910. Again in 1930 emphasis was placed on securing a complete count of Indians, with the result that the returns probably overstated the decennial increase in the number of Indians.

That a decline in numbers and a subsequent rise were ascribed by the Census Bureau itself as the consequence of its varying operations suggests how imprecise the figures are. With changes in procedure and definition, the population fluctuated as though suffering from recurrent disasters. In 1950 the approximately 345,000 Indians counted did not include about 75,000 persons who would normally have been reported as Indians on such documents as birth and death certificates (30,000 mixed-bloods, plus almost 45,000 enrolled in federally recognized tribes). In addition, at least 25,000 persons not classified as Indians were entitled to legal benefits as members of tribes with federal treaties but did not usually report themselves as Indians.

From 1960 to 1970 the growth in the number of enumerated Indians was 67,000 more than the increase as measured by births and deaths. The excess was too large to be explained by errors in registration, an undercount in the 1960 census, or net immigration from Canada or Mexico. Seemingly a major part of the large difference was due to a shift in self-identification; persons who were listed as white in 1960 chose in 1970 to be classified as Indians.

There has been an intermittent but generally accelerating growth in the indicated population, but what this means is difficult to say. There are several possible components: a real growth in numbers, undoubtedly a portion of the increase in the most recent period; a more nearly complete enumeration, based on the readier access to remote parts of reservations and the usually easier communication with Indians; a shift in self-identification, including the creation of "instant Indians" by various federal programs.

The 282 federally recognized tribes merge into a single composite only in relation to the relatively few laws and administrative procedures regarding all "Indians." Antipathies often persist from the continual wars of the past, and suits to validate one tribe's claims have often been against not only the federal or another government but also other tribes' competing claims.

There is no reason to expect consistent responses to the query, "Are you an Indian?" As an Indian, a person has been able to share the wealth of the tribe and acquire special access to education, employment, and medical care; and as a white he has evaded discrimination against Indians. Most writings on marginality stress the negative consequences of living in two cultures, but an individual can sometimes gain by alternately playing each of the two roles.

The Bureau's campaign to improve coverage was combined, it must be emphasized, with a newly instituted self-identification. "Indians" are no longer so classified in a census enumeration because they are so regarded in their community, because they are members of a recognized tribe, or because they have a certain minimum proportion of Indian forebears. They become Indian by their own declaration, in part reacting to an often reiterated assertion that it is in their monetary interest so to classify themselves. A less satisfactory way of enumerating members of a minority would be difficult to devise.

Classification of Europeans

The technical requirement that the question on ethnicity be put in a simple form—"What was your country of birth?" or something equivalent—meant that superficially valid responses were in a deeper sense false. Many of the proponents of immigration restriction, who became increasingly active from the 1870s to the 1920s, were motivated by antipathy to Jews and Roman Catholics. Some of the charges they made were obviously prejudiced, but it was impossible to test any of them against accurate data, for the United States had no useful statistics on religion.

For example, Jewish immigrants from Eastern Europe were listed by their country of origin in both immigration statistics and census data on the foreign stock, and it is difficult in retrospect to work out how many of the "Russians" were, more significantly, Jews. Indeed, there have been many private studies of the Jewish population; probably no American minority has shown more interest in itself. The surveys that attempted to estimate the number of Jews and their demographic characteristics, however, were generally poor substitutes for official data. Persons with "Jewish names" have been counted, but this procedure is probably even less reliable in this case than for gentiles. Counts have been made of children absent from school on Yom Kippur, the most solemn of Jewish holy days; from a comparison of their number with the average absence and an estimate of the size of Jewish families, one can guess how many Jews lived in the school district. Questions on mother tongue in the 1940 and 1970 censuses were used to extrapolate from those reporting Yiddish to the whole of the metropolitan Jewish population. Since its first volume in 1899-1900, the *American Jewish Year Book* of the American Jewish Committee has regularly published estimates of the population. Of such reports, one of the fullest and most informative was in the 1971 volume, written by Sidney Goldstein, a demographer who has specialized in the analysis of American Jewry.

Hostility toward the Catholics who immigrated from Southern and Eastern Europe derived in part from the ill will built up earlier against the Irish, who had begun to leave in large numbers after the famine of the 1840s, and thus became the first sizable Roman Catholic bloc in the United States. The Famine Irish, as they were called, arrived as paupers, lived in hovels, and for a generation or two helped perform the country's most menial tasks. When they climbed up, it was only—or so it was believed—to the lower middle class. According to private survey data, however, by the 1950s and 1960s the average Irish Catholic had risen to levels of education, occupational prestige, and income second only to those of Jews. That this was not recognized earlier was due to the lack of official statistics on religion: Irish Catholics, identified only by their nationality, were confounded with the so-called Scots-Irish, Protestants of whom most had immigrated earlier and remained low on the social ladder. The crucial distinction between the two types of Irish was made mainly from a series of polls by the National Opinion Research Center, since this private institution did ask respondents for their religion. Andrew Greeley used its data both to demonstrate the success of the Irish Catholics and to illustrate how this was achieved.

Conclusions

From this review of the national statistical agency's operations, one can conclude that each step toward keeping track of the population's ethnic composition was taken ad hoc, responding to pressures from Congress or the public. The sectors of the population specially noted in the first censuses had an exceptional relation to apportionment, which was and remains the primary purpose of the counts. During the nineteenth century and particularly its later decades, when political debate focused on immigration restriction, the schedules were amended to test how well newcomers were fitting in with their new country's culture. This proved—until very recently—to be a temporary concern, and one could have assumed that this would also be so of the subsequent measurement of discrimination and relative deprivation by race and nationality. In the 1930s and 1940s no one could have anticipated how salient an issue the counting of ethnic blocs would become, or how troublesome it would therefore be for officials supervising the operation.

As one would expect from something that developed rather haphazardly, ethnic counts have been far from satisfactory. Indeed, there have been very few instances when statistical data were deliberately manipulated to support a political position, but many of the decisions on how a group was to be defined, or how it was to be counted, have had political consequences. Ideally, an enumeration should take place in a political vacuum, for partisan passions about the results typically affect the route to those results. With the development of a welfare state, the financing of many local or private functions was shifted to the national capital and, with it, the same means of seeking preferment. It is the supreme paradox of our time that, not only in the United States but generally, the greater state control over the economy and society has brought about not the growing indifference to nationalism and ethnicity that every socialist since Marx anticipated but precisely the opposite.

It is not easy to lay down general principles by which one could decide which groupings are significant enough to warrant the extra cost of recording them. Understandably, census procedure has generally been to subclassify populations that are well known in America (thus, English, Scots, Welsh, and Irish, rather than merely British) but to ignore differences of equal or greater important in less familiar nationalities—such as that between Japanese Americans who originated in the main island (known in Japanese as *Naichi*) or in Okinawa, or Chinese Americans who derived from Canton or from Hong Kong (or, in many cases, via Hong Kong from Northern China).

The grossest category based on race is, of course, "nonwhites," which was introduced in 1960 as an economy measure. A two-category classification by color may have been defensible for national summaries, in which Negroes constitute the overwhelming majority of nonwhites, or for regions of the country with few Indians, Asians, or other non-Negro nonwhites. In the West, however, the figures made no sense; the state of Hawaii has incurred the additional cost of new summations. Even social analysts well aware of the limitations of the color dichotomy have sometimes been constrained to follow it, for if the denominators of rates were so given, the numerators had to be denoted in the same way. After a good deal of criticism, the Bureau of the Census responded only by abandoning the term and substituting for it "Negroes and Other Races," which (though it seems to mean the whole population) designates precisely the same sector as "nonwhites."

To say that the ethnic classification has not been consistent or logical is to point to the obvious. The issue is rather why this has been so. Four main factors are involved. The first, which with some charity we can label Science, denotes the effort to classify the population as accurately as possible, using all the techniques available to statisticians and demographers. The second is Law, the constitutional requirement that the Bureau of the Census count the population in order to allocate seats in the House of Representatives and, following the directives in particular pieces of legislation, to set the distribution of federal funds according to the relative numbers in each locality. A legal scholar, Thomas A. Cowan, held that Science and Law, at best complementary, are often at odds. America has become an extraordinarily litigious nation altogether, and the new laws and regulations have invited the third factor, Politics, to participate in each count as a major contender. Some of the dubious decisions of the bureau resulted from standard bureaucratic conservatism augmented by diverse interest-group pressures. The fourth factor, which can be called Expediency, is the constant effort to accommodate to fiscal and technical constraints. There was no "nonwhite" category insisting that it be classified as such; and demand for a "Hispanic" grouping was hardly more visible. There is no way of classifying ethnic groups that satisfies all of these governing principles—Science, Law, Politics, and Expediency. The Bureau of the Census has been engaged in a mission impossible, and not one entirely of its own choosing.

13

Europe's Nations and Subnations

Norman Davies's *Europe: A History,* a massive work of 1,395 pages, fascinates not only for the vast compendium of knowledge he has assembled but also, and perhaps even more, for the questions he raises. Of these, the leading one is the simplest: What is "Europe"? It is a rather modern concept, developed over several centuries as a secular synonym for "Christendom." Not only religion, however, but such civic institutions as public law made the array of nations, even with separate languages and mores, into what was seen as a single entity. As Edmund Burke wrote, "No European can be a complete exile in any part of Europe."

This ideal of European unity was, of course, fragile. Bismarck was not the only prominent statesman to label Europe "a geographical notion"; Jean Monnet, a pioneer in establishing pancontinental institutions, believed that "Europe has never existed; one has genuinely to create Europe." There has been a particular difficulty in setting the boundaries. Can one label Eastern Europe and Russia as parts of "Western civilization," and is not Britain, concentrated for centuries on its overseas empire, really peripheral to the mainland?

If the concept of "Europe" is difficult to pin down, this is no less the case with its constituent units. The word *nation* often, as in League of Nations or United Nations, designates a political entity. But in its original and second current sense, a nation is a people who have in common such characteristics as ancestors, history, and language. In synthesizing national histories Davies had to cope with the dilemma set by dual definitions of the nation/state. He cites as a striking example a history of Poland written by Tadeusz Korson, a Pole from Warsaw, and published (because of the Russian censorship) in Austrian Galicia. In his work the author carefully distinguished "Poland," or his concept of the "nation," from "the Polish-Lithuanian-Ruthenian-Prussian state."

At one time, it is true, Europe's nations were more or less adequately defined by their dominant ethnicity; in most contexts, that Spain included a sizable number who spoke Catalan or that Prussia contained Polish-speaking elements mattered little. In particular, the four multiethnic composites known as the Austro-Hungarian, German, Russian, and Ottoman empires were seen as stable political units. Those multiethnic empires disintegrated following the First World War, and some other European nations, most recently the United Kingdom, are apparently continuing the decomposition. On the other hand, the steps toward a federal Europe seemingly have weakened some national rivalries, such as between Germany and France. One might argue that Europe's countries are both too small and too large—too small to afford the efficiency of large-scale production and distribution, but often too large to give their heterogeneous populations a full sense of identity. There is a large library on each of two trends in Europe, centrifugal and centripetal, but the two tendencies are most interesting when seen not singly but in conjunction.

Austria-Hungary

Even well-educated Americans generally find the hodgepodge of Central Europe confusing. When the Soviet spy Gerhart Eisler was much in the news, a reporter from *Life* magazine interviewed his sister, Ruth Fischer, an ex-Communist then living in New York. Talking of their life as children, Fischer described their home in what had become Czechoslovakia, and the alert reporter was quick to recall her earlier statement that they had been brought up in Austria. With more forbearance than she usually evinced, Fischer offered a short course on Central European history, to which this ace reporter, speaking for a good portion of college-educated Americans, could only respond, "How complicated!"

Austria-Hungary was a prime example of what has happened to Europe's composite states. In the pre-1914 Habsburg Empire the German-Magyar core was intermingled with Czechs and Slovaks; Serbs, Croats, and Slovenes; Ruthenians and Poles; Italians, Romanians, and Jews. Most of these peoples, moreover, were not themselves wholly cohesive. Vienna's German-speaking elite was divided between *grossdeutsche* and *kleindeutsche* factions, promoting, respectively, the incorporation of Austria into a pan-German empire and or the maintenance of Austria's independence. Hungarians were sharply split by religion. Slovak intellectuals had gradually constructed a firmer base for distinguishing their language from Czech. Ruthenians, who spoke a language similar to Ukrainian, had been converted to the Uniate Church, hostile to the Orthodox faithful to the east.

These protonationalities started to take on a more definite form early in the modern era. By the first decades of the nineteenth century, a common device of Austro-Slav aristocracy and middle classes was to set up an ethnic organization (called a *matica* in Serbian), to disseminate their culture. If the editors of a literary journal, say, could not continue without help from a sufficiently numerous body of the well-to-do, such an association brought money and talent together. It would publish books in minority languages, found folk museums, and mount campaigns to challenge the monopoly of the German language in the universities.

In the Habsburg setting, the democratic aspirations of the revolutions of 1848 were often couched in ethnic terms, but after the fighting ended, little remained of the half-dozen constitutions expressing the rebels' high hopes for both political and minority rights. For a period Austro-Hungarian officials tightened controls over the empire's diverse populations, but eventually separatist ambitions were allowed to recover some of their earlier fervor. Indeed, ethnic aspirations were countered by the fact that people of all tribal strains shared to some degree in Austria-Hungary's affluence. Competition between Germans and Hungarians was mitigated by their apparent joint rule. Around 1880 about a third of Vienna's cosmopolitan population was Czech, mostly of the lower middle class with schools in their own language. Many of the Jews who migrated to the city from Polish Galicia rose quickly to high levels in business or in the arts and sciences. The administrative language of Galicia itself was Polish, and the province's governor was always a Pole.

By the summer of 1918, close to the end of the First World War, however, the Habsburg regime was dissolving. Not only were there massive desertions from the Austro-Hungarian army but some of the soldiers formed Czech, Polish, and South Slav legions ready to fight on the Allied side. Britain and France promptly recognized the nascent governments of "oppressed Austrian nationalities," as they designated themselves.

From Ethnos to Nation

Ethnic agitation rose to a climax following the war. The principal architect of the "right of self-determination" as the criterion for dismembering the four empires was the American president, Woodrow Wilson. He endeavored to convince such single-minded patriots as France's Georges Clemenceau that in building "a world made safe for democracy," one had to start with a "peace without victory." Of the famous Fourteen Points with which he set out his version of postwar moral reconstruction, points Six through Thirteen pertained to the adjustment of the populations and the boundaries of particular countries.

The Treaty of Versailles, signed in 1919, was an inharmonious mélange of Wilsonian utopianism and clauses manifestly designed to reduce Germany to permanent weakness. A series of subsequent covenants redrew the map of Europe. By the Treaty of St. Germain, Austria recognized the independence of successor states. The Treaty of Trianon carved off about three-quarters of Hungary's territory and two-thirds of its population. With the Treaty of Neuilly, Bulgaria agreed to massive reparations and loss of territory. The Treaty of Sèvres, drawn to deal with a Middle East still in the throes of alien occupation and natives' flight, was superseded three years later by the Treaty of Lausanne, which restored to Kemalist Turkey some of the territory the Ottoman empire had been forced to cede.

One recurrent clause of these treaties was the use of population transfers to effect a greater homogeneity in the new states. By the largest of such transfers, as set by the Treaty of Lausanne, Greece was compelled to accept a million ethnic Greeks forcibly expelled from Turkey, and Turkey had to welcome 400,000 ethnic Turks from Greece. Over 50,000 ethnic Greeks were also compelled to leave settlements in southern Russia to be "repatriated." Those ousted from homes where their families had lived for generations, having left with a fraction of what they had owned, arrived in "their" nation carrying mainly a well-founded hatred of their prior home country, a sentiment they undoubtedly disseminated among their new conationals. Moreover, despite the large number of persons forcibly resettled, they were too few to eliminate ethnic minorities. Poland's post-treaty population, for instance, included more than 30 percent non-Poles, Romania's 25 percent non-Romanians. And throughout Central Europe any who were denied the "right of self-determination" had to live in countries all in the full flush of exclusionary nationalism.

All these treaties were negotiated far from the populations subject to the deliberations, and on-the-spot arrangements were often made by coercive means. Several weeks after the armistice that ended the war, the United Kingdom of the Serbs, Croats, and Slovenes was proclaimed, with King Peter I of Serbia as monarch, and a week later Montenegro deposed its own king and joined the federation. From its inception the new state was at odds with Austria, Hungary, and Bulgaria, which wanted revisions in the relevant covenants, and with Italy, over other disputed territories.

Alexander I, king from 1921 to 1934, tried unsuccessfully to consolidate his rule under Serbian control. The Croat Peasant Party was outlawed, and the Croatian leader Stephen Radich was shot while attending a session of parliament and died from his wounds. When Croats set up an assembly of their own, the Serbs responded by suspending the constitution and dissolving the federal parliament. Vladko Machek, the new leader of the Croats, was arrested, acquitted, and re-arrested. In 1929, in a continuing effort to erase historic associations, the king changed the name of the country to Yugoslovia and broke up the traditional provinces into new "banats" with purely geographical names.

In 1934 King Alexander was assassinated by a Macedonian working with Hungarian terrorists. His successor, Peter II, partly resolved disputes with Bulgaria and Italy, and a projected concordat with the Vatican was abandoned in response to opposition from Croats and Muslims. On August 26, 1939, as a climax to the reforms, a democratic government of a federally organized Yugoslavia was instituted—and perhaps some of the optimism in European capitals was justified. Less than a week later the German invasion of Poland set off the Second World War, and all plans for changing the government were put on hold.

Battles were fought on Yugoslav soil, both between the major belligerent armies and between the countries' nationalities. A Croatian puppet state was organized under Nazi sponsorship; Soviet armies invaded Yugoslavia and installed Tito, leader of the Communist guerrillas, as premier; his government crushed the pro-Western opposition and executed its leader. Later Yugoslavia was expelled from the Cominform, but it remained a sufficiently totalitarian state to keep ethnic aspirations of non-Serbians under tight control. When journalists covering the war there wrote of mass slaughter of civilians and the fraudulent elections in former Yugoslavia, invariably they pointed to the region's long history of interethnic discord. As this pocket history of the recent period shows, one need not go back centuries to make that point. Within the memory of living persons there has been enough mayhem to have generated bitter memories.

The other Slav state carved out of the remains of Austria-Hungary was Czechoslovakia. The territories assembled by Tomás Masaryk, the country's first president—namely, Bohemia, Moravia, part of Austrian Silesia, Slovakia, and Carpatho-Ruthenia—had never before been united even as an administrative unit. Each acquisition of territory sacrificed both the rights and the good will of other peoples. Slovaks wanted a rather loose federation that they called "the Czecho-Slovak State," but with their superior military force Czechs centralized their own power in "Czechoslovakia." Almost a third of the new country's population comprised German speakers in Bohemia (or, by its other name, Sudetenland), and it was also a military invasion of Czech troops that incorporated the territory into the new state. A third area, the Duchy of Teschen, was claimed by Poland; it was important not for its population but for its coal deposits, heavy industry, and a rail line connecting Bohemia with Slovakia. An Inter-Allied Commission recommended that Teschen become an independent ministate, but the proposed plebiscite never took place; after a sharp dispute Teschen also became part of Czechoslovakia.

Czechs managed to hold on to the "homeland" they had assembled as long as the prosperity of the 1920s continued, but once the Nazis took power in neighboring Germany, once the Soviets invaded from the east, once the Slovaks saw an opportunity to establish their own country, the figment of Czechoslovakia disappeared.

Minority Rights

In President Wilson's draft of the League of Nations Covenant, the rights guaranteed to minorities were so broad that they all but negated the principle of national sovereignty that he also championed. Though the League's protection of minorities was no more effective than any of its other operations, because of its efforts, member states tried to identify specific ethnic groups more precisely than had been the rule.

Specifying the ambiguous identities of the elements of fluid populations was a formidable task. At the 1928 meeting of the International Statistical Institute, Alajos Kovács, an official of Hungary's Central Statistical Office, presented a paper titled "La connaissance des langues comme contrôle de la statistique des nationalités." Nationality, he argued, should be measured as it was in his country, by asking for each person's mother tongue. The flavor of his presentation can be judged from its peroration: collecting better ethnic data "would do more than serve the interests of science; it would also help ensure a durable peace by silencing the accusations and counter-accusations based on the imperfections of nationality statistics and the impossibility of checking on them."

Some fifty years later Mario Strassoldo, a political scientist at an institute in Trieste, wrote a book on the same subject, *Lingue e Nazionalità nelle Rilevazioni Demografiche*. What some decades earlier had been viewed as a problem of statistical methodology Strassoldo interpreted as an instrument with which each country could compile data that would present the image it wanted the world to see. As he illustrated from Austrian censuses, the mother tongue that Kovács had recommended was specified differently from one enumeration to the next. In most instances, as Strassoldo showed, such choices were without doubt part of a purposeful cooking of the data.

Political ends can be served by grouping languages into units one wants to aggrandize, or by dividing others into smaller units. In the old Austrian censuses Yiddish speakers were classified as part of the German majority, which thus became larger. In Germany's censuses the two dialects of Kaschub and Masurian were counted as separate from Polish, but no less distinctive German dialects were classified as German. Another way to minimize the size of an ethnos is to ask about minority languages only in particular areas. As Strassoldo pointed out, Italian surveys in 1961 and 1971 were limited to Bolzano and Trieste, though in other provinces there were many whose main language was Romansh, Provençal, or French.

A contrast between the 1910 census of Austria-Hungary and the 1921 census of Czechoslovakia indicates the cumulative effect of such manipulations. Between the two enumerations the number speaking German (including Yiddish) fell by 13.7 percent, the number of Hungarian speakers in Slovakia by 43.6 percent. Indeed, there were losses from wartime mortality and emigration, but a good part of these massive declines was a consequence of classifications by the two states in a manner favoring the nationality dominant at the time of each census.

Such fraudulent counting is well illustrated by an anecdote. A Hungarian immigrant to the United States, in some trouble with a federal agency, asked a friend to accompany him to its office, hoping that a native-born citizen might assist in settling the matter. After a satisfactory session, the Hungarian remarked to his friend that in fact the village he had given as his birthplace is not in Hungary, as he had reported, but in Romania. "But this should not cause any difficulty," he added, "for in fact it is in Hungary." He had merely moved Transylvania to the country where it really should be.

Western Europe

In many respects the difference between Western and Central/ Eastern Europe is considerable, but hardly concerning the strength of ethnic sentiment or the accuracy of the statistics used to measure it.

Most of the *Volksdeutsche* (ethnic Germans in Central/Eastern Europe), seen as a problem during the Nazi period, were expelled to Germany as soon as it became feasible, bringing with them the disruptive sentiments that could have been anticipated. Small enclaves of ethnic Slavs in Western Europe were the object of an analogous attention during Stalin's *Drang nach Westen*. Until they had their curiosity piqued by Soviet references to "the Wends," few diplomats or journalists had ever heard of these several tens of thousands living along the upper reaches of the Spree River and speaking a variety of Slavic dialects known collectively as Sorbian. During the Cold War the Soviets regarded them as an advance guard in Western Europe, and unlike the *Volksdeutsche* they have not been transferred "back" to their real homeland.

Norway, a country of less than four million inhabitants, used to be one of the few European states with no formal ethnic differentiations. After more than a century of agitation favoring it, when peace came in 1945 and the Nazi occupation was ended, the country adopted a second official language. Because the standard speech used by the educated middle class was close to Danish, recognition of "Landsmål" supposedly was patriotic; and because the new tongue was an amalgam of several dialects of peasants and fishermen, another appeal was based on democratic principles. In any case, the country's schoolchildren now must learn both Norwegian and the "language of the countryside."

Frisian is an ancient Germanic language surviving (barely) on the German islands off Schleswig-Holstein and among some inhabitants of the Dutch province of Friesland. According to a survey in 1969, most Dutch Frisians could speak the language, but more than 30 percent could not read it, and 69 percent could not write it. Differences by age and rural-urban residence suggested that a decline in numbers was continuing. Even so, in response to demands by a tiny nationalist clique, The Hague helped establish Frisian as the first language of "their" province. School administrators were required to begin children's education in that language and shift to Dutch only in the fourth year. Any periodical in Frisian that managed to get at least 250 subscribers could shift some of its costs to the central government, and by the 1970s there were four such publications. The province acquired a tax-supported regional museum and archival society.

Romansh (also called Rhaeto-Romance or Ladin) is spoken by tiny clusters of population, most in the Swiss province of Grisons (or, in German, Graubünden) but also in portions of South Tyrol and Friuli, the neighboring areas of Italy. In Grisons it is divided into four official and six school dialects, and the total number speaking all of these constitutes less than 1 percent of Switzerland's population. Yet in 1938 the Confederation recognized Romansh as Switzerland's fourth national language.

This formal recognition fits in with Switzerland's worldwide reputation as a never-never land where persons of diverse roots live together in perfect harmony. However, in another shift in Swiss language communities, francophones in the Jura region of the mostly German-speaking Bern canton demanded a canton of their own. As voiced by one militant whom I interviewed some three decades ago, their program combined documentation from the Thirty Years War of 1618-48 with tactical quotations from Lenin. The Rassemblement Jurassien and its journal, *Le Jura Libre,* derived the name and ideology from de Gaulle's Rassemblement du Peuple Français. Eventually, by a vote of six to one, the canton approved a compromise, but the militants rejected it: German-speaking inhabitants of the Jura should not have been given a say, which on the contrary should have been granted to the *jurassiens de l'extérieur,* francophones who had emigrated. In 1979 an independent "République et Canton du Jura" came into existence, but the Rassemblement Jurassien announced that it still would not rest until South Jura is reunited with North Jura into a single canton.

It was George Bernard Shaw, as I recall, who remarked that the movement to revive Gaelic resulted mainly in tying the Irish more closely to England, for they could neither truly regenerate their past culture nor have the time also to learn enough French, say, to escape their pervasively English environment.

Belgium

The best example in Western Europe to portray ethnic confrontations is Belgium. The country came into existence as part of the post-Napoleonic settlement, invented as a buffer to protect Europe against a possible resurgence of French invasions. Its borders with France, Germany, and the Netherlands have no natural features to mark the political demarcation. The most important cultural boundary, that between Romance languages to the south and Germanic languages to the north, runs through the middle of the country.

Dutch-speaking Flemings have always made up about two-thirds of the population, but until several decades ago only the French spoken by the Walloon minority was used in all governmental contexts and also by both the mercantile and industrial bourgeoisie and the Catholic prelates. Over the years this link between language and social status spread, and in the nineteenth century upper-class Flemings routinely spoke Dutch to the servants and French among themselves. For a Fleming to rise above his father's level, a prime requisite was to acquire (for example, in francophone units of the army) an idiomatic and accentless French; acculturation to Walloon culture was both a means of upward mobility and a symbol of its achievement.

In Antwerp's Archive and Museum of Flemish Culture a visitor can see vivid evidence of how ethnic differentiation worked in the past. A book on display tells of the *vervlaamsching* (the conversion to Dutch) of the University of Ghent. A yellowing French-language newspaper clipping quotes from one-time Prime Minister Charles Rogier: "The best thing the Flemish girls can do is to learn French as quickly as possible, so that they can become houseworkers in Wallonia, where because of their industry and cleanliness they are much in demand." Many of the individuals now celebrated as Flemish patriots were in fact bohemians who spent their lives defying the parochial norms of Catholic Flanders; a few generations after their death, that phase of their history is omitted.

Today the almost precise line separating the two language communities detours only in the environs of Brussels, where nineteen bilingual townships became the focus of sharp disputes. The last census to include questions on language was in 1947, and no more recent information is reliable enough to satisfy both factions.

When I spent some weeks in Belgium at the height of a controversy at the Catholic University of Louvain, I made a point of visiting the campus. Because Louvain (Flemish: Leuven) is in Flanders, nationalist students demanded that this be an entirely Dutch-speaking institution, and their rioting spread to demonstrations in other Flemish cities and to flamboyant speeches in Parliament. Two members of the faculty with adjacent offices, one Flemish and the other Walloon, had hardly spoken to each other for years; since I can make do in both French and Dutch and thus could be seen as neutral, both wanted to make certain that anything I might write about their differences would be "correct." I got more details than anyone could want about the alleged outrages of both factions. Ultimately, the campus remained where it was as a totally Dutch institution, and the francophone sector was moved some kilometers south to Ottignies as a brand new Université Catholique de Louvain. One difficulty concerned the library, which in spite of Nazi depredations still included priceless centuries-old items. The holdings were divided by their catalogue numbers, the odd to one side and the even to the other, and two committees, one from each side, were given the task of exchanging this for that. American professors who complain of committee assignments should know how fortunate they are.

Life in Belgium is often complicated by constantly revived memories of past injustices, not to say instances of present inconveniences. The new situation has many traps for the outsider. Towns have different—sometimes quite different—names in Dutch and French, and a motorist driving along one of the roads meandering back and forth across the language boundary may have to stop occasionally to find his way. A letter sent to the wrong town name, or to a *"rue"* rather than a *"straat"* (or vice-versa), may be returned for a better address.

Few persons in the bilingual country are now learning both languages adequately. Flemish students in secondary schools and universities, who once had to know French, are now taught in Dutch. They study French (or often rather English) as a foreign language; and Walloons, similarly, seldom acquire more than a smattering of Dutch. The conflict between two sectors of the population, of which at least one used to be more or less completely bilingual, has become one between two language communities, with a somewhat reduced communication between them.

Cyclical Nationalism

The intensity of European nationalism has risen and fallen in a cyclical pattern. The Romanticism of the early nineteenth century—

the historical novels of Walter Scott and his imitators, the accumulation of ballads and Märchen, the quest in language or folklore for cultural roots, the gradual accretion, in a word, of nationalist sentiment—was partly a reaction to the rationalist, somewhat arid cosmopolitanism of the Enlightenment. In spite of the subsequent vigorous competition among European powers that had thus acquired a more specific identity, they constructed an elaborate international system (consisting of the balance of power and the gold standard, among other institutions) efficient enough to maintain an almost uninterrupted peace from the Congress of Vienna in 1815 to the outbreak of the First World War in 1914.

Germany and Italy, the two countries of Western Europe where hypernationalism led to obscene abuses of power, were also the ones that had retained strong regional loyalties. The hostility between Prussia and the Rhineland, the virtually distinct civilizations of North and South Italy, have been a basic element of the two nations' modern histories. One reason for the excessive concentration of power in Berlin and Rome, one can hypothesize, was that there were considerable centrifugal forces to overcome.

With the defeat of the Axis in 1945, those who had viewed nationalism as essentially jingoism were in a position to declare themselves validated. Once the new wisdom had bestowed legitimacy on the right of self determination, this brand new prerogative set in motion a trend with no apparent end. Whether by supposed genetic stock, language or dialect, religion, or any other characteristic by which sectors of national populations are distinguished, the potential number of Europe's self-conscious subnational sectors is staggering. The farcical trend in the United Nations, overrun by delegates from postcolonial countries too lilliputian to exert a force in any other arena, suggests the possibilities. In Europe there is certainly a trend in that direction, a counter to the more prominent one toward some version of federalism.

In 1952 a plan of the French statesmen Robert Schuman and Jean Monnet created a West European coal and steel pool. This first step was followed by the Common Market, with its gradual elimination of tariff barriers and the free movement of labor and capital. It was set up essentially by France and West Germany, with four other countries as junior partners; not until 1973 was France willing to add Britain and other applicants to the roster. Then came the institution of a European Parliament, with vague but expansible powers, and a

Court of Justice, which was supposed to settle disputes among member states.

In 1999 an international currency was launched. The introduction of the euro, by which countries that are sometimes political adversaries gave up their right to control their monetary policies, was remarkable, and knowledgeable observers have differed greatly on whether the bold adventure will succeed. The EMU (for European Monetary Union) is still defined in dictionaries only as "a large flightless bird"—not the happiest omen. France and Germany together account for 55 percent of the output of "Euroland," and the other nine members carry far less weight. The European Central Bank, which sets interest rates and monetary policies, is located in Frankfurt, symbolizing Germany's dominant role.

How much national sovereignty should be sacrificed to a United Europe? The American political scientist Carl Friedrich projected the developing European federalism into "an emergent nation?" (though indeed with a question mark). Walter Hallstein, a German diplomat who wrote *Europe in the Making* (original German edition in 1969), began the work with a contrast between his country, accustomed by its history to a federal government and therefore well disposed toward a federal Europe, and France, a centralized state fearful of any collaboration that might reduce its *puissance et gloire.* According to Jean-Paul Fitoussi, a prominent French economist, "The Germans should go back to a more moderate role, that of shareholder and not that of chairman of the board. Germany's role is too visible." Antonio Martino, a former foreign minister of Italy, put it more bluntly: The pan-Europeans "wanted a Europeanization of Germany to prevent [a repetition of] the two disasters we had in this century, and instead we could get the Germanization of Europe."

To repeat the exclamation of the *Life* reporter: How complicated!

14

Names in Population Records

In several contexts agencies of the United States government have used persons' surnames to classify the population by ethnicity. As two important examples, names were used to set immigration quotas, and the Bureau of the Census used names as the defining characteristic of Hispanics. In these as in other cases, the procedure functioned poorly, for several reasons. Unaltered family names are not necessarily an accurate index of ethnicity, and in any case many Americans have changed them.

American Names

Whatever a person's original name, the odds are high that at some time it was changed to another. There have been, for example, a transliteration from another alphabet, a shortening, rarely a lengthening, an omission of letter combinations unusual in English, an adaptation to similar name, a transposition of letters, a translation, a shift in pronunciation, an entirely different name.

In Henry Mencken's massive work on the American language, he opened his discussion of surnames by citing the Social Security Board's 1939 roll of 43.9 million persons, beginning with 471,190 Smiths, 350,530 Johnsons, 254,750 Browns, 250,312 Williamses, 240,180 Millers, and 235,540 Joneses. Of the first fifty names, only one—Cohen—was not of British origin, and this fact in itself suggested that many surnames of other origins had been assimilated to the national norm. By an estimate that he cited, only about a third of Americans with English surnames had them because of English blood in the male line.

The revision of surnames was well under way before the founding of the Republic. In two eighteenth-century lists of German or Swiss immigrants living in Pennsylvania, one from the ship on which they came and the other at their place of residence, "scarcely a name is exactly the same on both lists." The discrepancies were often the consequence not of a decision by the subject but rather of the carelessness or semiliteracy of the clerk compiling the record. A single document, a will drawn in North Carolina in 1754, spelled the testator's name as both Willcox and Willcocks, and other documents designated him as Wilcox, Wilcocks, Welcox, Wellcocks, Welcooks. Poor Mr. W. was illiterate and had to depend on hardly more literate functionaries to spell his name.

The harassed clerks who registered the millions of immigrants being processed on Ellis Island were neither conversant with the languages they encountered nor meticulous in compiling their record. Between 1906 and 1924, naturalization courts required a certificate of arrival issued by the Immigration and Naturalization Service, and for that period it is thus possible to trace immigrants at two points in their lives. As one example, Milan Shimitz, a Serbian born in Hungary (by the criterion used to define nationality, this would have made him a Hungarian) became Emil Smith.

During the First World War (and, much less, also during the Second), German Americans tried to avoid an identification with the enemy. In the metamorphosis of their names, each German-language vowel was consistently shifted to a particular other vowel, and difficult consonants like the German *ch* disappeared. The endeavor to be seen as 100 percent American, as the common locution put it, though strongest among those of German background, was a factor also among immigrants from virtually all countries.

Under successive naturalization laws immigrants could formally adopt a new name when they applied for citizenship, and all fifty states set up suitable procedures. The many who took on a new name include a considerable number of well-known personages: Spiro Agnew, for example, was the son of Theofrastos Anagnostopoulos. One source lists 164 actors and actresses, 47 musicians, and 59 sports figures, all with their original names and the ones they then chose, sometimes first as professional noms de guerre, eventually as their legal designations.

Sometimes the name adopted was not part of an acculturation to America but rather a carry-over from the old country. In Polish the ending -ski indicates high status, and there are more persons of Polish forebears bearing this honorific in the United States than in Poland. Well-to-do Norwegian peasants had both a patronymic (that is, the father's given name plus -sen or -datter) and a "farm name" adopted from the estates on which they or their ancestors lived. This symbol of quality in Europe also proliferated among American immigrants from that country.

So long as Jews lived apart in ghettos, most had only one name. As a first step in their emancipation in modern times (and also to facilitate the collection of taxes and the imposition of conscription), most European countries required that they adopt a surname that remained constant through succeeding generations. Some local officials in Germany and Austria demanded bribes; those unable to pay were given ridiculous or obscene designations, and those who responded generously to the blackmail got names beginning with *Fein-* (fine) or ending in *-blum* (flower). In one of his stories Sholom Aleichem mocks the tendency to adopt highfalutin names with a character who was called Platon Pantolonovich Lokshentopov. A book on the names of Jews sums up its account: "Even the most religiously motivated and identity-conscious Jews have become acculturated as far as their names are concerned."

An article in *Aufbau* (August 6, 1943), New York's German-language newspaper for refugees from Nazism, was titled "Müssen Sie Washington heissen?"—Do you have to call yourself Washington? The most interesting result of a survey among its readers was the reasons they gave for what all saw as an important decision: to shift from a name that Americans could not spell or pronounce; to complete a break with the past, as by rejecting Deutsch (German); to avoid anticipated anti-Semitism; of soldiers, as officially counseled by the U.S. Army, to avoid special persecution if they were taken prisoner; to adopt the name of relatives who had immigrated earlier. Most were happy with their new names; a small minority said they regretted having taken the step.

With many Americans' interest in tracing their roots, genealogical societies have proliferated. Up-to-date manuals instruct their readers on how to track one's ancestors, using a range of possible sources. The Mormon church maintains a Family History Library, the largest in the world specializing in genealogical data, with records from more than fifty countries transferred to 2 million rolls of microfilm.

In general, the cultural shift from "the melting pot" to "multicultural diversity" had little effect on the names that immigrants or their descendants chose. A few black leaders marked their alienation from American society and their accommodation to Islam. The most prominent was Malcolm X, but even fellow members of the Nation of

Islam did not generally adopt new names. A black writer, well known as LeRoi Jones, changed his name to Imamu Amiri Baraka, a bit difficult for even his admirers to remember.

A compilation of names thus manipulated was the empirical base that the United States government used to compute two important criteria, how to judge aspirant immigrants and how to define "Hispanics."

Immigration Restrictions

In immigration records, those arriving in the United States have been classified by their country of origin. This was a rather loose designation of ethnicity not only for the multilingual empires of Central and Eastern Europe but also for less motley nations, for many of the early immigrants had little or no consciousness of belonging to a nationality. As he saw himself, such a person typically had four identities: he was a subject of a particular state (say, Russia); he spoke a particular language (say, Estonian); he adhered to a particular religion; and he regarded a certain province or even village as home. Even immigrants from nations that had become politically unified states sometimes did not necessarily identify themselves as natives of those. An "Italian," for instance, was more likely to look on himself as a Sicilian or a Calabrian, but it is not easy with the statistics available to quantify such a tendency. In a study of Italian immigration to Toronto, family names were used to specify the region of Italy from which immigrants came.

It was only after they arrived in the United States that many of the newcomers learned, initially from questions asked by immigration officials, to identify themselves as natives of "their" country. Having been taught that they belonged to a particular national stock, some submerged their provincialisms into a broader patriotism, their local dialects into a language. The first Lithuanian newspaper was published in the United States; the Erse revival began in Boston; the Czechoslovak nation was launched at a meeting in Pittsburgh.

Over the whole history of the United States, established residents seldom welcomed newcomers of a different nationality; the Germans and Irish who immigrated in the middle of the nineteenth century faced many types of discrimination. But the "new immigrants" who came from the 1880s to 1914—each year hundreds of thousands and then millions of East European Jews, southern Italians, and others seen as undesirable types—generated a restrictionist sentiment stronger than any before that.

Henry James, a second-generation American, left the United States first for France and then, permanently, for England, becoming a British subject a year before his death. A member of a distinguished family, James in a sense typified the reactions of many Americans of English stock. In 1904 he visited Ellis Island, and what he saw filled him with a "sense of dispossession," fully justifying his earlier decision to emigrate. Admission of these utterly alien masses was, in his view, a "mongrelization" of the native blood, a kind of "race-suicide."

The intensified goal of restricting the immigration of specific nationalities was sought first by denying entry to illiterates, but this did not bar nearly enough aspirant immigrants from Southern and Eastern Europe to satisfy nativists. By a stopgap measure that Congress passed in 1921, immigration from European countries was limited to 3 percent of the number of foreign-born of each nationality resident at the time of the last available figures, those of the 1910 census. A second law, adopted in 1924 as another temporary barricade, reduced the 3 percent to 2 percent and changed the base population to that enumerated in 1890, when the proportion of those designated as undesirable was much smaller. What was intended to be the permanent system, enacted in 1929, set quotas by whole population's "national origins."

The Census Bureau, with assistance of two experts paid by the American Council of Learned Societies, endeavored to calculate "the number of [white] inhabitants in continental United States in 1920 whose origin by birth or ancestry is attributable to [each] geographical area" designated in the immigration statistics as a separate country. Since it was impossible to divide the population into the discrete ethnic groups that were thus called for, the committee undertook instead to measure the proportionate contribution of various national stocks to the total white American gene pool. It began by dividing the country's original white population by national origin, principally from the family names at the country's founding. To the base derived from the first census were added immigration figures, such as they were, and—for lack of a breakdown by the ethnicity—an overall rate of natural increase.

The committee's "main source" for estimating the ethnic distribution in the founding population was a calculation by William Rossiter, a census official, who had estimated the national origins of the population from the surnames listed in the 1790 enumeration, as follows:

English	83.5 percent
Scotch	6.7
German	5.6
Dutch	2.0
Irish	1.6
French	0.5
"Hebrew"	<0.1
All others	0.1

As the committee itself pointed out, there was a "considerable element of uncertainty" in Rossiter's classification.

According to Rossiter, a larger proportion of non-British stock was found in particular areas, such as New York with 61.1 percent Dutch or Pennsylvania with 16.1 percent German. A probable reason for this finding is that residents of a community made up largely of Germans, for instance, retained their Germanic names, while many of those living among persons of English stock changed them to an English-sounding equivalent. The historian Albert Faust duplicated Rossiter's analysis of names in the 1790 census, but he then checked that roster with local data from several states. The total number of persons of German stock in the founding population was, by his reckoning, 375,000 (which, to be conservative, he reduced to 360,000) or 18.9 percent of the white population, as contrasted with the 5.6 percent that Rossiter had estimated. In his work Faust cited a paper by a well-known German statistician, Richard Böckh. For the years 1898-1904, when the United States classified immigrants by stock independently of their country of origin, Böckh calculated that, in addition to the 151,118 Germans from the German Empire, there were 289,438 from such other countries as Austria-Hungary, Russia, and Switzerland. The record did not improve over time. For instance, after the multiethnic empires of pre-1914 Europe had been broken up following the Allied victory in the First World War, those born in Germany, Austria-Hungary, or Russia were allocated to the new nations according to their names.

In short, the benign scholarship of William Rossiter, when put to use by the powerful restrictionist bloc of the electorate, was turned into the barrier its members had been seeking for several decades. By 1790 a good proportion of the population had assimilated to the English base, and their English names, a symptom of that acculturation, was interpreted as an index of national origins. Even small discrepancies in 1790, when increased geometrically from that date to 1920, made a considerable difference in the immigration quota each country was to be allowed.

The Creation of "Hispanics"

The Bureau of the Census, which generally has found it difficult to classify the American population by ethnicity, has had the most trouble with immigrants from Mexico. After experimenting with classifications by immigration status, race, and mother tongue, in 1950 the Bureau chose surname as its criterion. To the almost 7,000 Spanish names collected earlier by the Immigration and Naturalization Service were added some 1,000 others by specialists in Romance languages. Eventually one analyst supplemented the 7,718 names used by the Bureau with 11,262 others, including many from subcultural regions.

Since not only Mexican Americans were included in the categories that the Census Bureau used, the fortuitous consequence of these attempts to define "Mexicans" was the creation of a new statistical unit, "Hispanics" or, as some of them insist on being called, "Latinos." These persons are divided into five categories: Mexican, Puerto Rican, Cuban, Central and South American, and Other.

At first, it was more or less possible to distinguish the component elements of Hispanics by geographical location, but this became less and less satisfactory with the spread of all the subgroups to new areas throughout the country. Whatever differences exist between whites and blacks, or between whites and Indians, are masked within the Hispanic category, since those so classified may be of any race. The ethnic groups comprising the persons "of Spanish origin" vary greatly in median age, family type, fertility, educational level, type of occupation, proportion below the poverty line, median income, and almost any other social indicator on which there are data.

As a group the Cubans, who arrived last, have a higher level of living than other Hispanic populations; it is said that they dislike being classed with them. On the other hand, in the opinion of Manuel A. Bustelo of the National Puerto Rican Foundation in New York City, "The use of 'Hispanic' rather than specific ethnic groups has distorted realities. In many instances this has served to convey a more positive picture of overall advancement, while concealing the fact that Puerto Rican communities on the mainland are worse off than in previous years."

Once the surname became the index used to identify Hispanics, a Hispanic woman who married out of the group disappeared statistically and a non-Hispanic woman who married in was added. According to a study of Spanish-surnamed Californians, between a third and two-fifths married out. Martín is reckoned as the tenth most common name in Spain, but it was omitted from the Bureau's list because it occurs frequently also among those of English, French, or German origin. An indeterminate number of Hispanics had changed their names to an English-sounding one, and many Filipinos, who are classified as Asians, have Hispanic names. Using various coding techniques, the Bureau estimated that up to 63.3 percent of those designated as Hispanic were falsely classified. Of those who identified themselves as of Spanish heritage, those classified by name as non-Spanish went as high as 69.1 percent. By a rather relaxed standard, the Spanish surname was judged to be "a fair approximation of Spanish origin" in the Southwest but not elsewhere in the country.

In 1970 the census short form had no question related to Hispanic identity. One long form, distributed to 15 percent of the population, asked about birthplace, surname, and language; another long form, distributed to the remaining 5 percent, asked about Spanish origin. With four ways of counting Hispanics, the Census produced four estimates, ranging from 5.2 million to 9.6 million.

Since all of the objective criteria of membership in the Hispanic population were of dubious suitability, from 1980 on the Bureau depended on respondents' self-identification to set the dimensions not only of the Hispanic population but also of its several subunits: Mexican, Puerto Rican, Cuban, South or Central American, and Other Spanish Origin. There were new problems with self-identity, but it has had one important advantage over any objective measure: a subjective yardstick, based on how the respondent answers a question on ethnicity, is probably a better index of whether his behavior will conform to the norms that that subnation has set.

The supposed unity of Hispanics is based on the fact that they all, to one degree or another, derive from Spanish culture. Even if one ignores the acculturation to English, the varieties of Spanish differ significantly among the several subgroups, as is clear from studies of the distinctive "dialect" or "language" of Chicanos. Even commercial firms seeking customers among Hispanics often take care to differentiate among the several groups.

Not only is the whole Hispanic population a miscellany but none of the four units within it is really homogeneous. In the opening paper of Volume I of *Aztlán*, perhaps the best of the journals devoted to Mexican American interests, Fernando Peñalosa offered a tentative three-way classification of the population: "Americans of Mexican ancestry," who regard their forebears as of little importance one way or the other; "Mexican Americans," who are constantly conscious of their ancestry, usually with an uneasy blend of positive and negative feelings about it; and "Chicanos," who are committed to the defense of Mexican American subcultural values as they view them. "Attempts to form national alliances of Mexican American organizations have failed over the question, 'What do we call ourselves?'"

Why, in sum, has the Bureau of the Census established the category "Of Spanish origin"? Undoubtedly, the main reason is that it is convenient for summary tables. As another factor, some members of Congress or other politicians may have wanted to enhance their power by fostering a still nonexistent unity; in 1976 four Democratic members of the House of Representatives from Texas, California, and New York joined with the resident commissioner-elect of Puerto Rico to form a Congressional Hispanic Caucus.

When the first reports of the 2000 census were released, the news media published as the most striking item the "fact" that Hispanics were on the verge of outdistancing blacks and becoming the nation's largest minority group. The *Boston Globe* announced that "Boston became a majority-minority city in the 1990s for the first time as Latinos, Asians, and blacks arrived and as tens of thousands of whites left." On page 1 of the *Los Angeles Times,* similarly, readers were told, "For the first time ever, no racial or ethnic group forms a majority in California." This misunderstanding, stretching from coast to coast, derived from procedures in the 2000 count that may have invited such conclusions. For the first time, respondents were permitted to label themselves as of more than one race. And Hispanics were of all races; in the count of 2000, persons identified themselves as Spanish/Hispanic/Latino, 35.3 million, divided as follows:

White	48 percent
Black	2
Mixed race	6
Other	42

With overlapping categories, one can legitimately compare neither Hispanics and blacks nor Hispanics and whites; to do so is like asking whether more paperbacks or more love stories are published each year.

15

Jews as a Race

From the early medieval period to the eighteenth century, the rationale of anti-Semitism was almost exclusively religious. Jews had been responsible for Christ's death, and they celebrated an annual festival with the blood of a freshly murdered Christian child. The 150,000 Franks, Normans, and miscellaneous rabble who, in 1097-98, set off in the First Crusade to recover the Holy Land from the Muslim infidel did not succeed in that venture, but they did pillage Jewish communities on their way eastward, killing the inhabitants and destroying their synagogues. The Catholic Church sometimes protected Jews against the pogroms that punctuated the Middle Ages, for despite the doctrinal anti-Semitism some ecclesiastical authorities wanted Jews to witness their own humiliation by the triumph of Christianity.

Nor did the Reformation bring relief. Martin Luther himself wrote a book, *Of Jews and Their Lies,* that helped transfer the ingrained hatred to Protestantism. Jews, he wrote, were as obstinate as Egyptians, and since neither plagues nor miracles could improve the Pharaoh, Moses had to resort to the extreme solution of letting him drown in the sea.

So long as persecution was based on a mutable trait, it was possible for some to escape. How many Jews converted to Christianity or Islam is not known, of course, but over the centuries the proportion was sizable. When New Christians were tortured by agents of the Inquisition, the ostensible reason was doubt about the sincerity of their conversion; thus, a genuine conversion presumably protected former Jews from persecution. In Spain of the seventeenth and eighteenth centuries New Christian converts were barred from the highest offices because they lacked the requisite "purity of blood," but such an occasional reference to genetic integrity was an exceptional gloss on the dominant differentiation of Jews by their religion.

Once the European Enlightenment evolved into an effective counterforce to Christianity, one might have supposed that a denigration of Jews based almost entirely on religious antipathy would lessen and perhaps even dissipate altogether. However, the French philosophes, a main font of modern secular ideology, also initiated the modern version of anti-Semitism, a nonreligious hatred as strong as the animus it partly replaced. No pioneer of the movement was more typical than Voltaire, and hardly anyone in history was more obsessed than he with Jewry. In his *Dictionnaire Philosophique* he described Jews as "the most abominable people in the world," "a totally ignorant nation" whose "priests have always sacrificed human victims with their sacred hands." During Hitler's domination of Europe, one Henri Labroue, a history teacher, had no difficulty in compiling a 250-page book of Voltaire's anti-Jewish writings. The antipathy was taken over by the French Socialists, and no less a figure than Pierre-Joseph Proudhon held that "one must send this race back to Asia or exterminate it." From this source anti-Semitism became a significant strand in international socialist doctrine, prominent in Karl Marx and pervasive in Soviet society.

The race theories that proliferated in nineteenth-century Europe set a new, and more dangerous, stage in Jewish history. Since conversion now meant nothing, there was no way out. In spite of the shift from a religious to a genetic basis for fastening on the Jew as the prime scapegoat, there was sometimes an amazing continuity of anti-Semitic doctrine. For example, in the introduction to *The Destruction of the European Jews,* Raul Hilberg gives a list of anti-Jewish regulations from the canon law of the Catholic Church and, in a parallel column, the astonishingly similar decrees of the Nazi regime.

In spite of this continuity, the distinction between religious and secular Jewishness that the Enlightenment brought about necessitated some change also in anti-Semitism. Such a man as Moses Mendelssohn could bridge the widening gap between Jewishness and Judaism, but most of his children converted. Other Jews declared themselves to be agnostics. The identity of Jews, until then a simple matter, became more and more ambiguous, and it developed into a problem to which anti-Semites never found a full solution. Anti-Jewish laws and even myths had to be rewritten to close off the exits of conversion or apostasy, and a suitable revision did not come easily.

For example, sixteen members of the German Reichstag in the 1890s had as their unofficial platform the following doggerel:

Was er glaubt ist einerlei;

In der Rasse liegt die Schweinerei.

(What he believes is a matter of indifference; it is in race that the rottenness lies.) Yet the anti-Semitic legislation they would have liked to sponsor always foundered on the issue of how to identify their intended victims.

As another example, Karl Lueger (1844-1910), a leader of Austria's notoriously anti-Semitic Christian Social Party, was mayor of Vienna from 1897 to his death. Some of his best friends, he declared, were Jews, and some were employed in the city's services and even admitted to the city's Gymnasium and University; but a limit had to be set. *"Wer Jude ist, bestimme ich."* (*I* decide who is a Jew.) The identity of Jews was so ambiguous that it could be decided arbitrarily according to one man's whim.

The fateful question of who in Nazi Germany was a Jew took two and a half years to work out. The first formulation, in April 1933, was to divide the population between "Aryans" and "non-Aryans" according to whether or not they had at least one Jewish parent or grandparent. But the Japanese protested that, as non-Aryans, they were classified with Jews; and German critics held that the Jews themselves should be differentiated according to the amount of their non-Aryan blood. In September a second attempt was made in a decree setting qualifications for German citizenship, but this, too, also had to be discarded. The final decree was written at the highest Party level, by Staatssekretär Wilhelm Stuckart and his expert on Jewish affairs, Bernard Lösener. They worked under pressure, for in a decree that specified criminal sanctions, "Jew" and "German" had already been used as approximate equivalents of "non-Aryan" and "Aryan," but without precise definitions. But it took until November 14, 1935 for the citizenship law to reach its final form.

A Jew was defined as: A person with at least three Jewish grandparents; or a person descended from two Jewish grandparents who belonged to a Jewish religious community on September 15, 1935 or subsequently joined one; or was the offspring of a marriage with a three-quarter or full Jew contracted after that date; or was the offspring of an extramarital relationship with a three-quarter or full Jew and was born after July 31, 1936.

Defined as not a Jew but a *Mischling,* or person of "mixed Jewish blood," were the following: A person with two Jewish grandparents who did not adhere to the Jewish religion on September 15, 1935 and did not join it subsequently and was not married to a Jew on that date and did not marry one subsequently; or a person with one Jewish grandparent. These two subclasses were later designated *Mischlinge* of, respectively, the first and the second degree. They were not in principle to be destroyed but were subject to various types of less total discrimination.

Nor was application of these regulations simple. A new profession of "*Sippenforscher*" (genealogical researchers) came into being, for anyone who sought employment by the Reich or membership in the Party had to submit seven documents—the birth or baptismal certificates of four grandparents, two parents, and himself. A Party office was established to decide on doubtful cases, of which some were taken to Germany's highest court. In a few instances, a person with four "German" grandparents was classified racially as a Jew because he had adopted the Judaic religion. Court cases concerning *Mischlinge* were especially common and confusing. A *Mischling* of the first degree could be transformed into one of the second degree, and one of the second degree into a "German." "Pseudoliberation" resulted from a clarification of the law or correction of prior false evidence, and "true liberation" was awarded for "merit."

After Germany conquered large portions of Europe during the first years of the Second World War, the allies it acquired also issued new or revised decrees defining Jews who were to be victimized, and these laws introduced yet more complications. As just one example, the results of a series of laws in Hungary were especially bizarre: a person born in 1920 to Jews converted to Christianity, if his forebears had lived in Hungary for a century or more, was a Jew in 1938, a non-Jew in 1939, and again a Jew in 1941.

Though both Nazi Germany and these various partial imitators loudly proclaimed their classification as racial, in fact they continued the earlier religious categories. No attempt was ever made to classify the population by the shape of the nose (in accordance with a standard anti-Semitic stereotype) or by blood type. The change from past categorizations was only that persons were identified as Jews either by their own religion or by that of their parents and grandparents (or occasionally of their spouse). Though racial ideologues held that pollution persists indefinitely, even the fanatics who established the program did not consider tracing tainted blood back more than two generations.

What is a Race?

That the Nazis adopted Hitler's obsessive hatred of "inferior" races as a programmatic justification for the horrors they perpetrated led understandably to an overreaction. Anthropologists still debate, though less than they used to, about what is meant by "race," with some proposing that it would help eliminate racism if we discarded the concept altogether. From the fact that there are no "pure" races, as I have already remarked, they deduce that there are no races. But it is part of biological evolution that all classifications from phyla through genera and species down to subspecies are "impure"—that is, have both characteristic attributes and imprecise boundaries. At the boundary it is arbitrary whether we term certain unicellular beings "plants" or "animals"; therefore, by this kind of reasoning, neither plants nor animals exist.

One response to the ostensibly racial discrimination was to accept the propaganda and argue, in opposition to a palpable fabrication, that Jews do not constitute a race. Among persons with any regard for rational deduction from elementary evidence, given the history of this people and its distribution over the world, one would hardly expect anything but a wide range of all genetic characteristics. However, if one understands "race" to be a human group that shows a relatively high probability of inherited characteristics, and if one applies this definition to particular sectors of the world's Jewish population, then one finds discernible racial pockets. For instance, certain genetic diseases are more common among Ashkenazi Jews than among other Jews or gentiles. From such a finding one would conclude that, if one starts with the nineteenth-century concept of a prototype, Jews have no racial element in their being. But if one defines "race" rather as a probabilistic aggregate that modern biologists and physical anthropologists generally use, this is not the case.

Paradoxically, in spite of the usual aversion to the notion of a Jewish "stock" (to use a common euphemism), some Jewish intellectuals have argued for a biological genesis of Jewish superiority. The theory was spelled out in greatest detail by Nathaniel Weyl in his book, *The Creative Elite in America*: the smartest young men became rabbis, married the daughters of the best off, thus were able to bring up a large progeny. In contrast, the smartest Catholics became priests and lived as celibates. In short, in Weyl's words, "Jewish intellectual eminence can be regarded as the result of seventeen centuries of selective breeding for scholars."

The sociologist-philosopher Lewis Feuer wrote an interesting critique in his *Ethnicity, Identity, and History.* The smartest Jews, who had the greatest possibilities for advancement in the Christian or the Muslim world, were generally the most likely to convert. Among the forty-nine Nobel laureates listed in the *Encyclopaedia Judaica,* precisely one was descended from rabbinic forebears; of 28 famed rabbis of modern times, all but six were descended from rabbis. "Possibly selective breeding heightened the acumen of rabbinical intelligence," Feuer commented; "it may also have extinguished qualities of venturesomeness and originality." Intelligence is not a single characteristic, to be passed on like a blood type. The effects of heredity are far too complex to be understood through so simplistic a version of Judaic history as Weyl and others offered.

Races are a reality, and for some purposes it is appropriate to regard Polish Jews, for instance, as one race. They tend to have certain blood types, certain diseases, certain other genetic characteristics in higher proportion than other humans, and that is all that is meant by the designation.

16

Chinese Americans and Japanese Americans

Neither their numbers nor their nationwide significance would warrant a discussion of Chinese and Japanese in any but the most exhaustive review of American minorities. Their importance lies rather in their characteristics, which in a number of ways challenge generalizations based on larger nationalities. As Asian immigrants to a population predominantly of European origin, they were set apart by their religious beliefs, cultural attributes, and social organizations—as well as their race, under which all other attributes were often subsumed. These manifold differences tested America's open immigration policy and eventually broke it asunder. Not only were the Chinese the first immigrant group to be specifically excluded, but from this precedent there developed the criterion that all aspirant immigrants should be judged mainly by their places of origin.

The gross discrimination, the collective frustrations, to which Chinese and Japanese have been subjected ordinarily result in a pattern of poor education, low income, high crime rate, and unstable family life, with each of these reinforcing all the other components of a self-sustaining slum. Efforts to assist members of such "problem minorities" in achieving parity with the general population have seldom been altogether successful. However, these two minorities, as we shall note in some detail, themselves broke through the barriers of prejudice and, by such key indices as education and income, surpassed the average levels of native-born whites. This anomalous record, like the earlier one of Jews, challenges the premises from which the etiologies of poverty, crime, illegitimacy, and other social ills are typically deduced. That discrimination is evil in itself is beyond question by the norms of American democracy; the question is whether even the most debilitating discrimination need incapacitate a people if it is not reinforced by other pressures. In the large field of ethnic and race relations, hardly any theory or social policy would remain unchanged if one applied the new insights that the extraordinary success of Japanese and Chinese immigrants suggests.

Immigration from China and Japan

A scant century and a half ago, when contact between China or Japan and the West was close to nil, the ignorance of each other was almost total on both sides. The Chinese were forbidden to teach their language to a foreigner or to send books abroad. Japan was even more isolated, cut off for centuries from all touch with the rest of the world, apart from the so-called "Dutch learning" trickling through the port of Nagasaki. The first edition of the *Encyclopaedia Britannica* (1768) summed up the available knowledge about Japan in a single short sentence, giving its latitude and longitude.

With the push of Westerners to open the two countries to trade, their self-imposed isolation was reluctantly relinquished. In 1842, after a war that the British won over China with disconcerting ease, the Emperor's representatives signed the first of the treaties by which the ensuing century of national humiliation was given apparent legality. Only three years later the Chinese agreed that the troublesome foreigners should administer their own courts of justice and, in another move to keep them at arm's length, leased in perpetuity land on which the British at Shanghai could build their own homes and offices. Paradoxically, two reasons for the greatest resentment later on, extraterritoriality and foreign settlements, had been arranged by Chinese officials so harassed that they welcomed the lessening of their responsibilities.

Incursions by other great powers following Britain's initiative led to comparable trade concessions and slices of territory. Thus, during the major Chinese emigration to the United States, up to the establishment of the Republic in 1912 and partly also beyond, the country was in shambles, with a pathetic regime able to continue in its faltering steps mainly because the several imperialist powers found its weakness to their advantage and at the same time prevented each other from making the whole country a colony. In the so-called Taiping Rebellion, Chinese patriots attempted for more than a decade to overthrow the alien Manchu dynasty and, in a strange combination of forward-looking reaction, to lay a basis for modernizing the country by restoring the Ming emperor to the throne. Ultimately they failed, and the civil war weakened China still more.

The opening up of Japan began in much the same fashion. In 1854, when Commodore Matthew Perry of the United States Navy sailed up Suruga Bay for the second time and refused to leave until Japan ended the self-seclusion it had imposed two centuries before, this was a milder imitation of Britain's forcible acts against China. During one decade the harried Tokugawa officials signed no less than forty-four treaties with foreign powers giving them access to other ports, fixing tariff rates, and establishing extraterritorial rights for foreigners. The parallel with China needs no emphasis; the difference is that the counterpart to the Taiping Rebellion succeeded in Japan. The Meiji Restoration in 1868 also combined a revival of ancient prerogatives with ardent progressivism, a virulent xenophobia with an efficient determination to incorporate all the elements of Western culture that made Japan's enemies strong. The divergent paths of the two countries reached a climax in the Chinese-Japanese war of 1894-95. After her victory, Japan annexed Formosa and other territories, and China was able to pay the indemnity of $200 million only by borrowing from all the other imperialist powers, who thus got a firmer grasp on her economy.

The first effect of this contrast on migrants from China and Japan was the different views that the American public had of the two countries, and thus to some degree of those who had come from them. Within the bounds of general disinterest and misinformation, American images of China vacillated between two incompatible extremes, timeless stability and almost unlimited chaos, sage wisdom and superstitious ignorance, great strength and contemptible weakness, philosophic calm and explosive violence. The cycle of opinion concerning Japan was in part the same, if only because in Western minds the two countries were not sharply differentiated. More consistently, however, it was an alternation between admiration for Japan's stupendous achievement—the most rapid and efficient industrialization in world history—and fear of what this meant for American interests.

The nature of the two states influenced also the types of persons who emigrated from China and from Japan. According to the religious beliefs that prevailed in both cultures, only constant care by the living could keep the spirits of the dead content, and to forsake one's native village incurred the greatest of Confucian sins, a lack of filial piety. Chinese emigrants, perceived as outcasts and vagabonds, included a great many refugees and criminals. In both countries, moreover, the religious disapproval was at first reinforced by government policy. The prohibition of emigration from Tokugawa Japan was so strictly enforced that shipbuilders were forbidden to construct any boats except those suitable only for coastal traffic. But Emperor Meiji proclaimed that "knowledge shall be sought throughout the world, so that the foundations of the Empire may be strengthened." The emigration that the new regime encouraged took place largely under state auspices. The first to leave, 148 contract laborers who went to Hawaii in the year "Meiji One," or 1868, were treated so shabbily by their employers that an agent was dispatched from Tokyo to investigate arranged to have the most dissatisfied return home at Hawaii's expense.

In China, in contrast, persons who attempted to emigrate and minor officials who connived at their act were officially subject to death by beheading. Like most of the country's other laws, this one was not enforced except in the sense of enveloping emigration in crime and corruption. In Cuba in 1876, a joint commission with Chinese, British, and French members made perhaps the most thorough of many investigations of how coolies were recruited and how they were treated in passage and on arrival. Of the total of 40,413 Chinese coolies shipped to Cuba, 80 percent had been decoyed or kidnapped, 10 percent had died in passage. On their arrival in Havana, the survivors were taken to "man-markets," where they were "stripped and their bodies examined in the manner practiced when oxen or horses are being bought." Sold to the highest bidder, most went to sugar plantations, the rest to tobacco and coffee estates or other menial tasks.

In the decades following the American Civil War, some of the most principled opponents of Negro slavery were also the least willing to admit another slave population to the United States. Much of the fear and hostility expressed by proponents of exclusion derived from an at least partially correct estimation of the conditions of Chinese emigration. Not all the malevolence was based on prejudice but on increasingly solid evidence concerning some migrants, whose characteristics were too often generalized to the whole population, or to all Asians, including Japanese. Eastern Congressmen were often more unyielding in their hostility than colleagues from California. In 1874, President Grant expressed a widespread sentiment when he stated, "The great proportion of the Chinese immigrants who come to our shores do not come voluntarily, to make their homes with us and their labor productive of general prosperity, but come under contract with headmen who own them almost absolutely."

Government Control of Migration

The first law concerning the movement of Chinese into the United States was the treaty of 1868, negotiated by Anson Burlingame, America's first Minister to China. Its preamble reads:

> The United States of America and the Emperor of China cordially recognize the inherent and inalienable right of man to change his home and allegiance and also the mutual advantage of the free migration and emigration of their citizens and subjects, respectively, from one country to the other for the purpose of curiosity, of trade, or as permanent residents.

The treaty was arranged in order to facilitate American residence and trade in China. Its reciprocity, at the time a seemingly empty courtesy, became the exclusionists' main target over the next several decades.

Hostility to Chinese immigration existed throughout the United States, but the antagonism became strongest in California and spread from that state to the rest of the country. Gold was discovered at Coloma, California, on January 24, 1848. One week later Mexico signed the treaty ending its war with the United States and, in return for $15 million, ceded to its victorious northern neighbor a considerable territory, including California. The frantic gold rush, thus, coincided with an ardent postwar patriotism, so the effort of law-abiding citizens to hold their own against the riffraff attracted to easy riches, a problem throughout the frontier, was often expressed in nationalist terms. A special tax was imposed on foreign miners; though directed mainly at Spanish Americans and French, it was collected especially from Chinese, the quintessential foreigners who, almost accidentally, became the main target of California's first anti-alien legislation. The hostility that developed thereafter was based in considerable part on ignorance, which was maintained and reinforced by the extreme clannishness of the Chinese.

Governor John Bigler of California, campaigning for reelection in 1852, proposed that the influx of coolies be checked. The issue, thus drawn between free and indentured labor only a few years after the Chinese first appeared in California, was sharpened by a number of fortuitous events. *The Daily Alta California*, until then warmly pro-Chinese, got a new editor and reversed its stand. The number of aliens in the state increased greatly, by 1870 reaching some 210,000 out of a population of 560,000. About a quarter of the foreign-born were Irish, who competed with the Chinese as unskilled laborers and, presumably for that reason, were especially hostile to them.

Anti-Oriental bills were introduced in the California legislature over the next several decades, but the key decisions were made in Washington. The 1868 treaty, already quoted, provided that Chinese subjects resident in the United States "shall enjoy the same privileges, immunities, and exemptions in respect to travel or residence as...citizens or subjects of the most favored nation." Even before 1870, when Congress passed a law excluding the right of naturalization, foreign-born Chinese were usually barred from citizenship. Also in 1870, China agreed in an amended treaty that the United States "may regulate, limit, or suspend," but "may not absolutely prohibit," the immigration of Chinese laborers. In line with these provisions, the Chinese Exclusion Act of 1882 suspended immigration of Chinese laborers for ten years. That the bar had to be renewed each decade meant that anti-Asian agitation was given a recurrent focus, an issue around which to rally those striving for full and permanent exclusion.

Chinese going home would change places with seamen who deserted their ships. Others would claim to have been born in the United States, with the right to enter as citizens. When anyone who had established a legal residence died, his certificate was sold. According to an authoritative work by S. W. Kung, "It is no exaggeration to say that the Exclusion Act actually helped thousands of Chinese, Americans, and Europeans to make millions of dollars by taking up smuggling as a regular and profitable business."

The goal long sought by the exclusionists was finally achieved in the Immigration Act of 1924, under which aliens ineligible for naturalization were not permitted to immigrate. Exclusion was extended from Chinese to other Asians mainly by a series of partly inconsistent court decisions. In 1906, when the notorious political machine ruling San Francisco decided to segregate all Oriental children into a single inadequate school, this parochial affair developed into an international incident. President Theodore Roosevelt, who received an official complaint from Tokyo, dared not ignore it: after its amazing victories over China and Russia, Japan was a power that other nations respected. After an investigation on the spot by a member of his cabinet and almost two years of negotiations, Roosevelt signed a famous Gentlemen's Agreement, under which the Japanese government itself undertook to restrict emigration to the United States to nonlaborers or members of prior residents' families. In substance the difference from the Oriental Exclusion Act of 1882 was slight, but face was saved on both sides—at least until the Act of 1924.

Proscribing citizenship barred a class of permanent residents from their only legitimate route to political power. Moreover, the right to vote entails much more than making a choice on election day; citizenship is often a prerequisite to certain upper economic activities, and by a series of laws in Western states those ineligible for naturalization were denied legal access also to several middle-rank occupations.

Immigration Statistics

In the modern period, characterized by swollen populations and efficient mass transportation, a migration must be measured in the millions to be numerically significant. Immigration statistics, in general not a highly reliable source, were especially deficient with respect to the Chinese, for two reasons. The count of those departing was even less accurate than that of arrivals, and in many years more Chinese left the United States than came to it. And especially after the Exclusion Act was passed in 1882, a large but indeterminate number entered illegally. The issue was raised time and again in Congress, which took testimony on the many means used to evade the law, but with little consequence.

Despite the large and rapidly growing populations of China and Japan, emigration from these countries has been relatively modest. From 1820, when American immigration records started, to 1924, when the national-quota system was enacted, of the total of 36 million listed as entering the United States, only 1 percent were Chinese and 0.8 percent Japanese. Furthermore, these data on gross immigration overstate by a considerable margin the number who remained. It is difficult in retrospect to construe these figures as "The Oriental Invasion," the title of an article by a leading sociologist, or *The Japanese Invasion,* a book introduced by Robert Park, the foremost American sociologist of that period. The language was stronger in the brochures of nativist organizations, but exaggeration was characteristic also of official publications and scholarly works.

Many persons of Asian stock presently resident in the United States live in Hawaii, and from the time of its annexation as an American territory in 1898 to its admission as a state in 1959, confusion concerning its status in national statistics was a constant source of error.

In local accounts about the Islands, estimated proportions of Japanese who remained there were compared with those who departed "either to the mainland or back to Japan." Works that focused on the West Coast, on the other hand, counted in-migrants from Hawaii as new immigrants, thus counting many persons twice.

Whatever their number, most immigrants from Asia were young men. As already noted, for a very considerable period a normal family life was all but impossible for most of the Asians living on the mainland. Hawaii, on the contrary, became famous as an interethnic melting pot in the literal sense. However, as Romanzo Adams remarked in his classic *Interracial Marriage in Hawaii,* Japanese "married within their own group in higher proportion than any other of the peoples of Hawaii," for when the interest of the family is decisive, "marriage with persons of another race or people never takes place." The Hawaiian Chinese, on the contrary, often mated with women of other races, especially native Hawaiians, and how to designate the offspring from such marriages long remained a puzzle.

In sum, no set of official statistics concerning the Chinese and Japanese in the United States can be accepted at face value. The attempts to correct these data that various authors have made, however much an improvement, also reflect to some degree the irremediable gaps in the sources. With no firmly established population figures, the debate over Asian immigration was conducted in large part on the basis of rumored or fabricated "hordes" versus over-modest estimates by partisans on the other side.

Social Mobility

In Hawaii or on the mainland, most Chinese and, several decades later, most Japanese began as poorly paid unskilled laborers. The most important employers in Hawaii were the sugar plantations, which developed so rapidly that they soon dominated the whole economy. As early as 1865, a Dr. William Hillebrand was sent to China as royal commissioner of immigration; he chartered two vessels and transported some 500 workers on five-year contracts. Under Hawaiian law any district or police magistrate could sentence a laborer who willfully shirked his work to serve double the time lost from his contract. Later, when a fine or imprisonment was substituted for such an extension, the contracts became all but unenforceable, for the field workers generally had nothing to forfeit but their freedom.

The percentage of Chinese in Hawaii's population rose from 0.5 in 1853 to a high of 22.3 in 1894, and this rapid increase excited much opposition. Whether to permit further immigration of Chinese became a prominent political issue: planters pleaded their case in economic terms, while opponents charged that the too numerous Chinese were a danger to health and civil order. The dispute was resolved during the 1880s by substituting Japanese for Chinese. The same cycle was then repeated: initially welcomed as industrious workers, the Japanese were admitted in ever larger numbers until they, too, were seen as a political threat.

The Hawaiian Republic, established in 1894 with citizenship limited to Caucasians and native Hawaiians, was not viable. According to the 1896 census, there were 3,086 Americans plus perhaps twice as many Europeans compared to 24,407 Japanese and 21,616 Chinese. Under the new administration established in 1898, America's prohibition of contract labor was extended to the territory of Hawaii, but this formal regulation seemingly had little effect on actual working conditions. As one *Report* of the Commissioner of Labor on Hawaii noted, "It is perhaps inevitable that for a time the technical rights of laborers under American law will be disregarded.... It must be remembered that our legal codes were made for a country where social conditions prevail quite different from those in Hawaii."

During the first decades of this century, both Chinese and Japanese were able to move off the plantations, which eventually had to substitute more and more machinery to replace field labor. Alternative means of earning a living were generally a step up, though usually still a small one. The crucial prerequisite to becoming either an independent craftsman or a small businessman was the accumulation of a modest capital; one might wonder how this could have been amassed out of the meager wages paid to field hands. A typical budget of a Japanese worker in a Hawaiian sugar plantation was reconstructed from data from the years 1909-16. Out of the monthly wage of $18 the companies withheld originally 25 percent, or at this time $3.40, as a deposit against possible future charges. A continuing link to Japan was indicated by charges for stationery, lamp oil, and a portion of the contributions and gifts. Yet a frugal man could save $2.10 of the net monthly wage of $14.60. Whether in Hawaii or on the mainland, among both Japanese and Chinese, the same abstemious regimen was routine.

On the mainland the initial jobs of Asian immigrants were more diverse. Many Chinese were engaged in mining, either as especially prodigious independent prospectors or as helpers in the larger enterprises. They, and later the Japanese, were employed as field laborers or in plants that processed agricultural products. It was Chinese who built the Central Pacific Railroad. E. B. Crocker, the director of the company, at first doubted whether these short, slight men could do the heavy work required: he was persuaded to try out a batch only because the white workers kept deserting to seek their fortune in the gold fields. The experiment was a glowing success, and every Chinatown was searched for men who could be tempted by steady work at $40 a month.

The same capacity for hard work that recommended Asians to the employers of unskilled laborers enabled them to rise from this lowest level to one where their industry and perseverance were reinterpreted as unfair competition. Legal impediments in great variety were contrived to block the advance of Asians to middle occupational ranks. In Hawaii a 1903 law stipulated that only citizens or persons eligible to become citizens (that is, not Asians) were to be employed as mechanics or laborers on "any work carried on by this Territory, or by any political subdivision thereof, whether the work is done by contract or otherwise." In the western states, similarly, the noncitizenship of foreign-born Chinese and Japanese was used to bar them not only from professions and such licensed occupations as realtors and beauticians but, more fundamentally, from mining, fishing in coastal waters, and the ownership of agricultural land. Great ingenuity was expended in finding harassments applicable to other occupations. San Francisco, for instance, imposed a special tax on laundrymen who delivered their goods with a pole rather than by horse and wagon.

The reactions of the Chinese and the Japanese to this pattern of discrimination differed. In general, the Chinese retreated, the Japanese persevered, and this contrast affected much in the way of life of the two ethnic groups.

The retreat of the Chinese was by three routes: migratory, residential, and occupational. In some years the sojourners who had come with the intention of returning home in any case departed in greater numbers than those arriving. However inadequate, the population statistics reflect a decline in numbers and a gradual rise in the median age of those remaining. Second, the vast majority of the

Chinese in the United States established Chinatowns in the larger cities. Most fundamentally, the Chinese withdrew from economic competition. Only in the deep South did they act as middlemen, a typical role of the Chinese minorities elsewhere in the world, which often arouses hostility from both of the other sectors of the population. The usual business in the Chinatowns was devoted to one of two functions, either serving the Chinese community itself or offering exotic foods and commodities to visiting tourists. Those who settled in cities with too few Chinese to congregate into a special quarter also had a narrow range of specialties. They carried over the "women's work" that they had done in mining camps: cooking was transformed into Chinese restaurants, washing into Chinese laundries, and both into personal service with private families. By 1909, when the Immigration Commission of the U.S. Senate conducted its massive investigation of immigrant peoples, the threat from the Chinese had so much dissipated that it was not thought worthwhile to include them. "Such data as were obtained were secured incidentally to the investigation of other races."

Few generalizations are valid concerning the whole shifting labor force of Japanese. Typically they were paid less than other workers, except sometimes Chinese or Mexicans. Often they were hired in gangs through an agent, who for an additional fee also supplied the workers with Japanese food on the job. According to the Immigration Commission's detailed investigation, during the summer of 1909 about 40 percent were working as farm laborers, with piecework earnings about twice as high as other nationalities. Once their competitors had been eliminated from particular areas, however, Japanese field hands became "less accommodating and [did] less work in a day;...by strikes and threats of strikes and boycott, they raised wages." Apart from agriculture, Japanese worked for the railroads, canneries, lumber mills, mines, and smelters.

No matter what their first jobs were, most Japanese wanted to acquire a plot of land, and many accomplished this goal piecemeal through a succession of different types of tenure. By 1909, according to the Immigration Commission's estimate, throughout the West some 6,000 Japanese were farming a total area of more than 210,000 acres. The success of these farms derived in part from an unusual degree of specialization, but more fundamentally from the hard work and extraordinary efficiency of their owners or tenants. To block this advance, California enacted the first anti-Japanese land law in

1913. Even though President Wilson sent his Secretary of State to Sacramento to argue against it, the bill passed by 35 to 2 in the Senate and 72 to 3 in the House. Under its terms, persons ineligible for citizenship could not own agricultural land or lease it for more than three years. In a decision on the law's constitutionality, the U.S. Supreme Court held that, in the absence of a treaty stipulating aliens' rights, each state had the power to set its own legal structure. Over the following years California's initiative was followed by ten other western states. How much of an impediment these laws were to Japanese agriculturists is a matter of dispute. Their provisions were often evaded by various quasilegal means: land was bought in the name of native-born minor sons; partnerships were formed with whites who could front for both members. Though the legal impediments were sufficient to aggravate the already great difficulties in reclaiming land from the desert, by 1940 Japanese controlled a sizable share of agricultural production and distribution, particularly in Los Angeles.

In two crucial respects, thus, the Japanese were more vulnerable than the Chinese: they lived in small, often rural communities scattered widely throughout the West, and they were in constant and growing competition with white farmers, whose organizations amassed great political power during the interwar years. By December 7, 1941, when Japanese planes attacked Pearl Harbor, Japanese Americans had few influential friends and many strong enemies.

Community Organizations

The effects of residential and economic isolation were reinforced by the array of separate community organizations that both Chinese and Japanese established. These were of several types, some distinct to one of the nationalities and some set up by both. Among the Chinese the putative extended kin indicated by the clan names was often important in establishing links in Chinatowns abroad. In all of China, apart from those sinicized from Manchu or other foreign languages, there are only 400 or 500 clan names, of which a fraction were represented among Chinese Americans.

Virtually all of the pre-1945 immigrants from China came from one province—Kwantung—and within that province most came from the single district of Toishan. The Toishanese dialect, radically different from Mandarin, therefore became the dominant Chinese speech in America. Similarly, most of the Japanese immigrants to the United States came from six prefectures out of the total of forty-seven, the six that had constituted the most developed area of pre-Meiji Japan. Most of the migrants to Hawaii came from three of the same six prefectures or—a difference that the Japanese themselves made much of—from Okinawa. In general, thus, both the Chinese and the Japanese constituted more homogeneous groups, sharing more traits than was typical of immigrants originating over a wider range of their native countries.

In the United States those originating in each district of China, or each prefecture of Japan, established associations that in principle included all their compatriots. Then all of these local-based units joined together into federations, of which the most famous was the "Six Companies" in San Francisco, now known officially as the Chinese Consolidated Benevolent Association. Its president, popularly termed "the mayor of Chinatown," often speaks for the whole community in dealings with non-Chinese institutions. The parallel federations of prefectural kai were called the Japanese Association of America, of which there were four on the mainland (in Los Angeles, San Francisco, Portland, and Seattle) and two in Hawaii (with memberships originating in Japan proper and Okinawa). These associations acted as quasi-official representatives of the Japanese government, which gave them the right to endorse, for a fee that they kept, the legal documents that virtually all their members needed from time to time. After the Immigration Act of 1924 was passed and this function lapsed, the Japanese associations began to decline.

The functions of these federations, in part social or political, were also economic. Those just arriving from China or Japan were helped to establish themselves. This meant (as also with other nationalities) that persons from a particular locality tended to congregate in the same place in the United States and often in the same occupation. Neither those seeking employment nor the indigent typically sought assistance outside the ethnic community. For example, according to statistics compiled by the Federal Emergency Relief Administration, the per capita relief funds distributed during the depression of the 1930s to Negroes or whites was several times that going to Chinese or especially Japanese. During the initial evacuation of Japanese from the West Coast, a federal agency started a temporary relief program for the families that had been forcefully evicted from their homes. Even under these extreme conditions, they had little to do until a few Japanese, virtually none of whom had ever had any prior contact with a welfare organization, were referred to them for assistance or advice. "A humorous touch [!] was added to [such] situations when the social worker groped for elementary synonyms for 'social security benefits,' 'eligibility,' 'regulations,' 'resources,' and other stock-in-trade terms."

The help that the associations gave Japanese in agriculture was a crucial element in their getting established and surviving. According to the 1911 *Report* of the Senate Immigration Commission:

> The early Japanese farm organizations...aided their members in finding ranches, served to limit the competition for land by fixing a maximum rental that a Japanese should pay, assisted in marketing the crops and obtaining supplies, interested themselves where disputes arose between a landlord and a tenant, and disseminated scientific knowledge of agriculture and horticulture through publications of their own.

Perhaps the most important type of assistance was through a rotating credit association, called *hui* in Chinese and *tanomoshi, ko,* or *mujin* in Japanese. Like Negroes, Asians were able to get few loans from regular banks; but unlike Negroes, they used traditional institutions to amass the capital needed to establish small businesses. One system worked more or less like a building-and-loan association: subscribers paid in regularly, receiving interest for their deposits, and were eligible for interest-bearing loans when they needed them. Or, several Japanese women who wanted wrist watches set up a minor example of another type of cooperative. With several friends and acquaintances, they established a tanomoshi of ten members, each of whom contributed five dollars a month to the common fund. In successive months, thus, the members could each buy a fifty-dollar watch without having to seek credit outside the community. The cooperation is built on absolute trust (the Japanese word derives from *tanomu,* meaning "dependable"); nothing bound a person to pay his share except honor, but to default was rare.

Up to the Second World War, whatever differences there were between the Chinese and the Japanese in the United States, one could reasonably hold that their similarities were greater, similarities derivative from both the common elements of the two cultures and the parallel discriminations under American law. During the war, however, Chinese Americans benefited somewhat from the good will toward America's ally (the Oriental Exclusion Act was repealed), but Japanese Americans were stereotyped as potential or actual enemies of the United States.

Across a large part of the western United States, all persons of any degree of Japanese descent—a total of more than 110,000 citizens and aliens, men and women, grandmothers and babes in arms, simple gardeners and professionals—were transferred en masse to "relocation camps," where they were kept behind barbed wire and guarded by armed soldiers. No charge of disloyalty was brought against any person; the basis for the evacuation of a whole subnation was a loosely specified "military necessity." Indeed, in time of war extraordinary precautions are appropriate, but the FBI and naval intelligence officers had already rounded up everyone who, by the widest interpretation of national security, could be regarded as the slightest threat. These persons had been screened on the basis of specific evidence applied to particular persons, and those who might have constituted any danger were out of circulation before the mass internment.

The unprecedented act of setting up concentration camps in the United States was accomplished seriatim. Japanese Americans were first instructed to leave the coastal area and, on their own, to find new homes elsewhere. Depending on assurances from both military and civilian authorities, some three or four thousand of them moved to inland California counties. When these counties were subsequently included in the proscribed zone, this necessitated a second forced move. Less than a month later, officials decided to intern all Japanese Americans for the duration of the war. While permanent camps were being constructed, temporary "assembly centers" were hurriedly established at such sites as fairgrounds or racetracks, and from March to November of 1942 all Japanese Americans were congregated in these quarters. Over the same period, the movement began to the ten camps scattered through the Rocky Mountain area.

In their function and mode of operation, the places of sequestration were prison camps, but everything in them was overlaid with a thick patina of official euphemism. Camps were "relocation centers" or "projects"; inmates were "colonists" or "residents"; the wages they were paid—according to the level of skill, $12, $16, or $19 per month for 48-hour weeks—were "cash advances." The official reason for the evacuation, military necessity, was gradually displaced by a professed intention of shielding the Japanese from the wrath of the populace, a rationalization repeated often enough to convince even some of the prisoners themselves of "the soundness of 'protective custody.'" Under Milton S. Eisenhower, the first director of the

War Relocation Authority (the agency instituted to run the camps), the policy was to hold all Japanese in the camps as long as the war continued; and such long-term activities as "Work Corps" and "Producers' Cooperatives" were established. Eisenhower resigned after only two months and was replaced as director by Dillon S. Myer, who tried, on the contrary, to resettle evacuees outside the camps as quickly as possible. Well before November 1942, when the last Japanese in the West was incarcerated, outward movements of certain designated categories began: students allowed to attend colleges in the Middle West or East, field workers granted extended furloughs for agricultural labor, young men permitted—after a change in military policy—to volunteer from the camps for service in the armed forces.

In the words of one of the country's foremost constitutional lawyers, the incarceration of Japanese Americans in concentration camps during the war was "the most drastic invasion of the rights of citizens of the United States by their own government that has thus far occurred in the history of our nation." No evidence was ever offered to suggest that any inmate was guilty of anything. Part of the history of the internment was the failure of the nation's judicial system to provide equal protection under law. The most important cases were three that reached the Supreme Court to test the legality, respectively, of the curfew that had been imposed prior to the mass evacuation, the evacuation itself, and the detention in camps. In fact, all three cases pertained to the same issue, which the Court chose to consider seriatim. On the same day, December 18, 1944, the Court decided both that Fred Korematsu's constitutional rights had not been abrogated, since he had not been "excluded from the Military Area because of hostility to him or his race," and that Mitsuye Endo's detention, in a unanimous decision, exemplified the "racism inherent in the entire evacuation program." This kind of discrimination "bears no reasonable relation to military necessity and is utterly foreign to the ideals and traditions of the American people." During the two and a half years that the case took to reach this conclusion, however, the camps had been built and peopled.

In a shamefaced review of the policy after the war was over, blame was assigned to various groups or factors. A number of conservative or reactionary organizations, such as the American Legion and the Native Sons of the Golden West, had long agitated against Asians, and their denunciation of Japanese Americans grew far more fervent after Pearl Harbor. One can say that they set the mood, but they had no power to carry out what they advocated. President Franklin D. Roosevelt signed the executive order authorizing the evacuation; his attorney general, Francis Biddle, implemented that order with the assistance of such relatively minor figures as Tom Clark, acting as liaison between the federal government and the army. In California, the mainland state with the largest number of Japanese Americans, the attorney general was Earl Warren (later to become chief justice of the U.S. Supreme Court). Called to testify before a committee of the U.S. House of Representatives considering the evacuation, Warren came armed with maps to demonstrate that the Japanese Americans (like the less affluent of whatever ethnic stock) lived close to the airports, railroads, transmission lines, and other likely sabotage targets. True, there had not been a single act of sabotage in the more than six weeks since the war had started, but the attorney general used this very absence of evidence as proof of collective guilt:

> Many of our people in other parts of the country are of the opinion that because we have had no sabotage and no fifth-column activities in this State since the beginning of the war, that means that none have been planned for us. But I take the view that that is the most ominous sign in our whole situation. It convinces me more than perhaps any other factor that the sabotage that we are to get, the fifth-column activities that we are to get, are timed just like Pearl Harbor was timed.... If there were sporadic sabotage at this time or if there had been for the last two months, the people of California or the Federal authorities would be on the alert to such an extent that they could not possibly have any real fifth-column activities when M-day comes.

Most of the Japanese Americans put in camps incurred considerable losses by the forced sale of their property or its destruction during their absence. Under the compensation program set up after the Supreme Court's condemnation of the internment, payments totaling about $38 million were made to approximately 26,500 claimants. At the time of the evacuation, the Federal Reserve Bank estimated the property losses incurred by Japanese Americans at $400 million. Thus, the payments averaged 10 cents per dollar lost and claimed, less 10 percent for attorneys' fees—and less also a considerable deduction for the inflation during the interim (the last payment was made in 1965), for which no adjustment was made. Grudging justice was often so much delayed that the plaintiffs had died before their heirs received amounts barely sufficient to pay the legal costs.

Upward Mobility

One might have anticipated that the camp inmates would suc-
cumb to bitterness and apathy. Instead most lived out the Japanese
proverb, "Six times down, seven times up!" The Japanese American
community disintegrated during the war, and much of it was never
revived. The effect of this dissolution on the younger people was
ambivalent: the kin links and community organizations, indispens-
able means to advancement in the earlier period, could easily have
become constrictive after broader opportunities became independently available. Once the prodigious effort needed to overcome the
economic and psychological consequences of the camp experience
was successfully exerted, young men and women were not impeded
by family pressure, for example, to take over their father's store or
to continue in his skilled trade. The occupational traps of young,
second-generation Japanese working at Los Angeles vegetable
stands, the control that patriarchs of the first generation exerted on
their families, often unreasonable by American standards, the restrictive life in a Little Tokyo—all these elements of the prewar existence were reduced in importance or eliminated, together with much
of the agricultural economy, the Japanese associations, the consular
authority, and a good deal of the informal community solidarity.

This extraordinary thesis, that some Japanese Americans were lib-
erated (as well as damaged) by the partial destruction of their community, can seemingly be validated by two comparisons. The Japanese in Hawaii, who were not put in camps, advanced greatly during the postwar years, but their upward mobility seems to have been
less than that of the mainland Japanese. And while the high proportion of both Japanese and Chinese who moved up to become professionals reflects the extraordinary skill and energy of the two ethnic groups, the continuing high proportion of Chinese (but not Japanese) in service occupations may reflect, at least in part, a continuing pressure to remain in the traditional setting, living in a Chinatown
and working, say, in a Chinese restaurant.

Whatever validity there may be to this paradoxical hypothesis, it
is certainly the case that by most indices of economic and social
well-being Japanese and Chinese rank higher than any other ethnic
group identifiable from census statistics. According to data on religion collected in private polls, Jews and some Protestant denominations or Catholics have had a faster rise or a higher status, but the

number of Asians included in these typically quite small samples is so tiny that the comparisons are hardly meaningful. The contrast between Asians and other racial minorities is especially strong. The key factor is the significantly higher level of education, which helped bring about markedly lower rates of unemployment, a higher proportion in upper-level occupations, significantly greater incomes, and a better style of life as indicated by housing. Whether Japanese or Chinese ranked higher along such dimensions depends on which of these criteria one uses; but by most indices Japanese showed a slightly better position, as in education, or a much better one, as in income. An even larger proportion of Chinese than Japanese were in the top occupational grouping, but their average was brought down, as already noted, by the relatively large percentage of service workers.

Since 1970 both Asian minorities have had higher levels of education and income than native-born whites, and their occupational distribution was especially distinctive. Proportionately almost twice as many Chinese, and almost one and a half times as many Japanese, were classified as professional or upper-level technical workers than the national average.

As we have noted, the first steps up were taken as a consequence of unrelenting hard work and abstemious habits of consumption, but not even the most self-denying man could ordinarily save enough even for a small business or an artisan's shop. The principal clue to these initial advances was that the self-discipline of individuals was supplemented by various types of organizations designed to further their joint efforts. While this cooperation may have been reinforced by the factitious unity resulting from the surrounding hostility, it derived basically from old-country institutions. As younger men were able to seek more profitable and pleasant work, moreover, many of them avoided the jobs that had become stereotyped "Chinese" or "Japanese."

Social Pathology

Extraordinary as have been the positive achievements of Chinese and Japanese, the lack of a countervailing negative record is in a sense even more surprising. Of course, statistics on various types of social pathology are notoriously poor, and many of the series do not include separate totals for the two Asian groups. But of all types of crime, delinquency, dependency, or social disorganization about which we have usable statistics, the recorded incidence is typically lower for Chinese and Japanese than for any other ethnic category in the American population, including again native whites of native parents. The meaning of these statistics, however, is not always the same with respect to the two communities. The extremely low rate of Japanese crime reflects reality, but the comparable rate for Chinese is at least partly spurious, a consequence merely of the fact that criminal acts in a Chinatown generally do not get into the general statistics.

Japanese community norms have generally been strong enough to offset factors "causing" crime among members of other groups. In Seattle, for example, where Japanese used to live in a high-delinquency slum, of the 710 boys sent to a special school for delinquents over the period 1919-30, only three were Japanese— and those three lived in a portion of the neighborhood isolated from other Japanese. As a kind of punishment, the English section of the Japanese-language Los Angeles paper used to publish a "police blotter" listing by name, for instance, a licentious minister and an abortionist. Moral offenders who ignored this public reproof were sometimes helped to return to Japan.

Several elements of Chinese and Chinese American cultures coalesced to produce an environment especially prone to lawbreaking. So-called secret societies, a traditional form of organization since the first century B C E , were always an incipient threat to the Chinese state, quiescent for long periods but then the center of revolutionary-criminal behavior. During the almost three centuries of the Ching dynasty, with the alien Manchu controlling the central regime, the illegal or quasilegal organization of local affairs proliferated both in China and abroad.

In the United States their antigovernment spirit was transferred to the tong, an institution specific to Chinese American communities (the word comes from the Cantonese pronunciation of *t'ang*, "brotherhood"). Just as the prohibition of emigration was circumvented in China by criminal bands, so indentured immigrants, forbidden by American law, were brought in by extralegal methods. No loyalty was felt to the Manchu Empress at one end or to Washington or Sacramento at the other. Behind a facade of benevolent precepts, the Chinese companies and tongs of California began as early as the 1850s to supervise and oppress their countrymen. Later, open force was substituted for more subtle pressures, and spheres of influence were defined in open battles. Rival tongs had on their payrolls full-time gangsters who used knives, hatchets, guns, and in at least one instance machine guns in their internecine wars. According to a standard work on Chinese Americans by Rose Hum Lee:

> Tongs are synonymous with racketeering, white slave traffic, narcotics, gambling, murders by "hatchetmen," blackmailing, extortion, intimidation, threats, and destruction of property.... Their persistence testifies to the continuance of many of the older practices.

Police found it hard to protect the gangs' victims, for Chinese were reluctant to appear as witnesses. "To do so meant death.... Possibly the American courts thought justice was being meted out, but among the Chinese it was known that in reality the interpreter was judge and jury. And...the interpreters were under the influence of the larger family guilds" or, later, of the tongs themselves.

The same family cohesion that gave illegal organizations their structure also helped furnish them with their victims. In their native setting, Chinese have been embedded in nuclear and extended family, "house," and clan. Cut off from these normal surroundings, the immigrants sought substitutes, sometimes illegal ones. The relatively high rate of drug addiction among Chinese, though a transfer of a Chinese culture trait, has been especially marked among unsuccessful sojourners, lonely men who know they will spend the rest of their lives in barren rooms, doing menial work in laundries and restaurants.

With the ambiguous evidence, the present status of tongs (or, as they are now euphemistically termed, merchants or district associations) is a matter of dispute. According to Betty Lee Sung, for example, the activities of the remaining organizations are "apt to be for social, cultural, or recreational purposes," with the functions even of the Chinese Benevolent Association "reduced to the ceremonial." Rose Hum Lee, on the contrary, noted a decline after the tong wars of the 1920s but then "a revival following the arrival of young male adults after World War II." Some of the factors influencing the trend have been more or less fortuitous. The Chinese who moved away from Chinatowns, of whom there have been more in recent decades, were usually able to escape the gangsters' domination. And with the increased average age among the sojourners and the balancing of the sex ratio among young Chinese, organized prostitution declined from a lack of sufficient custom. It would seem that organized crime has shifted mainly to the importation of narcotics, though the evidence is not firm.

The most visible disruption in the Chinese communities is the renewal of rampant gangsterism and open warfare among the rival organizations. Large numbers immigrated of so-called Hong Kong Chinese (usually, in fact, persons from other parts of mainland China who merely left in the port of Hong Kong). They received little help from the cities where they settled, for most of the newcomers spoke a different dialect and knew very little or no English. They usually had little skill in any occupation; some were ardent propagandists for Maoism, in contrast to the still strong support for the Kuomintang among the older generation. Many of the Hong Kong Chinese felt that they were subject to discrimination by both whites and resident Chinese, and they reacted with bitterness and sometimes extraordinary violence.

It is often assumed that the characteristics of the two Asian minorities derive mainly or entirely from their family life. But it has often been surmised that intergenerational conflict is likely to be stronger between foreign-born immigrants and their native-born offspring. One might suppose that the typical tensions would be aggravated in the Asian American family, because of the greater distance between the Asian and the American cultures, and thus between the two generations. The immigrant generation, ineligible for citizenship and in other respects relegated to a low level of American society, were likely to be denigrated by their children. The deference due to older persons under Confucian norms is so excessive by American standards that the second generation was bound to resent the obligation. From puberty on Asian American children are subjected to a straiter discipline than the usual American child ever knows. According to Dorothy Thomas's compilation of life histories, "Dad was strict to the point of tyranny"; "This revolt process then went down to my next sister and so on down the line." The commonest conflict concerned the choice of a spouse: parents wanted to continue the home-country practice of selecting a wife or husband, while the young people wanted to marry for love. The notion that the low incidence of social pathology is due to effective child rearing in Asian American families, in short, is inadequate.

The explanation would seem to be rather that the parents' responsibility for rearing their offspring is to some degree borne by the whole community. A dramatic example is the reaction of the Japanese Americans in Sacramento to a few delinquents who had been arrested for shoplifting. The local chapter of the Japanese American

Citizens League (the post-1945 successor of the prewar Japanese associations) organized a Japanese family guidance council. At public meetings that it sponsored, probation officers, psychiatrists, and other "experts" addressed virtually the whole of the Japanese American community. The pressure was only partly on teenagers; the council's principal effort was to arrange for whatever services might seem appropriate when parents were unable (or unwilling) to control their own children. In the view of the council's officers, negative publicity was itself salutary, for it brought parents back to a sense of their responsibility not only to their family but to the community.

The Future

Tradition has sometimes shown an amazing longevity. In the early 1960s, the central altar figure of Pei-ch'i in a Buddhist temple in Marysville, California, was still protecting the settlement against the Yuba River. A rather long list of such vestiges would include also partial revivals. Still in the 1920s, few Chinese in California observed American holidays and Sundays, celebrating instead the festivals of their native culture.

As early as the 1880s, a San Francisco festival celebrating the birthday of Goon Yum ("Queenly Sound"), the goddess of mercy, ended by offering her meats dripping in fat—an oblation that those newly arrived from China found strange for a vegetarian Buddhist goddess. When a Buddhist priest, the fourteenth generation that succeeded to the hereditary position, moved from a temple in rural Japan to one in suburban Honolulu, he found that the temple building and its surrounding property were not owned by the priest, as according to tradition, but by an abstract entity called "the Mission," whose members, following the congregational principle of American Protestantism, also controlled many of his activities.

Around the time of the Second World War (when China was being praised as an ally), the younger generation lost their disdain for what they had deemed medieval superstitions and began to enjoy them as much as their parents and grandparents. According to a Chinese American journalist, "they are becoming decidedly conscious of the color and symbols of these old-China festivals and on occasions are even inviting their American [!] friends to join them in their celebration." These shifting contrasts in generational attitudes and tastes are another instance of Hansen's about third-generation nativism.

According to a survey of Japanese and Hawaiians of Japanese origin, a good majority in both countries believed that children should be reared to respect discipline; but when this abstract desideratum was contrasted with teaching respect for the truth, many more Americans chose the latter. As one would expect, American respondents considered old-country ceremonies less important than did Japanese, and women ranked themselves higher in the United States. On the most basic difference between "traditional" and "modernist" points of view, man's attitude toward nature, Japanese ranked surprisingly low and Americans much higher. But many more Americans than Japanese expressed both a belief in religion and a higher regard for religious institutions. Many American respondents reacted positively to the concept of "democracy," but they also had more faith in leaders defined as "good" and more often declared that public interests override private ones.

The question was asked, "If you were not a Japanese, which of the following nationalities would you like to be (choose as many as you like): Chinese, Korean, Filipino, native Hawaiian, Portuguese, local haole [i.e., white Hawaiian], Arab, Jewish, Russian, German, French, and English?" The responses differed between the three generations of Japanese Americans and—more or less the same thing—between those with three levels of education. The Issei said they would rather be white, certainly not Chinese (for them the Chinese-Japanese war was a vivid memory). The self-assertion of the third-generation Sansei, on the other hand, was expressed in a reduced proportion choosing haole and an increased proportion choosing every alternative.

The remarkably high rate of interracial marriages, when projected into the future, was extrapolated to the creation of a new racial type, sometimes termed "cosmopolitan." In cultural rather than biological terms, however, there has been a greater persistence of ethnic boundaries; many Chinese, for example, are part Polynesian, white, or whatever but feel themselves nevertheless to be members of the Chinese community. "When asked if their social activities were usually with other Chinese families, 100 percent of the immigrants and 71.7 percent of the local mothers replied in the affirmative." And the two largest subgroups, Japanese and whites, have remained distinct also biologically, with only their edges blurred by occasional interracial breeding.

The acculturation of Asian Americans means, among other things, that after one or two decades they try to imitate some of the more irresponsible extravagances of other Americans, approaching the national average in political immaturity, crime and delinquency, desertion and divorce. Having partly broken out of the patterns that shaped them to their anomalous virtues, both groups will become more differentiated and thus, to some degree and in some respects, less worthy of emulation. Let us hope, however, that they are not to be completely melted into the national pot, but that they will rather continue to train their members in the courage, perseverance, and dignified self-esteem that have marked these peoples' history in the United States.

17

Social Consequences of Religion

Two of the principal founders of sociology are famous for their analyses of just this question. In his best known essay Max Weber argued that "the Protestant ethic" contributed to the rise of capitalism, and he continued his research with memorable analyses of the world's other major religions. In Émile Durkheim's *Suicide*, he contended that because Catholics have a more cohesive moral community than non-Catholics they are less likely to take their own lives. These prototypes represent two of the principal frameworks for analysis pertaining to what is now called the sociology of religion: historical monographs on how transcendental faith affects mundane activities and, on the other hand, statistical analyses of the mode of behavior of various denominations. The impetus from such grand beginnings, however, has not evolved into a corpus within hailing distance of Weber and Durkheim.

The Place of Religion in American Culture

Before the founding of the Republic, the faiths to be found in the several colonies were remarkably diverse. In addition to the established Roman Catholic Church and the Church of England, there were the Congregational Church (divided between Independents, who repudiated the Church of England, and Nonconformists, who did not), the Dutch Reformed Church, the Baptists, Lutherans, Friends, Mennonites, Methodists, Presbyterians, and several smaller sects. Just as the founding of a new nation required that a limit be set on the former colonies' political authority, so the instilling of a national unity meant that none of the churches could retain the local monopoly that some of them had enjoyed. All were disestablished, and the obligation to pay tithes was abolished.

What this separation of church and state meant in effect was gradually specified in a number of Supreme Court decisions related to the

Constitution's First Amendment. It so happened that suits brought by the small denomination of Jehovah's Witnesses became the principal vehicle of this clarification. Of the forty-five suits that that church took to the country's highest court, it won thirty-six. With the most important of these decisions, *Cantwell v. Connecticut* (1940), a unanimous Court incorporated the relevant clause of the First Amendment into the Fourteenth, thus extending to religious dissidents all the legal protection afforded to racial minorities.

By one official doctrine, thus, religious faith was held to be irrelevant to civil society. Immigrants encouraged to acculturate in every other sense were guaranteed the right to maintain their own faith. This doctrine has become troublesome with the immigration of Muslims, for in Islam church and state are not only not separate but they are hardly distinguishable. Among the orthodox, *sharia,* the code of conduct based on the Koran, sets the conduct of both religious and what in the West are termed secular activities.

Yet no one really believes that in the United States adherence to a religion exists, as it were, outside the boundaries of society. When John F. Kennedy was campaigning for the presidency, he was asked to comment on the pertinence of his Roman Catholic faith to the post he was seeking. Some of his political opponents charged that any Catholic American has a double loyalty, both to the Constitution and to Rome. His reply, given on a number of occasions, was a full and unequivocal assurance that there is no relation between being American and being Catholic. The Jesuit journal *America* commented:

> Mr. Kennedy doesn't really believe that. No religious man, be he Catholic, Protestant, or Jew, holds such an opinion. A man's conscience has a bearing on his public as well as on his private life.

How much the public position of religion has changed is suggested by the debate between Republicans seeking the party's presidential nomination in 2000. When asked what political authority most influenced him, George W. Bush responded with an improbable "Jesus Christ," and several of the other aspirant candidates felt it necessary to echo this piety. Charles Krauthammer, a notable commentator on the political scene, remarked that all of the candidates had referred to God a total of twenty-one times, a performance he thought unseemly. "For those who take religion seriously, it is sacrilegious. For those who are secular, it is scary."

Statistics on Religion

In the United States, contrary to a number of other Western nations, there is no consensus on the usefulness or legitimacy of official statistics on religion. Plans to include a question on religious affiliation in the 1960 census were abandoned in response to objections from the American Civil Liberties Union, various Jewish organizations, the liberal Catholic weekly *Commonweal,* the Protestant magazine *Christian Century,* and some Christian Scientist congregations. In favor of including the question were professional societies of demographers and sociologists, the Jesuit weekly *America,* and various other Catholic organizations. Protestant groups were divided or, more often, indifferent. In sum, most Americans were unconcerned, social scientists were in favor of the proposal, and it was opposed especially by Jewish organizations.

The Bureau of the Census, made aware that the issue might become troublesome, announced that such a question would not be included in the census but instead only in a survey, pointing out that the law that requires everyone to respond to questions in the former does not apply to the latter. It conducted its one and only survey on religion in March 1957, with the following results:

Religion	Number of Adherents (–000)	
Protestant	78,952	
Baptist		23,525
Methodist		16,676
Lutheran		8,417
Presbyterian		6,656
Others		23,678
Roman Catholic	30,669	
Jewish	3,868	
Other religion	1,545	
No religion	3,195	
Not reported	1,104	

Since the Census Bureau's single foray into this perilous territory, the principal source of data on religious affiliation are the compilations of figures furnished by church organizations, rather than by communicants, and published in the *Yearbook* of the National Council of Churches. These statistics are supplemented by periodic surveys by Gallup and other polling organizations. Some of these furnish information on matters not usually considered; for example, a survey funded by the Lilly Endowment asked questions on the average size of congregations and the average contribution per church member.

The many small sects meeting in stores converted into churches, which lack the means of compiling accurate statistics, are often suspected of grossly exaggerating their membership. One might suppose, on the contrary, that these tiny temples are often overlooked in whatever national statistics are collected. In either case, the probable accuracy of whatever statistics are collected varies greatly from one denomination or sect to another.

The paucity or even lack of reliable data about a significant attribute of the population has important consequences. As an example of how the lacuna can affect public perceptions, take the record on Irish immigrants. For many decades the typical picture of the Irish American was a Catholic, mired in the working or lower-middle class, of low to medium income. Underlying this image, however, was an amalgam of Catholic Irish and the Protestant Scots-Irish, with many of the latter living in the Appalachian region at close to the poverty level. Using data on religion gathered by the private National Opinion Research Center, the priest-sociologist Andrew Greeley was able to show that as early as the 1950s and 1960s Irish Catholics had risen far and, thus, that the typical representation from official statistics had been grossly misleading. The excellence of his book, *That Most Distressful Nation: The Taming of the American Irish*, derives in considerable part from this private source of data.

There is a widespread feeling that religion is a private matter, not a legitimate matter for surveys under any auspices. Some denominations (e.g., Mormons) refuse to be counted altogether. In others some communicants may share the widespread opinion that such data are often used to reinforce stereotypes and prejudices, and thus that persons given a label (Jew or Catholic or whatever) may suffer from discrimination. In its 1957 survey the Bureau of the Census collected data not only on religious affiliation but also on a number of social and economic characteristics of the respondents. These statistics were never published, a truly rare occurrence in the Bureau's history. In response to a letter from me, the Chief of the Bureau's Population Division wrote merely that "a decision was reached in the Department of Commerce not to issue any further details." Indeed, the strong opposition from Jewish organizations was probably based less on an aversion to the publication of mere numbers than to any association of being Jewish with being wealthy or powerful; for such a linkage, it was feared, would stimulate anti-Semitism.

There is no consensus on the meaning of a church "member." Most Protestant denominations include only those who have been confirmed and are currently enrolled in a specific congregation. As defined by Roman Catholics, Protestant Episcopalians, and several Lutheran denominations, however, membership includes all who have been baptized, thus encompassing infants and children as well as any adults who have drifted away without declaring their alienation. How to define a "Jew" has been the subject of a small library; in most counts by synagogue officials, as well as in the larger surveys reported periodically in the *American Jewish Year Book*, irreligious Jews are included. The justification offered is that it is important to know the number not only of observant Jews but also of any persons who may join, or rejoin, Judaic institutions.

A Christian Country?

At least on the surface, paradoxically, the United States is both a Christian country and one in which no formal association is permitted between church and state. Its citizens pledge allegiance to one nation "under God"; its currency is marked "In God We Trust"; its legislatures begin their proceedings with a prayer. But the directive in the First Amendment that "Congress shall make no law respecting an establishment of religion, or prohibiting the free exercise thereof" does not mean what it clearly states but rather, as interpreted by the Supreme Court, that throughout the culture there is a high wall, an unbridgeable legal gap, between the secular and the religious. Neither religious nor irreligious persons can be content with so ambiguous a status.

Following in Max Weber's footsteps, one can make a plausible argument that ethical principles of the Western democracies flourished in the soil that Christian norms had prepared, or that the Ten Commandments embody a doctrine that makes for a just society; but such vast propositions are hardly a basis for labeling the United States a Christian society. To follow Durkheim's example, on the other hand, and relate religion to its presumed secular consequences, one must begin with statistics on the supposed cause and effect. But in the United States official data of this kind do not exist, and the significance of other statistics is often far from clear.

Mainstream Protestant churches have changed radically since the 1957 survey, and to label a person a Methodist or a Lutheran or whatever tells us little or nothing even about beliefs and practices once associated with those faiths. A fascinating article in the *Wall Street Journal* (February 10, 1999) gives some details on how complicated religious identity has become in the United States. Three responses to one question, "What is your religion?" are indicative: "I'm an Episcopalian, and I think of myself as a practicing non-Jew"; "I'm a Mennonite hyphen Unitarian Universalist who practices Zen meditation"; "I call myself a Christian Buddhist, but sort of tongue-in-cheek." The article continues:

> Jews flirt with Hinduism, Catholics study Taoism, and Methodists discuss whether to make Passover seder an official part of worship....The melding of Judaism with Buddhism has become so commonplace that marketers who sell spiritual books, videotapes, and lecture series have a name for it: "JewBu."

Religion and Morals

From the point of view of a social analyst, perhaps the main function of any religion is to instill a moral code in its practitioners. Undoubtedly, most members of whatever faith regard themselves as good people and see their religion as part of the reason for their virtuous life. Take, for instance, William F. Buckley's work about himself, *Nearer, My God*, in which he presents a very attractive picture of a coherent extended family governed by a stern but just patriarch. I would like to accept his implicit claim that the Catholic faith was a cause of his family's virtuous record. But there is another prominent American family that in a dozen ways is reminiscent of the Buckleys—closely tied to one another through several generations, differentiated from the surrounding milieu by their adherence to the Catholic Church, and—unlike anything one can say of the Buckleys—sometimes represented by rather disreputable members. From this quite inadequate sample of only two, the Buckleys and the Kennedys, one can draw the tentative conclusion that it was not Catholicism alone that made the Buckleys a model.

It is a commonplace assertion that religion and morality are very nearly inseparable. Certainly most Christians and most Jews are worthy citizens, but does the correlation really denote a cause-effect relation? Is it not more likely that decorous persons, because they seek their neighbors' approval, both attend church or synagogue and in other respects behave as the neighbors expect them to? Edith Wharton, that astute commentator on American society, commented:

> The Wetheralls always went to church. They belonged to the vast group of human automata who go through life without neglecting to perform a single one of the gestures executed by the surrounding puppets.

Indeed, even the thesis that membership in a church induces commendable behavior would be hard to demonstrate. One thinks of greedy televangelists, of priests who happen to be pedophiles, of politicians who religiously—one might say—make sure that they are seen entering church doors every Sunday.

Much of what many Americans deplore in their culture has been advanced, sometimes even initiated, by the mainstream religious institutions, indeed especially the Protestant ones but, lagging a bit behind, also the Catholic and Judaic. When the serious infirmities of the family, to cite a primary example, are described as one disastrous effect of the decline in religious faith, those who so instruct us seldom mention that some clergy of various denominations have been influential in setting the free-wheeling deportment that results in the propagation of fatherless children and "marriages" between homosexuals.

It is difficult to find instances where faith was clearly the cause of estimable behavior. A book by Philip Hallie, *Lest Innocent Blood Be Shed*, is a fascinating account of a French Calvinist village during the German occupation; all the residents followed the example of their pastor and offered refuge to Jews fleeing their Vichy or Nazi oppressors. Such examples are fascinating in part because they are so rare; few persons of any faith had the courage to oppose the Gestapo. But it is only when faced with perilous choices that the full import of a faith, any faith, becomes evident.

One of the recurrent themes in American law is whether religion has any place in public schools. DeKalb County, Alabama, had a ruling barring from public institutions of learning all prayer or mention of God. At a time when President Clinton (in his effort to find an escape from the travails of the Lewinsky scandal) was calling for prayer on national television, the county had been forced to hire a special monitor to search out illegal praying in its schools; a history teacher had been threatened with dismissal for ending a speech with the Lord's Prayer. The spectacle typifies dozens of ludicrous court decisions, following challenges that such organizations as the American Civil Liberties Union initiated throughout the country—typical except for the fact that in July 1999 the 11th U.S. Circuit Court of Appeals ordered a reversal of the decision barring any hint of religion in public schools.

The issue of school prayer has become in microcosm a platform from which adversaries have argued on whether it is the decline of religion that brought about a parallel decline in American morals. I find the argument on both sides unconvincing. When I attended the public schools of Jersey City, the principal gave us a reading from the Bible to introduce each weekly assembly. Every Friday morning he would pretend to read (for he undoubtedly could recite the passage, as I can still today) the following:

> Why take ye thought for raiment? Consider the lilies of the field, how they grow; they toil not, neither do they spin. And yet I say unto you that even Solomon in all his glory was not arrayed like one of these.

Most students did not listen to the familiar words, but a few of them must have wondered (as I did) at the choice of text, which seemingly advised them not to study, nor to read, for they would in any case be smarter than King Solomon.

How the farcical compromise came about that resulted in the continual repetition of this single passage I do not know. But a decision to permit the reading of the Bible in any other school would also, I am sure, be subject to some sort of bargaining, with an eventual settlement almost as absurd as this. At the time I attended its schools, Jersey City was governed by the corrupt machine of Frank Hague, a pious Catholic who would hardly have opposed prayer in schools. Moreover, since the city's population was made up largely of Irish, Italians, and Poles, the Catholic Church had a strong influence on any civic matter in which it took an interest. Even under such circumstances presumably it had been deemed expedient to avoid unnecessary dispute on what secularists defined as a constitutional issue, and I am sure that those who today fight to get prayer in public schools would also, if they were successful, be obliged to settle for half a loaf.

The supposition that the reading of such a passage, or the institution of any similar gesture, could affect the country's moral climate is, I maintain, ridiculous. To fuss about whether prayer may be permitted in schools is irresponsible, for it is fatuous to believe that this would of itself affect the behavior the students. I find the zealots of the ACLU distasteful, but I cannot muster much sympathy for those on the other side of this interminable controversy.

A Nonreligious Christian Country?

One of the most important of ancient truths embodied in any religious faith used to be that its verities were unique, that all competing creeds were in error and, as in many well documented instances, should be obliterated. The notion that virtue flows from Christian faith, in other words, must be countered by the long history in the Western world of persecution not only of Jews, the principal victims, but of a wide variety of dissidents. It is a mixed picture, and to associate a creed with only the more attractive half is inadequate.

How much of the near universality of religion in American life is genuine, how much a facade? It is not a question to which one can find a full answer, but it is nevertheless interesting to pose it.

The word "hypocrite" derives from the Greek for an actor, hence one pretending to be what he is not. The contrast between appearance and reality is retained in the meaning of the English word, together with a denigration absent in the original Greek. The first reference to "hypocrisy" in the *Oxford English Dictionary* is dated 1225, and the first for "hypocrite" 1540. Many of these early citations pertain to religious faith, and this emphasis is retained in the same dictionary's definition of the current words: a hypocrite is "one who falsely professes to be virtuously or religiously inclined." Today the allusion to religion seems a bit dated, and for the *American Heritage Dictionary*, lacking the long tradition of the *OED*, hypocrisy is "the practice of professing beliefs, feelings, or virtues that one does not possess; falseness." In an age of faith, that is to say, "hypocrisy" pertained mainly to ostensible religious belief, and the shift from it was to another set of rules.

The reign of Victoria is often pigeonholed as the pinnacle of hypocrisy. At that time someone claiming virtues he lacked may have been referring to religion, or it may have been to sexual behavior. By the 1960s, however, American proponents of new freedoms could find few sexual inhibitions to demolish. Yet hypocrisy certainly did not vanish. A large sector of American society still wanted to be regarded as conventionally moral members of a church, and the decline of religion in more meaningful senses seemingly affected this conventionality rather little.

In many ways the country's quasi-official Christianity is a facade. Behind it is the growing certainty of today's Americans that all peoples, all cultures, all religions, all ethical systems, are equivalent. The principal reason that Protestant and Jewish doctrine (and, to a lesser degree, Catholic as well) is so thin is that we have all been taught—and really learned, for a change—to be universally tolerant. If everything is equally good, there can be no such thing as a moral choice; ethical doctrine is obsolete.

The curious notion that all moral systems can be judged only by the standards included in them, what is generally known as "cultural relativism," was a gift from anthropologists. After having been proposed by various individuals, it became an official doctrine of the discipline in 1947, when the executive board of the American Anthropological Association submitted a joint statement to the UN Commission on Human Rights (*American Anthropologist*, 1947). If the principle of human rights were to apply to all mankind, they declared, it would have to include a respect for the cultures in which the individuals were embedded. To assist in such an expansion of the concept, they offered "some of the findings of the sciences that deal with the study of human culture," as follows:

1. The individual realizes his personality through his culture, hence respect for individual differences entails a respect for cultural differences.

2. Respect for differences between cultures is validated by the scientific fact that no technique of qualitatively evaluating cultures has been discovered.

3. Standards of values are relative to the culture from which they derive so that any attempt to formulate postulates that grow out of the belief of moral codes of one culture must to that extent detract from the applicability of any Declaration of Human Rights to mankind as a whole.

Perhaps the most significant element of this manifesto is its date, 1947, when the seemingly innumerable horrors of Nazi Germany were still being brought to light.

18

A Closing Word

The material of this book embodies a seeming contradiction. On the one hand, I have avoided technicalities that a demographer should know, addressing the work rather to the general reader. On the other hand, I have everywhere emphasized the deficiencies of population data—the errors, the omissions, the imputations, the half-hidden aggregations and classifications. Unless it was his role to adjust the data in order to mitigate these faults, most professional demographers would have little interest in them. They know that, like everything else that humans create, population and ethnic statistics are far from perfect; but their usual reaction is to take it for granted that they are as good as they can be made and that, therefore, one can use them as they are.

A nonprofessional who encounters statistics such as those discussed in this book would usually be unaware of all the compromises made in the process of generating them. He might have read of cities' suits against the Bureau of the Census and recall that the principal issue was whether sizable proportions of certain sectors of the population had not been included in the count. This is a significant fault, but it is one that the Bureau has tried, in part successfully, to correct. The homeless may be overlooked, so an especial effort is made to locate them. Aliens who have entered the country illegally may try to avoid contact with any official, so advertisements are posted that being enumerated in a census will not bring them to the attention of the immigration officials. Undercounts are the type of errors that one can correct to some degree, for there is a real number, the actual population of the United States, that one can approach in various ways.

True, the Bureau sometimes invents not only the characteristics but also the existence of those not found in quarters labeled "occupied," but this is an exceptional practice that many demographers deplore. A person is a person, but an *employed* person is so defined not only by his actions but also by how the statistical bureau interprets them. We all know that over the country's history the proportion of the population living in cities has grown steadily, but if we try to elaborate this fact with details, we find that the definitions of "urban" and "rural" were changed every decade or two. If we ask the Bureau of Indian Affairs how many Indians there are, and is the current number larger or smaller than a generation ago, we will get an *official* response that may astound us: there are several ways of counting Indians, and thus there is no single figure that can be designated the total number. In 1970, when the Bureau first used self-identification to specify racial and ethnic groups, it compared its findings with those published by other federal agencies; the differences ranged from 5 to 27 percent.

In short, most of the statistics discussed in this book reflect not the real entities, but rather statisticians' interpretations of them. These interpretations differ from one statistician to another, and thus over time. Every professional who uses them knows (or ought to know) this, but the general reader for whom this book was written does not. A work for the nonprofessional should not only point out deficiencies in official data but stress that they should be taken into account whenever one has occasion to cite them. This is what I have tried to do.

One of these deficiencies pertains not only to the data discussed in this work but rather to virtually all that are used in the social disciplines. When data are collected from one person after another and then coalesced into statistics about categories, a number of misunderstandings are likely to follow. When someone is identified, or identifies himself, as literate, he has in common whatever is understood by "literate," and the criterion has been inconsistent over both time and space. But then a profile is developed about the characteristics of "illiterates," and all who share the identifying attribute have bestowed on them all the others. Objections have been raised against the official use of "racial profiles," but not against profiles in general.

The reason is obvious: everyone manages from day to day by assuming that persons in his environment can be classified as members of a finite number of sets. We could not cope if the infinite variety of humans were the substance of our life's context. But we should keep in mind that our perceptions are flawed not only with respect to such sensitive matters as race, but altogether.

Appendix

Some of the chapters in this book are thoroughly revised and up-dated versions of earlier papers, in which the scholarly paraphenalia here lacking can be found. These articles are listed here, with a full reference:

"Age and Sex," *Society* (May/June 2001) 46-52.

"American Efforts to Reduce the Fertility of Less Developed Countries," in Nick Eberstadt, ed., *Fertility Decline in the Less Developed Countries* (New York: Praeger, 1981).

"Chinese Americans and Japanese Americans," in Thomas Sowell, ed., *American Ethnic Groups* (New York: Urban Institute, 1978).

"Concepts of Ethnicity," *Harvard Encyclopedia of American Ethnic Groups* (Cambridge, MA: Harvard University Press, 1980).

"Jews as a Race," *Midstream* (Feb.-Mar. 1988), 35-37.

"Marxism and the Population Question: Theory and Practice," *Population and Development Review*, Supplement to vol. 14 (1988), 77-101.

"A New Look at Malthus," *Society* (Nov./Dec. 1998), 60-65.

"On the Subnations of Western Europe," in Nathan Glazer and Daniel P. Moynihan, eds., *Ethnicity* (Cambridge, MA: Harvard University Press, 1975).

"Parents vs. State," *American Scholar* (Winter 1997), 121-127.

"Politics and the Measurement of Ethnicity," in William Alonso and Paul Starr, eds., *The Politics of Numbers* (New York: Russell Sage Foundation, 1987).

"Population Policy and Age Structure," *Policy Studies Journal*, 6 (1977), 146-155.

"The Social Roots of Hunger and Overpopulation," *Public Interest*, no. 68 (Summer 1982), 37-52.

"Staying Alive: Some Home Truths about Population," *American Scholar* (Winter 1988), 51-68.

Index

abortion, 83, 84, 113-21; in China, 99; in India, 102; in law, 115-18; partial-birth, 119 "acceptors," 92-93
acculturation, 151
action research, 87-88
Adams, Romanzo, 208
affirmative action, 133, 155, 156
Africa, 39, 91, 95, 127
African Americans. *See* black(s)
age, 3-4, 19-20, 23; groups, 27-28; structure and population growth, 24
AGE, 31
aggregation, 1-5
Agnew, Spiro, 186
agriculture, 211-12; Russian, 67-72
AID, 93-94
Aird, John, 99-100
Alabama, 233-34
Aleichem, Sholom, 187
Aleuts, 3
Alexander I, 175
America, 228-29
American Association for the Advancement of Science, 85
American Association of Retired Persons, 31
American Civil Liberties Union, 229, 234, 235
American Council of Learned Societies, 189
American Indian(s), 23, 105, 132-33, 140, 150, 151, 162-66; identity of, 163-65; instant, 163; population, 164-66, 238
American Jewish Committee, 166-67
American Legion, 216-17
Americans for Generational Equity (AGE), 31
anthropology, 236

antibiotics, 38
anti-Semitism, 195-200
antinatalism, 24, 88
Appalachian region, 141
Aquinas, Thomas, 113-15
Argentina, 43, 140
Armand, Inessa, 68-69
Aryan, 197
Ashkenazi, 199
Asia, 39
assimilation, 126, 133-35, 143, 151-52
Aufbau, 187
Augustine, 114
Australia, 135
Austria, 187
Austria-Hungary, 127, 172-73, 177
Aztlán, 193

baby boom, 24-25, 86
Bakunin, Mikhail, 77
Bancroft, George, 149
Bangladesh, 19, 40, 92
Banks, J. A., 80
Baraka, Imamu Amiri, 188
Barbour, Haley, 11
Bauer, Otto, 60
BEA (Bureau of Economic Analysis), 4
Bebel, August, 61, 74
Becker, Gary, 91
Beedham, Brian, 99
Belgium, 127, 128, 130, 180-81
Bentham, Jeremy, 49
Berelson, Bernard, 96-97
Bernal, J. D., 74
Bernstein, Eduard, 59, 60, 61, 77
Besant, Annie, 63, 82
Besemeres, John, 68
Bhawan, Nirman, 102
Biddle, Francis, 217
Bigler, John, 2-5

bilingualism, 1
Billig, Wilhelm, 74
birth control, 61-65, 81-82, 120; programs, chap. 8.
administration of, 90; for health, 91; in less developed countries, 84-86; rational choice and, 91-92
birth rate, 21; crude, 21
birth strike, 63, 64
Bismarck, Otto von, 30-31, 171
black(s), 127, 132, 134, 135, 137-38, 141, 142, 146, 147, 148, 151, 153-54, 158-62, 187, 193, 204; English, 141, 162; fertility, 22, 25-26; self-identity, 160-62; subcategories of, 159-60
Black Panthers, 147
Blackmun, Harry, 115-16
Böckh, Richard, 190
Bogue, Donald, 91
Bohemia, 176
Bonar, James, 45, 50
Bork, Robert, 117
Boston Globe, 193
Boulder City, 108
Brackett, James, 74
Bradlaugh, Charles, 63, 82
Brass, William, 95
Brazil, 92
Breton, André, 153
Britain, 16, 171; unemployment rate, 4
British, 202; Labor Party, 65; Society for Population Studies, 50
Brown v. Board of Education of Topeka, 134, 154
Brussels, 180
Buchalter, Lepke, 110
Buckley, William F., 232
Buddhism, 223
Bukharin, Nikolai, 60
Bulgaria, 174
Burch, Thomas, 115
Bureau of Economic Analysis, 4
Bureau of the Census. *See* United States
Bureau of Indian Affairs. *See* United States
Burgdörfer, Friedrich, 74
Burke, Edmund, 171
Burlingame, Anson, 205
Bush, George W., 228
Bustelo, Manuel A., 191

Caldwell, John, 86
California, 205-06
Calvin, John, 114
Cambridge University, 49
Canada, 127, 131
Cannan, Edwin, 85
Cantwell v. Connecticut, 228
Cape Colored, 143
Capital, 54-55
Carmel, CA, 13
Carolina Population Center, 48
Carr-Saunders, Alexander, 81
Castro, Josué, 74
category, ethnic, 146
Catholic University of Louvain, 180-81
Catholicism, 73, 88, 114-15, 120-21, 167, 195-96, 200, 227-301, 232
celibacy, 89, 120-21
census(es), 9. Bureau. *See* United States, Bureau of
Census. Soviet Union, 23. United States, 3, 229
Census Advisory Committee on the Spanish-Origin Population, 147
Central Pacific Railroad, 210
Césaire, Aimé, 153
Ceylon, 37
Chamberlain, Basil Hall, 29
Chandrasekhar, Sripati, 102
Chang, Chung-li, 81
Chao, John, 93
Chapel Hill, 12
Charles, Enid, 40
childbirth, 37
child rearing, cost of, 84
children, value of, 29
China, Chinese, 18, 19, 29, 40, 42, 86, 89, 142, 149; 202-04, 207-08; abortions in, 99; emigration from, 203-04; family, 81; family-planning programs, 98-101; fertility, 81, 97-98; mortality, 99; one-child program, 98-101; population, 98-101; wages in, 100
Chinatowns, 211
Chinese Americans, 201-25, 208-12, 218-19, 219-23; acculturation of, 223-25; community organizations, 212-215, 219; family, 208, 221-23, 224; secret societies, 220-22; Benevolent Association, 221; Exclusion Act, 206-07; immigrants to US, 26, 168

Christian Century, 229
Christian Scientists, 229
citizenship, 11, 186
Clark, Tom, 217
classification, 1
Clemenceau, Georges, 174
Clemens, Orion, 106
Clemens, Samuel, 106
Clift, Virgil A., 160-66
Clinton, William J., 233
Club of Rome, 40
Coale, Ansley, 79-80, 95
Cohen, Joel, 41
cohort, 20
Cole, G. D. H., 65
Colombia, 92
colorblind standard, 154-55
Cominform, 175
Commission on Population Growth and
     the American Future, 43, 88
Common Market, 182
Commonweal, 229
communism, 64
Communist Manifesto, 71
"compulsuation," 103
*Condition of the Working Class in En-
     gland, The*, 53-54
Condorcet, Marquis de, 45
Confucianism, 222
Congress of the United States. See
     United States.
Congress of Vienna, 182
Conquest, Robert, 72
consolidation, 140-41
contraception, 88-89; in less developed
     countries, 88-89;
methods, 94
Cook Island, 93
coolies, 204-07
country of birth, 148
Cowan, Thomas A., 169
Cozzens, Donald, 120
credit associations, 214
Crèvecocur, J. Hector, 149
Croats, 175
Crocker, E. B., 210
crusades, 195
Cuba, 204
cultural pluralism, 152-53; relativism, 236
Current Population Surveys, 146
Czechoslovakia, 127, 172, 173, 176,
     177, 188

data, open, 17-18; secret, 17-18
Darwin, Charles, 51
Davies, Norman, 171
Davis, Kingsley, 87 DDT, 37-38
de Gaulle, Charles, 179
Declaration of Human Rights, 236
Declaration of Independence, 9, 154
demographic transition, 35
demographics, 17
demography, 15-17; formal, 16; histori-
     cal, 35; social, 16
Denton, Sally, 109
dependency, 28-30; ratio, 28-29
Derogy, Jacques, 64
diglossia, 1-2
diseases, 38-39
disestablishment, 227
divorce, 108
Doe v. Bohen, 117
Doerr, John, 59
Donaldson, Peter, 48
Donceel, J. 114
dozywocie, 29
Dreyfus, Alfred, 61
Driver, Edwin, 87
Drysdale family, 91
Drysdale, George, 64
Dublin, Louis, 83
Durkheim, Emile, 227, 231
Dutt, R. Palme, 74

East India Company, 49
Easterlin, Richard, 24
Eberstadt, Nicholas, 86
economic areas, 4
Economic Commission for Europe, 10-11
Economist, 98-99
editing, 13-14
education, 12-13, 51-52, 86, 219
effective demand, 59-60
Egypt, 92
Ehrlich, Paul, 23
Eisenhower, Milton S., 215-16
Eisler, Gerhart, 172
Ellis Island, 189
Emergency Relief Administration, 213
employment, 4-5, 23 *See also* unem-
     ployment.
Encyclopaedia Judaica, 200
Engels, Friedrich, 53, 62, 71, 77
England, English, 64-65, 80, 124, 149,
     168

Enlightenment, 196
errors in population statistics, 11-13
Erse revival, 188
Eskimos, 29
Espenshade, Thomas, 84
Ethiopia, 41
ethnic, category, 143, 146; classification, 169; community, 143; group(s), 126, 131-33; origins of, 139-43, 145, 146; identity, 138
ethnicity, American, 149-58; concepts of, 125-31; counts by, 167-69; hidden, 135-36; measures of, 145-49; and race, 148, 155-56; rise of, 135-39; statistics on, 157-58, 237-38
ethnos, 173
euro, 183
Europe, European(s), 28, 31, 47, 83, 135, 151, 171-83; classification of, 166; marriage pattern, 47; Monetary Union (EMU), 183; Parliament, 182-83
evolution, 2, 51, 129

family, 24, 26-27, 33, 105; allowances, 82-83; in China, 81
family-planning programs, 97, 104; in Costa Rica 96-97; in Hong Kong, 96-97; Mauritius, 96-97, Puerto Rico, 96-97;
Taiwan, 96-97; Thailand, 96-97; Trinidad, 96-97; "success" of, 92-98, 104; theory of, 88-92
Family History Library, 187
Faroe Islands, 93
Faust, Albert, 190
FBI. See Federal Bureau of Investigation fecundity, 79
Federal Bureau of Investigation, 110
Federal Bureau of Narcotics, 110
Federal Reserve Bank, 217
federalism, 182-83
fertility, black, 22; in China, 81; maximum, 79-80; trends, 41-44
Feshbach, Murray, 23
fetus, maturation of, 113-14, 116, 118-20
Feuer, Lewis, 200
filial piety, 29
Finland, 40
First World War, 182
Fischer, Ruth, 172

Fishman, Joshua, 1
Fitoussi, Jean-Paul, 183
Fleming(s), Flemish, 130, 180
food supply, 39-41
foreign stock, 133
Fourastié, Jean, 36
Fourier, Charles, 55, 77
Fourteen Points, 174
France, 16, 30, 36, 45, 64-65, 82-83, 84, 89, 172
Frazier, Franklin, 138
Frémont, John C., 106
Friedrich, Carl, 183
Friesland, 178
Frisian, 178
frontier, 26, 105-11

Gaelic, 179
Galicia, 173
Galileo, 21
Gallup poll, 230
gambling, 109-10
Gandhi, Indira, 103
Gandhi, Mohandas, 101, 103
Gandhi, Sanjay, 103
Gannet, Henry, 4
Gates, William, 108
genealogy, 187
generational conflict, 30-32
genocide, 129
George III, King, 9
German(s), 151, 190; Americans, 186
German Ideology, The, 54
German Social Democratic Party, 61-62
Germany, 30-31, 172, 176, 182, 187, 197; censuses of, 177; Nazi, 236
gerontology, 30
Gesarimov, Genadv, 75
Ghana, 94
Gibraltar, 93
Glass, David, 83
Glazer, Nathan, 156
Godwin, William, 45-46
gold rush, 205
Goldstein, Sidney, 167
Goon Yum, 223
Gorbachev, Mikhail, 72
Gordon, Milton, 134-35
Grant, Ulysses S., 204
Greece, 174
Greeley, Andrew, 155-56, 167, 230
Greenland, 93

gross national product, 96-97
Grossman, Henryk, 60
group, ethnic, 146
Guarani, 1
Guillard, Achille, 15
Gutman, Herbert, 157

Hague, Frank, 234
Haiti, 39
Hajnal, John, 41-42, 47
Haley, Alex, 152-54
Hall, Charles, 55
Hallie, Philip, 233
Hallstein, Walter, 183
Hansen, Alvin, 83
Hansen, Marcus Lee, 136-137, 139-40, 223
Hawaii, 12, 132-33, 142, 148, 168, 204, 207-09, 213, 218, 223, 224
Heraud, Guy, 128
Herskovits, Melville, 139-40
Higham, John, 156-57
Hilberg, Raul, 196
Hilferding, Rudolf, 60
Hillebrand, William, 208
Himes, Norman, 81
Himmelfarb, Gertrude, 52
Hippocratic Oath, 116
Hispanic(s), 12, 143, 147, 169, 191-94;
   families, 192
   miscounts of, 192
historical demography, 35
Hitler, Adolf, 196, 199
Hobbes, Thomas, 125
Hobson, J. A., 60
Hogben, Lancelot, 40
Hollick, Frederick, 82
Hoover Dam, 107-08
household, 26-27
Humbert, Eugène, 64
Humbert, Jeanne, 64
Humphrey, Hubert, 154-55
Hungary, Hungarian(s), 172-73, 174, 198
Hutter, Jakob, 79
Hutterites, 79-80
hypocrisy, 235-36

Illinois Department of Human Rights, 156
immigration, 22, 185-86; by country of origin, 188; of Chinese, 201-04;
Cuban, 191-93; Irish, 230; Japanese, 201-04; Jewish, 166-67, 173; Mexican, 191-93;"old" and "new," 188; Puerto Rican, 191-93; restriction, 166, 188-91; of Spanish origin, 191-93; statistics, 207-08
Immigration Act of 1924, 206
Immigration and Naturalization Service, 186, 191
Immigration Commission, U.S. Senate, 211
imperialism, 60-61
imputation, 13-14
income, family, 22
India, 38, 40-41, 42, 89, 91, 97-98, 101-03, 127; family-planning programs, 101-03; population, 101-03
Indian(s), 129; American. See American Indian(s)
Indian Reorganization Act, 140
Indonesia, 92
INED, 83
infanticide, 89
Inquisition, 195
International Planned Parenthood Association, 102
International Statistical Institute, 18, 176
Ireland, Irish, 146, 151, 167, 168, 179, 230
Isaacs, Harold, 137
Islam, 187-88
"islands and peninsulas," 96-97
Isle of Man, 93 Israel, population of, 139
Italy, Italian(s), 16, 83, 84, 128, 182, 188; unemployment rate, 4

James, Henry, 189
James, Patricia, 50
Japan, Japanese, 4, 29, 38, 89, 168, 202-04, 207-128; 218-19; emigration from, 203-04
Japanese American(s), 12, 168, 201-25, 219-23; acculturation of, 223-25; camps, 213-18; community organizations, 212-15, 219; family, 203-04; 208, 224; land laws, 211-12
Japanese American Citizens League, 146, 222-23
Japanese Association of America, 213
Jehovah's Witnesses, 228
Jews, Jewish, 22, 195-200, 218, 229-31, 233-34 German, 46; identity of, 197-

99; immigrants, 166, 173, 188; names of, 187; population, 166; religion of, 195-96
Jones, LeRoi, 188
Journal of the American Medical Association, 118-19
Jura, 179

Kallen, Horace, 134, 157
Kautsky, Karl, 61, 62, 72, 77
Kennedy, Anthony, 117
Kennedy, John F., 228, 232
Khanna study, 97
knowledge-attitude-practice (KAP), 91
Koran, 228
Korematsu, Fred, 216
Korson, Tadeuez, 171
Kovács, Alajos, 176-77
Krauthammer, Charles, 228
Kulischer, Eugene M., 18
Kung, S. W., 206
Kuomintang, 232
Kwantung, 212

labor force, 28
Labroue, Henri, 196
Landsmål, 130, 178
language(s), 1, 130
Lanoky, Meyer, 110-11
Las Vegas, 109-10
Latin America, 42-43
Latinos. *See* Hispanics
Latter-day Saints. *See* Mormons
Lausanne, Treaty of, 174
League of Nations, 176
Lee, Rose Hum, 221
Lenin, V. I., 60-61, 179; on abortion, 68; on agriculture, 67-71; on free love, 68-69; on imperialism, 60-61; on neo-Malthusianism, 68; on population, 68 less developed countries, 18, 29, 37, 42-43, 55, 76, 84-86, chap. 8, 88-92; contraceptives in, 88-89
least developed countries, 39, 47
Levinson, Daniel, 27
Li, Wen, 96
Liebknecht, Wilhelm, 61
life, beginning of, 119-20
Life, 172, 183
Lilly Endowment, 230
Lincoln, Abraham, 106
Linné, Karl von, 2

Linnaeus, Carolus, 2
literacy, 238
Lithuania, Lithuanians, 188
Locke, John, 76
Lombard, Peter, 114
Lord, Eliot, 106
Lorimer, Frank, 70
Los Angeles, 212, 220
Los Angeles Times, 193
Lósener Bernard, 197
Low, W. Augustus, 160-61
Lowry, Ira, 157-58
Loving v. Virginia, 154
Lubell, Samuel, 153
Luciano, Lucky, 110
Lueger, Karl, 197
Luther, Martin, 114, 195
Luxemburg, Rosa, 60, 61

Machek, Vladko, 175
MacRae, Norman, 99
Mafia, 110
malaria, 37-38
Malcolm X, 187-88
Malthus, Thomas Robert, 15, 45-52; economic theory of, 56, 59; and education, 51-52; *Essay*, 45-52; interpretations of, 47-48; library of, 49-50; life of, 47-48, 49-50; and Marx, 48, 53-54, 55-57, 59-60, 62, 63, 104; politics of, 50-52; and religion, 46, 51-52; revived interest in, 50
Mamdani, Mahmood, 92, 104
Maoism, 222
marriage, 108-109; age at, 80
Martino, Antonio, 183
Marx, Karl, 48, 53-61, 76, 77, 135; anti-Semitism in, 196; class theory of, 58, 67; crisis and adjustment in, 58-61; economic theory of, 53, 58-61; and Engels, 53-54, 56, 71; and Malthus, 48, 53-54, 55-57, 59-60, 62, 68, 104; population theory of, 53-55, 60-62, 62-65, 67; underconsumption in, 58-61
Marxism, 43, 76, 90; on population, 74-76, 98
Masaryk, Tomás, 176
Massachusetts, 21
matica, 173
maturity, 27-28
Maulding, Parker, 96-97

Mayr, Ernst, 2
McCarran, Pat, 110-11
McCarthy, Joseph R., 110
Medicare, 29
Mehta, Ved, 103
Meiji Restoration, 203-04
melting pot, 133, 151, 187
Mencken, Henry, 185
Mendelssohn, Moses, 196
Mexico, 129, 205-06
migration, 139-40; consolidation of, 140-41; illegal, 10; international, 10-11; promotion of, 141-42
Mill, James, 49
Milton, John, 26
minority, group, 126; rights, 176-78
Mischling, 198
Mississippi, 11
Mombart, Paul, 40
Monnet, Jean, 171, 182
Montagu, Ashley, 129
morality, 232-35
Morgan, Lewis Henry, 54
Morgenstern, Oskar, 97
Mormons, 142, 230
morning-after pill, 118-19
Morris, Roger, 109
Morris, William, 61
mortality, by age, 28-29, 35, 38; by sex, 37; child, 35; decline, 35-39; infant, 35, 39; in less developed countries, 37
Moses, 195
Mosher, Steven, 99
Moynahan, Daniel P
Mozambique, 41
multicultural(ism), 187
Muslims, 228
Myrdal, Alva, 83
Myrdal, Gunnar, 83, 134, 138

names, American, 185-94; change of, 185-86, 190
Narain, Raj, 103
Nasser, Gamal Abdal, 90
nation, 149, 171
Nation of Islam, 187-88
National Association for the Advancement of Colored People (NAACP), 160
National Council of Churches, 229-31
National Fertility Study, 94

National Institute of Demographic Studies (INED), 83
National Opinion Research Center (NORC), 146, 167, 230
National Review, 118
nationalism, 125, 127; vs. internationalism, 181-83
National Socialism, see Nazism
Native Sons of the Golden West, 216-17
natural resources, 85-86
Nazi(sm), 83, 101, 128, 129, 135, 175, 176, 181, 187, 197-99, 233-34, 236
négritude, 153
"Negroes and Other Races," 168
Nehru, Jawahalal, 42, 90, 101
Neo-Malthusian League, 91
neo-Malthusianism, 63-64, 82
Netherlands, Dutch, 130, 178-79
Neuilly, Treaty of, 174
Nevada, 100-11; population of, 106-07
New Christians, 195
New Deal, 138-39, 162
New Economic Policy (NEP), 71
new industries, 59
New Republic, 118
Newcomb, Theodore, 136
Nigeria, 95
Nisbet, Robert, 139
"nonwhites," 132, 168, 169
Norway, Norwegian, 130, 14
Notestein, Frank, 15

obstetrics, 37
O'Donnell, Thomas Joseph, 115
Office of Federal Statistical Policy and Standards. See United States
Okinawa, 213
old persons, 28-30
opportunity costs, 84
optimum population, 85
Oriental Exclusion Act, 207, 214
Origin of the Family, Private Property, and the State, The, 54 Otter, William, 50
Ottoman empire, 172
Owen, Robert, 55, 77
Oxford University, 49

Paine, Thomas, 51
Paraguay, 1
Park, Robert E., 132, 138, 20
partial-birth abortion, 119

Paul VI, 120
Pebble Beach, CA, 13
pedophilia, 120-21
percentages, 21
Perevedentsev, V. I., 74
Perón, Juan, 43
Perry, Matthew, 202-03
Peter I, 175
Peter II, 175
Petersen, Renee, 16
Petersen, William, 50
Petty, William, 15
Philippines, 22
Piskunov, V. P., 74
Pius XII, 115
Planned Parenthood v. Casey, 117
Poland, Pole(s), Polish, 29, 127, 171-72, 173, 174, 186 polygamy, 142
Popov, A. IA., 74
population, 9-10; age structure, 107; forecasts, 41-42, 86;
growth, 88; optimum, 85; policy, 88; pyramid, 20; stable, 25; stationary, 25; structure, 19-33; transfers, 174
Population Association of America, 87
Population Commission, United Nations, 73
Population Crisis Committee, 92
Population Reference Bureau, 48
Populists, 67, 70-71
Powell, Lewis, 117
prejudice, 136
privacy, right of, 115-16
promotion, 141
pronatalism, 82-84, 90
Protestant ethic, 227
Protestantism, 232
Proudhon, Pierre-Joseph, 55, 196
Prussia, 172
Pucinski, Roman, 156

Quebec, 127
Quetelet, Adolphe, 16
quickening, 114, 118

race, racial, 3, 128-30, 134; crossing, 142-43; definition of, 199-200; and ethnicity, 148, 155-56; profiles, 3-4, 238
Radich, Stephen, 175
rates, 21
Ravenholt, R. T., 93-94

Reagan, Ronald, 117
regions, 4, 130-31
registration areas, 10
Rehnquist, William H., 115
religion, 132, 227-37; statistics on, 229-31
Rentenberg, 30
residence, 12, 133
Riabushkin, T. V., 73
Ricardo, David, 104
Robin, Paul, 64
Roe v. Wade, 115-16, 117
Rogier, Charles, 180
Romania, 174
Romansh, 130, 179
Romanticism, 181-82
Roosevelt, Franklin D., 217
Roosevelt, Theodore, 206-07
"roots," 153
Rossiter, William, 189-90
Royal Economic Society, 47
RU-486, 118
rural, 5, 238. *See also* urban
Russell, Bertrand, 73
Russia, 67, 171, 172, 174; agriculture, 67-74; ethnic composition of, 69, 174
Ruthenian(s), 173

Sacramento, 222-23
Saint-Simon, Conte Claude de, 77
Samoa, 39
San Francisco, 210, 213, 223
Sanger, Margaret, 74
sanskritization, 147-48
Sapir, Edward, 130
Sartre, Jean-Paul, 153
Saudi Arabia, 40
Sauvy, Alfred, 30, 104
Scalia, Antonin, 119
schism, 141-42
Schuman, Robert, 182
Scots, 168
Scots-Irish, 230
Scott, Walter, 181-82
Seattle, 220
Second International, 61-62, 63
Second World War, 175, 223
Selassie, Haile, 41
self-determination, 173, 182
self-identification, 166, 192
Senate Immigration Commission, 214
"senior citizen," 32

separation of church and state, 227-28
Serbia(n), 173, 175
Service, Robert, 69
Sèvres, Treaty of, 174
sex, ratio, 25-27; vs. gender, 25
Sharon, William, 110
Shaw, George Bernard, 179
Siegel, Bugsy, 110
Siegel, Jacob, 27
Simpson, Alan, 31
Singh, Karan, 102-03
Sippenforscher, 198
"Six Companies," 213
Slav, 173
slavery, slaves, 106, 150, 1
Slovak(s), 172-73, 176
smallpox, 38
Smith, Adam, 51-52, 76
Smith, Tom, 146
Smulevich, B. IA., 74
smychka, 70
social mobility, 80-81, 147-48, 208-12
social pathology, 219-223
Social Security, 28-29, 30, 32, 33; Board, 185
socialism, 55-56, 61-65, 72, 74, 196
Société de Démographie Historique, 50
Sorbian, 178
South Korea, 94
Soviet Union, 16, 18, 21, 69, 196; agriculture, 70-72; birth control, 73-76; economy, 69-71, 75, 100; ethnicity, 75-76; fertility, 72; forced-labor camps, 72; New Economic Policy (NEP), 71; peasantry, 70; population, 73-76; pronatalism, 74-75; terror, 70-72
Sowell, Thomas, 155-56, 158-59
Spain, Spanish, 1, 172, 195
Spanish-American War, 22
species, 2
Srinivas, M. N., 147
St. Germain, Treaty of, 174
St. Kitts-Nevis, 93
St. Lucia, 93
Stalin, Joseph, 69, 71-72
Stanford University, 99
statistics, 20-21, 237; on ethnicity, 157-58, 176-78
Stenberg v. Carhart, 119
Stephen, Leslie, 47
sterilization in India, 101-02

Sternberg, Fritz, 60
Steshenko, V. S., 74
Stone, Harlan F., 154
Stopes, Marie, 65, 91
Strassoldo, Mario, 177
Strong, Anna Louise, 71-72
Struve, Peter, 67
Stuckart, Wilhelm, 197
Stycos, J. Mayone, 91
subnation(s), 126-27, 131-32
Sudetenland, 176
Sullivan, Andrew, 118
Sumner, William Graham, 136
Sung, Betty Lee, 221
Supreme Court, 216, 217, 227-29, 231
Swahili, 141
Sweden, 38, 139
Sweezy, Paul, 59-60, 77
Switzerland, 128, 130, 131, 179
systematics, 2

Taeuber, Irene, 89
Taiping Rebellion, 202
Taiwan, 95-98
Tanovic, Becir, 156
tax burden, 33
taxonomy, biological, 2
Tennyson, Alfred, 128 Terzich, Robert, 156
Teschen, 176
Thailand, 94
third-generation nationalism, 136-37
Thirty Years War, 179
Thomas, Dorothy, 222
Thorez, Maurice, 64, 74
Thornton, Russell, 164
Tito, 175
Tocqueville, Alexis de, 126
Toishan, 212
tongs, 220
totalitarianism, 18
Transylvania, 178
Trianon, Treaty of, 174
Tsui, Amy Ong, 48
Tunisia, 94
Turkey, 174
Turner, Frederick Jackson, 105
Twain, Mark, 106

Ulam, Adam, 76-77
unemployment, 4, 55. *See al so* employment.

United Kingdom, 172
United Nations, 18, 182; Commission on Human Rights, 126; Economic Commission for Europe, 10-11; Population Commission, 73; statistics on ethnicity, 131-33
United States, Agency for International Development (AID), 93-94; Army, 187; Bureau of the Census, 93, 105, 132-33, 143, 147, 157-58, 160, 161, 162, 164-66, 185, 189, 229-30, 237-38; Bureau of Indian Affairs, 162; Chinese Exclusion Act, 206-07; Congress, 150; Constitution, 149-50, 154, 164, 228, 231; Declaration of Independence, 9, 154; Emergency Relief Administration, 213; House of Representatives, 193; Immigration Act of 1924, 206; Naval Intelligence, 110; Office of Federal Statistical Policy and Standards, 157; Office of Strategic Services, 110; Oriental Exclusion Act, 207, 214; Senate Immigration Commission, 214; Supreme Court, 216, 217, 227-28, 231; War Relocation Authority, 216
Université Catholique de Louvain, 181
University of North Carolina, 12
unproductive consumers, 59
upward mobility, 180, 218
urban, 5, 238. See also rural
Urlanis, B. TS., 73, 75, 76
USSR. See Soviet Union.
Utah, 142

Valentei, Dmitri I., 73, 75-76
van de Walle, Etienne, 9
Vatican, 175
Venezuela, 38
Vermeersch, Jeannette, 64
Versailles, Treaty of, 174
Victoria, Queen, 235
Vienna, 173, 197

village commune, 67
Vincent, Paul, 16
Virginia City, 106-07
vital statistics, 10
Voogelin, Charles, 140
Voegelin, Florence, 140
Volkedeutsche, 178
Voltaire, 196
voting, 136

Wall Street Journal, 232
Wallace, Alfred Russel, 51
Walloon(s), 180
Warren, Earl, 217
wealth flow, 86
Webb, Sidney, 77
Webber, Alan, 48
Weber, Max, 227, 231
welfare, 30, 31-32; state, 31
well-being, growth of, 59-60
Welsh, 168
Wends, 178
West Indians, 158-59
Weyl, Nathaniel, 199-200
Wharton, Edith, 233
White, Burton R., 115
Wilkins, Roy, 160
William, Julius Wilson, 159-60
Wilson, Woodrow, 174, 176, 212
Wirth, Louis, 126
Wolfe, Bertram, 61, 69
World Health Organization, 38
World Population Conference, 1954, 73
World War I, 181
World War II, 175, 223

Yiddish, 177
Yugoslavia, 127, 175

Zangwill, Israel, 133-34, 139
Zasulich, Vera, 67
zero population growth (ZPG), 23-25, 43, 83
Zero Population Growth, Inc., 23-24
Zetkin, Klara, 63